IF IT HAD NOT BEEN FOR THE
LORD

WENDELL M. MANIGAULT JR.

Palmetto Publishing Group
Charleston, SC

If It Had Not Been for the Lord
Copyright © 2019 by Wendell M. Manigault Jr.

First Edition

Printed in the United States

ISBN-13: 978-1-64111-411-0
ISBN-10: 1-64111-411-8

PROLOGUE

Coming up as a child, everyday life wasn't sweet. Some days it was good, some days bad, but through all adversities, I still held my head high. In my past, there were many mazes that I was mysteriously thrown into. My transition into manhood was like putting a puzzle together with no picture on the box to refer to. I had no direction, so I put the pieces together the best way I knew how. Growing up, you could say the model of our household was another day, another penny. A tree is known to stand the test of time, and through my journey I learned that a mother is known to do the same. My mother was the tree that nurtured my life, and as her seed, when I saw her leaves begin to wilt, I felt that it was my responsibility to in return nurture her as she nurtured me. Consequently, I learned that being in the streets was like being at a masquerade ball; I was just a vulnerable adolescent in a large mob of people, some with masks, some without. The people with masks were the people who I saw do shady things, and to me, couldn't be trusted. The people without the masks, I considered to be trustworthy. Behind the masks were the faces of some crooks, liars, and even killers. Although I was affiliated with all, I would eventually learn that even the unmasked were masked. It's funny how I had my life perfectly mapped out, and God did, too. Fortunately, the two plans didn't coincide. I've had many chances, but unlike many people, God gave me a second chance at life. Now walk with me through this journey as I show you why I say, If it had not been for the Lord.

CHAPTER 1

What's happening? My name is Wendell M. Manigault Jr., aka Lo Mann. I was born November 15, 1985, in the city and state of North Charleston, South Carolina. Back in the late eighties, my family and I were living in my great-grandparents' three-bedroom, one-bath home. Prior to my great-grandfather's death, my ole lady (mother) was one of his primary caretakers. After my great-grandfather's passing, his offspring unanimously made a decision to illegally evict my ole lady, and me and my eldest sibling, who were just toddlers, from the home without following the correct legal steps for eviction. In fact, my great-grandfather's offspring inconsiderably gave my ole lady two-weeks' notice to vacate the premises. By the grace of God, my family and I were able to find and relocate into a two-bedroom, one-bath apartment in a small public housing complex called Three Oaks Apartments at such short notice. In our household, both parents were present, in addition to three uncles (which are the brothers of my ole lady), my eldest sibling Kesia, and myself, with two younger siblings on the way.

As I was saying, coming up as a child, my everyday life wasn't sweet; some days good, some days bad, but through all adversities, I still held my head high. While living in Three Oaks, every adult who lived in our apartment was employed, except for two of my uncles. In those days, my ole lady was working at a nursing home facility; my ole man (father) was working at a restaurant as a cook; and my employed uncle was working at the cemetery as a grave digger. The other two uncles who were not employed worked odd jobs whenever they found employment, making just enough money to have in their pockets. Even though most adults were working, we were still struggling, because economically my ole lady was holding the fort down by her lonesome. As I recall, there were times when my ole man and uncles gave a few dollars here and there, but like I said, economically my ole lady was pulling the load.

Growing up in our household, there were times when my ole lady would fuss with my uncles and ole man about not getting any help with the finances, she would say, "There is no reason the bills can't be paid on time when every adult who is living here is able to work and help. Y'all always depend on me to do everything. If I don't do anything, nothing gets done—and y'all call y'all selves men. If dis is what y'all call being men, then all of y'all are a sorry excuse of a man. I shouldn't have to pull the load by myself, especially when y'all living here. Dat's sad I have to wake up in the morning, go to work all day, then turn around, come home from work, and do more work, while y'all laying on y'all ass all day. There is gonna be some changes. If y'all can't change up what y'all doing, y'all gonna have to pack y'all shit and get the hell out."

Not only that, when it came time for my ole lady to go to work, she didn't have much help in the babysitting department either, because either everyone in the house had something to do, and did not feel like watching my siblings and me, or they were too intoxicated for us to be under their supervision. When push came to shove, my ole man or uncle would watch us, but when they got in their mode, and didn't feel like watching us, they didn't. Whenever Plan A didn't work, my ole lady had to resort to Plan B, which was to contact one of my older female cousins on her side of the family. If all else failed, my ole lady then contacted a woman who was a long-time family friend named Miss Willamina Reese, or our grandparents. Our grandparents—my ole man's parents—played a big part in our lives; they were always there for my siblings and me. To my knowledge, my grandparents were always there for all of their grandchildren, but they helped my ole lady out a lot with my siblings and me because my ole man wasn't fulfilling his duties as a father. By no means am I saying my ole man neglected his children, because he never did, but he wasn't there economically, so my grandparents picked up the slack. Don't get me wrong, if my ole man was doing what he was supposed to do, our grandparents would have still been there for us. During our upbringing, my eldest sibling and I witnessed several domestic disputes between our parents that I believe children shouldn't have to witness. However, out of all the disputes that occurred between my parents, there are two incidents that stuck with me. The first incident that occurred began with an argument that escalated into a fist fight. In fact, they began brawling as if they were strangers. Due to my ole man throwing the first blow, my ole lady began striking back out of self-defense. As my parents were brawling, they noticed that I was standing there, and I distinctly remember hearing my ole lady say to me, "Go ahead back in the room. We just playing." I said to myself, "How could y'all be playing, when I clearly see y'all throwing blows at one another?" After my ole lady told me that they were just playing, my ole man then said to me, "Get out the room," but I did not budge. At the end of my parents' brawl, I looked at my ole lady as she stood at the bathroom sink, and said, "Your mouth is bleeding." Then she replied, "I know. I missed and hit my mouth on the bed while me and your daddy been wrestling."

Again, I just saw my parents fighting one another, but my ole lady kept lying as if I was stupid. With my ole lady still being upset, she told my ole man he had to leave because she wasn't putting up with that nonsense anymore; she could do bad by herself. Then my ole lady said, "Either you leave, or I will call the police—your choice." During that heated argument, my ole lady told me and my eldest sibling that my ole man sold our brand new VCR for drugs. My eldest sibling and I stood there speechless, like, "Huh. Wow, Daddy on drugs." My ole man was livid. Ultimately the cops were called, but my ole man fled the scene before they arrived.

Nearly twenty years later, my eldest sibling confessed that she knew where our ole man was the whole time. It was said that our ole man ran out the back door on to the rooftop, as me, my ole lady, and the officers searched for him. The reason my eldest sibling did not say anything is because my ole man told her not to, and she is a daddy's girl.

The second incident that occurred between my parents resulted in violence also, but this time around, my ole lady was the aggressor. On the day of the incident in question, my ole lady went to work and left my siblings and me under our ole man's supervision. Most of that day, my ole man was present in the home, but throughout that day, he was under the influence of alcohol. As I reflect on that day, I can't remember what my eldest sibling and I were doing, but I do remember she and I in our room. And to our knowledge, our ole man was still in the living room. Eventually my eldest sibling and I came out of our room, but what brought us out was the cry of our younger sibling Jasmine. My eldest sibling and I heard the cry from our room, but we thought my ole man was still in the apartment.

The second thing my eldest sibling and I noticed was the ongoing crying; it sounded like no one was attending to our younger sibling. And it was then that my eldest sibling and I noticed that our ole man wasn't there. Needless to say, we began searching the apartment for our ole man, then she and I went to the neighbor's apartment, but he was still nowhere to be found. After minutes of searching for my ole man, my eldest sibling and I called off the search, and decided to contact my ole lady to ask her if she knew where he was. In response to our question, my ole lady said, "He should be home with y'all, because that's where I left him." We both replied, "Well, he ain't here. We searched the apartment, and went to Miss Ann's apartment, but we still didn't find him." Just to make sure we wasn't tripping, my ole lady told my eldest sibling and I to look around one more time, but still my ole man was nowhere to be found. At the latter end of that conversation, my ole lady said, "I'm on the way. Lock the door, and don't let nobody in until I get there." Keep in mind, my ole lady worked in downtown Charleston, which is approximately fifteen to twenty minutes from where we lived in North Charleston, so you could imagine how infuriated she was, having to leave work for non-sense. By the time my ole lady arrived at the apartment, my ole man was approaching the door with a case of beer in his possession. As soon as my ole lady stepped out of the car, she asked my ole man, "Where were you?" and he replied, "Nowhere. I was here all day." In the act of this incident, my ole lady asked me and my eldest sibling if our ole man had been there, or if he'd left. Then she asked my ole man, "Where did you get this case of beer from, if you was here all day?"

As the drama unfolded, my ole lady said to my ole man, "So you mean to tell me I leave you in dis house with Kesia, Mann, and the baby while I go to work, and you leave my damn chirrun in the house by deyself just so you can go get some beer." By this time, my ole lady had already begun battering my ole man with her fist until he dropped; then she went in the kitchen, came back with a spatula, and began battering him again. The butt-whooping my ole lady distributed was that same good-ole-fashioned butt-whooping we all are familiar with; you know, those lashes that land so accurately—or in this case, those powerful counter punches—and the words that are discharged along with every single blow.

However, the drama did not stop there. I say this because the case of beer that my ole man purchased, she then cracked open and poured into the middle of the street as she stated, "Instead of you waiting until I get home to go to the store, you leave my babies in dis house to go buy some damn beer. If you want to drink that bad, drink it off the ground, or buy more."

After that incident, my ole lady took me and my siblings on Stall Road to Miss Willamina's house, where we stayed until she came home from work. At the time of this chaos, my eldest sibling and I were between the ages of nine and seven. She and I were attending Pepperhill Elementary School. She was in the fifth grade, I was in the second grade, and our younger sibling was an infant. Despite what my eldest sibling and I were exposed to, our parents always sat us down and taught us right from wrong; they would always express the importance of not becoming the aggressors, or victims of domestic violence, be it verbally or physically—considering what we witnessed between the two. "Let no one verbally or physically abuse you," said our parents, "because that's not love, nor is it right." It was also said to us, "Don't do what y'all see us do. Do better than us." By no means were my parents implying that we needed to be better than them, because all human races are equal. However, they were simply implying that we needed to do better than what they had done.

Another valuable lesson my parents expressed to us was the importance of education. In fact, I can recall them saying, "Stay in school, get an education, and make something out of yourselves. You can be whatever you want to be in life, be it a doctor, lawyer, athlete, etcetera, but you must keep in mind that education comes first." Oftentimes in those sessions my ole lady said to me and my eldest sibling, "If it wasn't for the help of the Lord and the government, I don't know where we would be, or how we would survive. I'm working two jobs, living from paycheck to paycheck, just to maintain, and as y'all can see, I'm doing everything by myself so that we can make it. That's why I always teach the importance of education."

As I reflect on the past that only seems like yesterday, I realize that my eldest sibling and I lacked for nothing as far as life lessons were concerned. In fact, my parents also spoke about the streets, stating how trouble was easy to get into, but hard to get out. They also instructed us to stay away from drugs, alcohol, and the wrong crowd. Being that my parents knew what this wicked world has to offer, they explained to us that if we were to go into the world and do something we weren't supposed to do, chances were, we'd end up behind bars. In fact, they went on to say, "And that's not what y'all want, because in jail, you can't walk around and do as you please. You basically have to do what you are told."

Beyond the lessons that my parents taught, my ole lady always drove me and my eldest sibling around different communities of North Charleston and downtown Charleston, showing us drug addicts, drug dealers, prostitutes, alcoholics, and the homeless, letting us know that that was how our lives could turn out if we didn't take heed to the wisdom and knowledge that was given to us.

"Always respect others," said my ole lady. "No matter who they are, because respect will take you places where money won't." Aside from that, my eldest sibling and I were brought up in church, attending every service you could imagine; my ole lady made sure of that. We all attended lovely Mountain Baptist Church, which is the church where my deceased great-grandfather pastored. If my eldest sibling and I did not attend our family church, my ole lady felt comfortable allowing us to ride a local church bus that drove in different communities of North Charleston to pick up the youth for Sunday service at this church located off of Remount Road.

To conclude this chapter, I want to close with a question: Isn't it absurd how my parents taught me and my eldest sibling right from wrong, considering the negative behavior they displayed in our presence? Despite how absurd it may seem, I count it as a blessing, because in my opinion, there is no other way to learn about the facts of life than being in chaos.

CHAPTER 2

Here comes the bride, here comes the bride—or should I say, here comes a lie, because that's what my parents were living. Although I don't remember my parents speaking to me and my eldest sibling about marriage, I do remember attending their wedding. Being that my parents were about to get married, they were excited, but I wasn't, because I was totally against it. True indeed, I was just a young lad, but the things I'd witnessed within our household between the two led me to believe they weren't compatible. I also believed that my ole man wasn't husband material, and that's only because I'd witnessed him display negative behavior towards my ole lady. On January 24, 1994, my parents got married in a three-bedroom home instead of a church. In fact, it was in my grandparents' home, the parents of my ole man. The attendees included my eldest sibling Kesia, myself, my younger sibling Jasmine, my grandfather (my ole lady's father), my great-grandmother (my ole man's grandmother), my grandparents (my ole man's parents), my ole lady's friend, and the bishop (my ole man's father's brother-in-law).

The bishop read the vows, and my parents recited them to each other in turn. I looked towards my ole lady, shaking my head silently, thinking, *No, don't do it*. Despite my silent gesture, my ole lady disregarded my objection, and carried on with the ceremony. After their vows were finished, the bishop then said, "Should anyone here present know of any reason that this couple should not be joined in Holy Matrimony? Speak now, or forever hold your peace." Truth be told, I wanted to speak, Lord knows I did, but I held my peace, because I knew what the outcome would have been.

Before the bishop announced the wedding ceremony was finished, I looked at my ole lady one last time and shook my head, having hoped she wouldn't follow through with the marriage, but she did. In all honesty, it was disappointing to witness my parents join in Holy Matrimony, but there was nothing I could have done, so I just accepted the change. As my parents rode off in the sunset and began living their newlywed lives, things were great. There were no arguments, or fighting; we all were happy, and got along just fine. One day my parents told me and my eldest sibling to get dressed because we were all going somewhere. Once my family got squared away, my ole lady drove to Ladson, where we arrived at a mobile home lot. As my family and I were getting out of the car, out came a salesman.

"Is it okay to tour your mobile home?" said my parents.

"Sure," said the salesman. "They are open."

As my family and I toured the mobile homes, my parents asked my eldest sibling and I if we liked this one specific trailer, and we replied yes. "Are we moving?" we asked.

"We don't know," said our parents.

In that moment, my eldest sibling and I began choosing rooms. And of course, she and I chose the same room, but then our parents butted in and said, "The oldest gets the room that's next in size to the master bedroom, and the second oldest gets the room next in size."

After my family and I toured the mobile homes, my parents had a sit down with the salesman, and my eldest sibling and I sat in the lobby. Sometime later, my parents came out of the salesman's office, and we all left. During our ride home, my ole lady turned the radio off and began talking to me and my eldest sibling. "We don't know if we will be able to purchase that home, but if so, there are going to be some changes." The changes my parents spoke about consisted of us having "responsibilities"—chores. For example, we had to keep our rooms clean, keep the bathroom clean, keep the living area clean, and keep the kitchen clean. With those responsibilities came allowances that my parents promised me and my eldest sibling that if we kept up with our chores, we would be able to receive an allowance. My parents also told us that if they were able to purchase this home, that meant we would be attending a new school. On that note, my parents told us, "We send y'all to school to get an education. Those teachers got theirs. Y'all are there to get y'alls." Then they went on to say, "If y'all can't get y'all education within the time frame that's given, that's on y'all, because we ain't paying for summer school—not when y'all can get an education free."

In addition to that, my parents said, "The domestic disputes that occurred between us [referring to themselves] in the apartment will not occur in the new home." After that lecture, my parents asked me and my eldest sibling if we understood all that was said. We said we did, then they turned the radio back on, and left it at that.

CHAPTER 3

This was still in the early nineties—1994, to be exact—and the mobile home my family toured eventually became ours after my parents, who were first time homeowners, made a down payment. Shortly thereafter, our mobile home was transported to an upscale trailer park called Trailwood, where my family and I ultimately resided. Days after my family and I got settled into our new home, my parents sat me and my eldest sibling down and asked if we remembered the talk they had with us. Then they told us to tell them what was said; they also asked if we understood all that was said. Having remembered and understood all that was said, she and I were exempt from the lecture our parents often gave. It was summer around this time. In that new home, my family and I did things as a unit. We ate dinner together, watched television, and partook in extracurricular activities.

My eldest sibling and I were also fulfilling our duties in terms of chores. In addition to that, my parents kept their word about no longer displaying negative behavior in our presence. Aside from that, my parents taught us how to be responsible. For example, my ole lady taught my eldest sibling how to conduct herself as a young lady, expressing that girls were to be seen, not heard.

My ole man taught yours truly how to conduct myself as a young man, expressing how I had to learn to stand on my own feet because this world wouldn't give me anything it didn't owe. Those lessons my parents taught me and my eldest sibling were just the tip of the iceberg; take my word for it, it gets realer than reality. Any time the bills were due my ole lady took me and my eldest sibling along with her most of the time, demonstrating to she and I how to make bill payments. For example, If my ole lady made payments with a money order, she demonstrated how to purchase a money order either from a gas station or a check cashing store; then she showed us how to fill out the money order and make the payment. On the other hand, if my ole lady used a check, at times she filled it out in our presence, then gave it to either me or my eldest sibling to make the payment. However, if my ole lady used cash she once again gave it to myself or eldest sibling to make the payment. Along with the responsibilities that were demonstrated, my ole lady coached us on how to manage our finances and save. In fact, any time my ole lady spoke to me and my eldest sibling about managing our finances and savings, she would say, "It's best that y'all learn to manage y'all finances while y'all young. That way when y'all are older, with responsibilities, y'all will know how to manage y'all finances in terms of y'all bills, and learn how to save not just for extracurricular activities, but a rainy day." Within the first year of living in our new home, my parents oftentimes had me and my eldest sibling in the kitchen as they prepared dinner. As my parents prepared dinner, they allowed us to partake in the process. For example, my parents allowed me and my eldest sibling to measure or mix the ingredients, grease the pan and/or cake bowl, season the meat, be it chicken, pork chop, etc.

On other occasions, if not the same, my ole man taught me how to operate a charcoal grill. He taught me how to clean the bowl, clean the charcoal grid, clean the cooking grid, apply protection for the charcoal grid, and how to fire up the grill. Truth be told, I wasn't interested in learning how to cook. That's why I don't know how to cook anything other than breakfast, minus grits, but my eldest sibling took a liking to it, so our parents allowed her to be more hands on with the preparation and cooking process.

Despite my lack of interest in cooking, it was evident that I enjoyed, and remembered how to operate a grill, courtesy of my ole man. As time went on, I learned a profitable trade from my ole man at the age of eight. My ole man took me along with him to the store, where he then purchased the equipment and accessories needed to complete the task. Early that next morning, I woke up to the sound of my ole man's guttural voice commanding that I get up, grab a bite to eat, get dressed, and meet him outside. Needless to say, I obeyed my ole man's command, and met him outside. The second I stepped outside, gazing at the morning dew, there he stood, gearing up to instruct me on how to operate the lawnmower he'd purchased the day before.

During training, I learned about the filter, the oil tank, the gas tank, the primer, and the crank. Once I learned about those specifications, my ole man briefly demonstrated how to mow the lawn. Afterward, I was then allowed to take over. At that moment, I made an error, but courtesy of my ole man, I was able to perfect my lawnmowing craft each row thereafter. Several cuts later, I took what I was taught and began to nurture my entrepreneurship, mowing the lawns of other residences within the community, charging seven or eight bucks per yard.

In the thick of attending those life classes my parents held, my eldest sibling and I were still able to enjoy our summer break. Unfortunately for all students, including me, our summer break was winding down, and the new school term was rapidly approaching, so me and my eldest sibling got ourselves prepared for the new school term at our new school. The night before, of course our parents did what parents do best—lecture. *Brrring, brrring, brrring.* Oh, how I hated the sound of those bronze bells repeatedly hammering in the morning, alerting all students, teachers, and staff members that school was in session.

Although it was still summer, the first day of school had arrived. I was in the third grade, attending Wendell B Goodwin Elementary School, and my eldest sibling was in the sixth grade, attending Brentwood Middle School. In the area where my family and I lived, my eldest sibling was privileged to ride the public school bus to and from school daily, but I had to walk close to a mile to and from school daily because the school had no active bus routes.

At the beginning of school, my eldest sibling and I were performing well; she and I were fulfilling our duties in terms of focusing on academics, be it engaging ourselves in group activities, completing class work assignments, homework assignments, etc. She and I also abided by our teachers' rules. My eldest sibling and I got acquainted with our new schoolmates, who became good friends of ours. In the course of fulfilling our duties at home and in school, our parents could not have been any prouder, because she and I were direct reflections of the valuable lessons they taught. Everything that my family and I spoke about was applied to our lives, and abided by us all, and for once it felt like everything was falling in place.

As my parents were working as a married couple to keep our family afloat, there was no drama. If you didn't know any better, you could have mistaken us for the Huxtables. During this time, my family and I celebrated my youngest sibling's first birthday. Then Christmas and New Year's came along, and my family and I celebrated that as well. The year 1994 was truly a great year for me and my family. And what better way to end the year than on a good note?

At the beginning of the new year, 1995, everything was still intact with my family. My parents kept their end of the bargain as promised, and my eldest sibling and I were still fulfilling our duties as instructed. As time progressed, there was a disruption in our family, and it was all because of me. The best explanation I can give for disrupting what my family and I were building was my age. I was your typical male adolescent, who was coming out of his shell. And considering that my head was already hard, it got harder the more outspoken and playful I became. Instead of me staying consistent with fulfilling my duties, I began acting out in school—and that's when the problem emerged.

Back in those days, I woke up in the mornings with good intentions of having an excellent day, but somewhere down the line, it did not work out as planned. The acts I got myself in trouble for were senseless acts, such as being talkative, being a class clown, and mouthing off at the teacher. Because I was acting out, the teacher spoke to me a lot about disrupting the class. In fact, I was labeled the ringleader, who always caught the blame for my classmates' reactions. Any time class was in session, I oftentimes told jokes and made the class chuckle. The instant everyone began chuckling, of course I caught the blame, and as a result, I began mouthing off. The moment I got blamed, I told the teacher, "You can't blame me for anyone else's actions. Everyone is responsible for their own actions. I didn't force anyone to laugh—they laughed on their own—so if I get punished, it's only fair that everyone else gets punished also."

As the teacher and I argued with each other, he said, "If you keep this up, I will contact your parents." Considering what the ramifications would be, I told the teacher, "Call 'em. I don't care."

The teacher decided to move my desk in front of the classroom, facing directly towards the chalkboard. You would have thought that would have made a difference, but it didn't; I was still acting out, committing silly acts. Instead of pulling myself together as instructed, I was making silly facial expressions as the teacher taught the class; I also gathered a few spitballs and chopped him in the back of his head.

As I reflect on that incident, I don't know what enticed me to commit that act. I guess it was an idle mind, but in my mind, it was a brilliant idea. The instant I launched the first spitball, I quickly turned back towards the chalkboard and glued my eyes to the textbook. Moments later, I then launched the second spitball, due to the success I'd had with the first launch. As I got set to throw the third spitball, I got busted. The teacher caught me red handed.

"Why did you do that ?" asked the teacher.

"Do what?" I replied. "I ain't did nothin'."

"You just threw a spitball at me."

"It wasn't me," I replied.

"I just caught you," said the teacher. "Who else could it be?"

"I don't know," I replied, "but it wasn't me."

Out of frustration, the teacher ordered that I turn back around and face the chalkboard as I was told; the teacher also threatened to place my desk in the hallway if I continued to disrupt the class. Generally with a case like this, the teacher would issue a verbal warning, but if the student failed to comply, the next step would be a parent-teacher conference, in person or over the phone. And if that didn't work, the teacher would then issue a written referral that consisted of in-school suspension, out-of-school suspension, de-tention, or possibly expulsion. If my parents had knowledge about the incident in question, I would have gotten my butt whipped and grounded, but fortunately there was no disciplinary action taken for my crazy antics.

As time went on, before the end of the 1994-95 school year, I made a complete turnaround as far as my behavior was concerned. I also maintained fairly good grade averages in all subjects except math. However, instead of making me repeat the same grade, the school held me back in the beginning of the 1995-96 school year un-til I brought that math grade up to par, then I was promoted to the fourth grade a month or so later.

CHAPTER 4

Woohoo! Finally, the wait was over. There was no more rising early in the morning, no more classwork assignments, homework assignments, quizzes or tests, and most of all there were no more teachers, administrators, and principles. After four extensive quarters of hard labor, school was no longer in session. *Hell-o, summer break. I have been awaiting your arrival*, I thought.

In the summer of 1995, I partook in a lot of extracurricular activities, just as I had during past summer breaks. During this break, I spent the summer roaming the streets with loved ones and peers in my community, as well as other communities, playing sports (baseball, basketball, football), or messing around with the damsels. I even spent nights at the homes of my loved ones or peers. I also took separate trips with my loved ones, one of my partners and his loved ones, and my church. The trips I took with the church were to Carowinds theme park, and Morris College for Bible school.

To you who may not be aware of Morris College, here is a little history: Morris college (MC), located in Sumter, South Carolina, is a four-year, co-educational, liberal arts, private, historically black college founded and operated by the Baptist educational and missionary convention of South Carolina. Morris College was founded in 1908, initially as a grade school, high school, and college. The college is named after Reverend Frank Morris because of his outstanding leadership throughout the African American communities of South Carolina. The college's first president was Dr. Edward M. Brawley (1908-1912). Morris College awarded its first bachelor's degree in 1915 under the administration of college president Dr. John Jacob Stark. Morris College offers bachelor degrees in twenty areas of study. The college is accredited by the Southern Association of Colleges and Schools to award four different types of bachelor's degrees: bachelor of arts, bachelor of fine arts, bachelor of science, and bachelor of science in education. To effectively accomplish the purpose and philosophy of Morris college its academic programs are organized into six academic division which oversee their respective departments. For further information, log on to Morris College website, and there you will find a boatload of information.

The other trips I took with my partner and his loved ones were to Carowinds theme park again, and Six Flags in Atlanta, Georgia. Aside from those trips, there were other trips that I took along with my in-home and immediate relatives who were my ole man's siblings, and their offspring. The trip I took with them was to this navy outdoor recreational area, called Short Stay.

Throughout the years, we oftentimes vacationed there, where we were lodged in two- or three-bedroom waterfront villas that were completely furnished. However, instead of interacting with other families who were vacationing as well, or participating in Short Stay's organized sports and games, my loved ones and I chose to vacation amongst ourselves. In no way, shape, or form were we being antisocial towards other families. In fact, my loved ones and I spoke to other families in passing, but it was important for us to spend quality time amongst ourselves, in order that we continued to build and maintain important family bonds that required constant attention and nurturing. During our weekend getaways at Short Stay, we had cookouts, competed in family friendly games, such as Taboo or spades, and shared stories about our family history, some of our grandparents and their generation, or our parents and their generation, and how both generations' upbringings were different from ours, the younger generation.

If we weren't all together, the parents and the grandparents would all be in one of the villas we'd rented. Me, my siblings, and cousins would all be in the other villas that our parents individually rented. In the early part of the day, my loved ones and I engaged in outdoor activities, including swimming, shooting hoops, and fishing. Upon my loved ones and I taking a dip, our parents surveyed the area for safety precautions. Thanks to our concerned parents, we were permitted to go for a swim.

Later that day, my cousins and I headed to the playground to shoot hoops. On our way to the park, my cousins and I were all fired up about competing against one another in a game of basketball. However, the younger cousins, including me, were in for a rude awakening, simply because our elder cousins were being a bunch of jackasses. The instant my cousins and I stepped foot on the court, they began selecting their draft picks, but as it got down to the wire, the younger cousins went undrafted in the final round. As a result, I expressed to my elder cousins how I felt, and although I do not quite remember what all I said, I do remember giving them a piece of my mind. Nonetheless, my elder cousins paid me no mind as they positioned themselves for tip off.

Immediately after the game ended, my cousins and I went back to our villas, where a cousin of mine and I ran into his ole man, who informed him that he'd made an attempt to go fishing but caught nothing. My cousin asked if he could cast his line into Lake Moultrie, but he was prohibited from doing so due to the lake's rip current. If time permitted, I could go on for days about the trips I took, and the extra curricular activities, but unfortunately it doesn't.

Throughout this same summer, I went yard sale hopping with my ole lady on the weekends, from dawn to dusk. I also went to work with her some days during the week. On the days I went to work with her, I would lend a helping hand by passing out newspapers to the patients, transporting patients to and from their rooms for breakfast and lunch, and to attend therapy. I would also fill the patients' pitchers with ice and water so they would have something to drink.

As the summer went on, I was stopped one day by this elder gentleman who lived across the street from us. He said, "Hey, young man, come here." Initially I was surprised, because I always hailed the gentleman, but he never spoke or waved. I had this perception of him because of how he looked, so for him to stop me was unreal . Despite what I thought about the gentleman, I wanted to see what he needed. He asked if I could assist him with his housekeeping, which consisted of washing dishes, cleaning the counter and table, sweeping the floor, and taking out the garbage. With all things considered, I told him I would help with his housekeeping duties, and from that day forward, I took it upon myself to check in on him periodically throughout the week.

Immediately after I'd helped him, I ran home to inform my ole lady about my good deed. "Mama, you know that ole white man who live across the street?" I said. "He stopped me and asked if I could assist him with his housekeeping. I was surprised, because he never spoke or waved whenever I hailed him." Then my ole lady asked, "Did you help him?" and I replied, "Yes, ma'am." I also told her that the gentlemen had given me a token of appreciation. In that moment, my ole lady instilled a valuable lesson in me. She said, "I'm proud of you, but always remember that any time you help someone, don't do it looking for something in return. Do it from the kindness of your heart. It's okay to accept a token of appreciation, but it's also okay to say, 'No thank you, I did this from the kindness of my heart.' You may not understand it now, but you will understand it by and by."

The gentleman whom I assisted was a war veteran who served in the US Armed Forces. During his service to our country, an incident took place, and unfortunately he had to have both his legs amputated. However, despite what the gentleman endured, he was able to readjust to civilian life, and carry on with what independence he had left.

As you can see, my itinerary was booked for the summer; in fact, my itinerary was booked throughout the year. Everything that I have mentioned took place either in the summer, or throughout the years of 1994, '95, '96, and '97. As time went on, things began to crumble within our household; it seemed as though my family was relapsing. For example, my eldest sibling was going through changes; I continued acting out in school; and the verbal and physical abuse that took place between my parents resurfaced. Little by little, my siblings and I began to witness the domestic disputes between our parents as displayed in our old residence. As we sat there listening to our parents argue, my eldest sibling and I quickly learned that the topics of their arguments had not changed. To my knowledge, I thought everything was going good, until I witnessed my ole lady bicker about my ole man not fulfilling his duties economically, and running the streets.

I can recall my ole man giving an amount that he thought was reasonable, whether that was twenty bucks, fifty bucks, or none. And as a result, my ole lady made a fuss about that, stating what bill was due, and the amount owed. The instant that statement was made—it never failed—my ole man oftentimes asked to see the bill, or bills that were due. According to my ole lady, both she and my ole man agreed to split the bills down the middle, but apparently my ole man wasn't holding up his end of the bargain. Needless to say, his lack of financial assistance created an issue between them, so much so that she began arguing about how he came up with all kinds of excuses not to pay the bills, considering their agreement. My ole lady said, "It is okay if you come up short sometimes—that's understandable; I can work with you—but when you come with an excuse every week, that is when we have a problem."

In response, my ole man said, "There is nothing I could do if my check came up short. If I can't give nothing, I can't give nothing. What do you want me to do? I can't squeeze blood out of a turnip."

Immediately after, my ole lady said, "I'm not asking you to squeeze blood out of a turnip. I'm asking you to be a man, take care of your family, and bring your money home, instead of blowing it in the streets and paying the drug man."

As my parents went back and forth, my ole man said, "This is my money. I work hard for this, and if you think I'm about to give the white man all of my money, and walk around broke, you stupid."

Due to my ole man's lack of financial assistance, there were times when we didn't have any food to eat. And if we had something to eat, it was peanut butter and jelly sandwiches, egg and rice, or Mama would spend her last few dollars for gas to purchase us something to eat. As I reflect on those days, I can remember my ole lady giving me fifty cents to pay the gas station clerk for gas because her tank was almost empty.

Despite the hardships and long suffering my loved ones and I endured, I must say my ole lady always managed to keep her faith in God, in addition to paying her tithes and offerings. And whether my loved ones and I realize it or not, it was my ole lady's prayers, and the power of God, that protected and provided for us when we didn't even know it.

CHAPTER 5

Several months prior to the end of 1996, our summer break ended and school was back in session. I was still attending Wendell B Goodwin Elementary School; the only difference there was my promotion to the fifth grade. In the first semester, my fifth grade year was not quite the same as my third and fourth grade year in terms of my academics and behavior. I started off on the right track, but as time went on, my academics and behavior took a turn for the worse. The behavior problem I had affected my grades tremendously because I was so busy being a class clown/slacker, and not completing classwork or homework assignments. I was given verbal warning, but since I failed to comply with the rules, I was then issued written referrals for detention, in-school suspension, out-of-school suspension, and a parent-teacher conference. My parents took disciplinary actions as well, giving me a butt-whooping and putting me on restriction.

On top of the academic and behavioral problems occurring at school, things were no different at home, because I was acting out there as well—or should I say, I was rebelling towards my parents, more so my ole man. The issues that led to my rebellious acts was the verbal and physical abuse that occurred between my parents. In a previous chapter, I touched on the domestic dispute that occurred between them, and I noted how they brought their disputes to a screeching halt. But as time went on, the drama between the two resurfaced. Due to their domestic disputes, my ole man and I went head-on many days, because I did not agree with him abusing my ole lady, verbally or physically. In fact, I can recall striking my ole man on several occasions the instant he put his hand on my ole lady and eldest sibling.

One of the incidents that led to me striking my ole man was an argument that occurred between him and my eldest sibling, but it wasn't so much of the verbal dispute between the two that grabbed my attention; it was the tone of my eldest sibling's voice as she yelled out, "Lo Mann!" In that moment, I immediately girded up my loins to see what the ruckus was about, and the second I stepped out of my bedroom into the hallway, I witnessed my ole man grabbing my eldest sibling by the neck, choking her. At that point, I politely asked my ole man to quit putting his hands on her, and in response, he said, "You better take your behind back in the room before I tear your ass up next."

As my ole man proceeded to choke my eldest sibling, I again asked him to stop, and for the second time, he replied, "Boy, you better take your ass in that room." Once I realized that my ole man wasn't letting up on her, I snapped, and in that split second, I struck him in the eye. The instant I struck my ole man in the eye, he paused and stood there for a moment, fiercely staring me in the eyes—then he vanished. If I didn't know any better, I would say that my ole man was contemplating whether he should have put his foot in my rear end or not; what say ye?

Within our household, there were many disputes between both my parents, verbal or physical, that led to criminal domestic violence.

And the arguments that my parents would have were the same as the others. Any time my parents had a dispute, I always prepared myself for the worst, because I knew what arguing could lead to between the two. For example, if I was in the same room as my parents during their dispute, I stood by my ole lady just in case things got violent. In fact, if I was in another room, I went to where they were, and did the same thing.

One night while in the kitchen, my parents got in a verbal dispute, then seconds later my ole man threw an object at my ole lady, forcing her to take cover. In return, my ole lady threw a cordless phone at him, forcing him to take cover as well. As my ole man got up from ducking, he began walking towards her, enraged and cussing like a mad man. Once my ole man got in arm's reach of her, he immediately extended his arms and grabbed her. I said, "Get your hands off my mama!" He then replied, "Get your behind out here." My ole lady looked at me and said, "Go head in the room. I'm all right." But I refused to budge.

Despite my efforts to try and break up the fight, both of my parents did not listen, so I took matters into my own hands. Before I knew it, I jumped in between the two, and swung on my ole man. Immediately, he and I began brawling. During our dispute, my ole lady was trying to break us up, yelling out "Stop!" repeatedly, but he and I paid her no attention; in fact, I kept swinging recklessly at him as he slung me to and fro, trying to gain control. Ultimately my ole lady broke up the fight, then sat me down in the living area and began asking me questions.

"What's wrong with you? Why did you do that?"

I replied, "'Cause he put his hand on you."

"Don't I always tell y'all, 'Honor thy mother and thy father, and thy days may be long upon the land.'"

After I answered her questions, she went on to say, "That is your father, and you are to respect him, even if he does something you do not agree with, because you are the child, and he is the adult."

During that lecture, my ole man added his two cents, considering he was still upset with me, so I kept my mouth closed as both of my parents spoke. With all things considered, my parents weren't telling me anything wrong, but I did not want to hear anything they had to say, because neither one of them were practicing what they preached. As the days went by, I continued to misbehave at home, as well as school. In addition to that, disputes between me and my ole man continued, either because of arguments he'd have with my ole lady and eldest sibling, or my mischievous acts.

As for school, I unfortunately had to attend summer school due to my behavioral issues and lack of cooperation in terms of not completing classwork or homework assignments.

CHAPTER 6

It was now the summer of 1997, and as you know, this summer was a little different than the other summers, considering I had to attend summer school. On top of that, I also partook in activities that I shouldn't have been, because a.) I was underage; b.) It was not the right thing to do; and c.) It led to the path of destruction.

Prior to getting enrolled in summer school, I, of course, was lectured by my parents, who said, "It does not make sense for us to pay seventy-five dollars for summer school, when you had four quarters to get an education for free. Then they went on to say that it would be their first and last time paying for summer school. "In fact," they said, "if you flunk again, you have to repeat the same grade until you get it together." Ultimately, I began attending summer school at Ronald E Mcnair Elementary School, Monday through Thursday, I believe along with three classmates with whom I attended school. Despite having to attend school over summer, I still enjoyed my break, partaking in extracurricular activities after school and over the weekend.

During that time, I was at the age where I wanted to experience new things that neither my parents nor God would have approved, so I did. I made the choice to have sex, smoke marijuana, drink alcohol, and hang out with drug dealers. At the time, I was only eleven years of age. I grew up without an older brother, and my ole man was not much of a role model, so I looked up to my older cousins and peers who were in the streets. Now that I am older, and able to reflect on the activities that my cousins and peers partook in, I have come to realize that they were far from role models. But they were cool— they were living the life that I desired to live, and they were showing me love that I failed to acknowledge I was already getting from my ole man, despite his flaws. So I followed their lead.

Granted, they participated in activities I chose not to involve myself in, but for the most part, I willingly followed their footsteps. For years, my parents were clueless about the activities in which I engaged myself, due to their work schedules, and the freedom I gained at a specific relative's house. But the time ultimately came where the truth unfolded, and I could no longer stay under the radar. In the course of time, I completed the summer school course, passing both subjects with an eighty-five average, and I got promoted to the sixth grade. After completing the summer school course, my parents congratulated me, stating how proud they were of me. Then they said that now I'd been promoted to sixth grade, I needed to be more attentive; I was entering middle school, and that was a whole new arena. As time kept winding down for the summer, I proceeded to enjoy my break, but eventually school started back, and I began my sixth grade year at Brentwood Middle School.

At the beginning of the year, things were great; the teachers were easy to get along with, and so were my classmates. As for my academics and behavior, they both were excellent; in fact, I was completing classwork and homework assignments, participating in class activities, and being attentive, respectful, and obedient. Truth be told, if you would have entered into any of my classes, you would have thought I was an angel—I was shocked and appalled at my behavior, and how well I was doing.

As hard as I tried to put my best foot forward, and do the right thing, I went astray in terms of my behavior. I also bumped heads with a student and the assistant principal. The story behind the incident that occurred was senseless. Let me explain. One day, this gentleman with whom I attended gym class wanted to confront me about a damsel he was courting at the time. In all honesty, I barely spoke to either of them. The most I ever said was "What's up?" However, one day the young lady was eyeballing me seductively, so I did the same in return. Days after, she approached me and said, "Oh, can't speak?" So I said, "What's up?" in response to her question. She and I conversated briefly, then exchanged numbers, and later that night I gave her a call.

As we had a casual conversation, I questioned her about the status of her relationship with the gentlemen she was courting. The young lady replied that she and the gentleman were no longer dating. She said, "I don't know why he is telling y'all that we still talk, when we don't." Further into our conversation, she informed me about him contacting her after school, inquiring about what was going on between me and her. She told me the gentleman had said he was going to roll on me the following day at school. Immediately, I chuckled at the gentleman's threat, then I told her she better get her lil boyfriend before he got beat on.

Without question, the gentleman confronted me that following day in our gym class. A partner of mine called me into the bathroom stall, and that was where I was confronted—but the gentleman wasn't there by himself; he brought an entourage. As soon as I entered the bathroom stall, the gentleman asked, "You talking to my gal?" Without hesitation, I replied, "Yeah." Then the gentleman said, "Leave my girl alone." In response to his demand, I said, "For one, that ain't yo gal. Two, if you got a problem with us conversating, you need to check her, not me."

Out of nowhere, the gentleman struck me in the nose, so I immediately grabbed him by the neck and arm, then pinned him against the wall.

As I held the gentleman against the wall, I repeatedly asked, "Do you quit?" He replied, "Yeah," but as I was letting up, someone snuck me from behind and put me in a choke hold. Once he got a good grip, he tried to toss me on the floor as he and I tussled. After brawling with this unknown individual, I eventually landed on the floor, and in that split second, the rest of the gentleman's entourage jumped in. Once I was able to see who'd put me in a chokehold, I noticed it was a friend of mine; in fact, it was the same individual who'd called me into the bathroom stall. In addition to putting me in a chokehold, this friend of mine, along with the others, jumped me. They didn't attack me for long, because another partner of mine entered the bathroom stall in the nick of time.

As my partner broke up the fight, he was enraged, saying, "Get off dat man! It don't take all y'all to fight one man." The instant the other partner of mine stood in my defense, the gentleman and his entourage let up, and thanks to that same partner, there were no bodily injuries other than epistaxis, also known as nose bleeds. Truth be told, I saw no signs of epistaxis while I was in the gym bathroom stall; in fact, my nose did not start draining until I exited the gym, but I still was unaware of it until I encountered my first period teacher.

The moment I left the gym, I fled to the school's hallway, where I ran into my teacher, who frantically asked, "Why is your nose bleeding? What happened?" I informed her about the fight, stating, "I got jumped by a group of students." My teacher immediately began interrogating me. "Who was behind the attack?" Due to my stubbornness, I failed to cooperate with the teacher, principal, and administrators, but they got to the bottom of it the moment they searched their files and saw the class I was attending that period.

Without delay, the teacher said, "Any time something like this happens, you need to inform a teacher or an administrator, instead of walking out of the classroom, because if you do not, you could get yourself into a lot of trouble."

After speaking with the teacher, the principal found out what was going on, and got involved. Unfortunately, I, the victim, was issued a three-day suspension because it was my word against the gentleman's word. Once the school contacted my parents, I was sent home, so my ole lady came to pick me up. When my ole lady came to the school, I explained to her what happened, considering that she'd already spoken with the teachers and administrators. After I'd explained what happened, she wasn't upset or anything; she understood. In fact, she said, "Try to stay away from that crowd, and so-called friend of yours who was involved."

Later that day, my ole man and I discussed the incident, and he basically told me the same thing my ole lady had said, so I served my three-day suspension in peace. During that three-day suspension, I got my mind right a tad bit in terms of making wise decisions, and I can assure you that I kept my distance from the so-called friend of mine. Throughout the rest of my sixth grade year in 1998, things were looking up for me. My grades were up to par, and my behavior was outstanding, but days before school was out, I landed myself in some trouble that led to expulsion. Brace yourself, because the information I'm about to share with you is a low down dirty shame.

During the last days of school a classmate whose locker was next to mine said, "I got something to show you," and asked me to come a little closer. As I approached him, he pulled out a magazine that contained content of an explicitly sexual nature. Being that I was visually drawn to the images, I grabbed the magazine and began flipping through the pages. In the act of browsing, I was unaware that the teacher was walking towards me and my classmate. By the time the teacher crept up between us, he and I were caught red-handed. Allow me to rephrase that—I was caught red handed with the magazine in my possession.

Straightaway, the teacher asked, "What are you guys looking at?" but the classmate and I did not respond. Then she said, "Hand it over. Let me see what you guys are looking at."

As much as I did not want to hand over the magazine, I gave it to the teacher anyhow, and boy, was she infuriated.

"Where did you guys get this?" she said. "And who does it belong to?"

Initially, the classmate and I glanced at one another, then I replied, "It's mine." Before I could blink my eyes, I was escorted to the principal's office, and without question, I was expelled. On the last day of school, I came back to pick up my report card, and the instant I opened it I learned that I'd been promoted to the seventh grade. Truth be told, I thought I'd blown it, considering the expulsion, but looking at those grades, and the bottom statement saying I was promoted to the seventh grade, was a relief.

CHAPTER 7

After that troublesome year, the summer of '98 had arrived, and I was estatic because we finally got a break from school, which was much needed. In the summer of '98, I became more adventurous when it came to being in the streets. I began running the streets more often that summer than any others. Any time I camped at my aunt and uncle's house, I was afforded the freedom that wasn't permitted in my parents' household. For example, in my aunt and uncle's household, my cousin had the liberty to come and go as he pleased. In fact, there were times when he and I hung out during the wee hours of the morning, and camped at other relatives' or peers' houses without them inquiring our whereabouts. On the nights I camped at my aunt's house, my cousin and I ran the streets from dawn till dusk, smoking marijuana and drinking alcohol.

In addition, my cousin and I hung in the Wildwood community on Eagle Drive in North Charleston at a partner of ours' granny's house, along with several others partaking in those same activities. He and I were also messing around with the damsels either in that same community, Northwoods Mall, and/or Walmart. During that summer, there were some positive activities that my cousin and I engaged in, such as fishing, hunting, and gardening. This cousin

I'm referring to, I looked up to him as a big brother. In fact, he was one out of the two whom I looked up to as big brothers. Like I have mentioned before, I didn't do everything my cousin did, but I have done most of what he did.

I had no experience engaging in the activities my cousin introduced me to, so he actually took time out and taught me how to fish, hunt, and plant. On the days my cousin and I engaged in outdoor activities, he and I were at nearby locations within the community. In fact, whenever my cousin and I went fishing, it was at a local pond several feet away from an immediate relative's home. If my cousin and I went hunting, it was in the wooded area that surrounded our home, which wasn't legal, because we lived outside of the South Carolina Department of Natural Resources game zones. Whenever my cousin and I planted, it would be in our yard, because our grandfather left acres of land behind.

I enjoyed every moment of those activities, because I was being taught something new by someone whom I looked up to. Although inexperienced, I caught on quickly with hunting and gardening, but fishing was a tad bit difficult. The issue I struggled with was casting out my line. Every time I made an attempt to cast my line, I failed miserably, either because the line went a short distance, or it would wrap around the fishing rod. After several failed attempts, however, my cousin, who stood by, took notice and said I was releasing the sinker too soon. He again sat down his rod and demonstrated how to cast my line, but I still was having difficulties. My cousin thought it was in my best interest for him to cast it out for me, and then for me to reel it back in. Although I caught nothing, you couldn't tell me I wasn't one of the best darn fisherman there is. Despite some of what my cousin and I did, that summer was fun. I enjoyed the time I spent with my cousin, and I appreciate what he taught me; we had a blast.

As the summer break was coming to an end, my parents hit me with some news—some unexpected news, I should say. There was talk about my parents sending me to live with my grandparents. It was said that due to my disruptive behavior at Brentwood Middle, I would no longer be attending that school. I would be transferring to Alice Birney Middle School, since I was moving in with my grandparents. The reason my parents sent me to live with my grandparents is because my grandfather was a strict disciplinarian; they figured if I was under my grandparents' care, I wouldn't misbehave. Truth be told, I, too, thought my grandfather would have been strict, but he wasn't; he was more lenient on me than I expected. In fact, I was allowed to do whatever I wanted, as long as I respected my grandparents and abided by their rules.

When my parents told me I was moving, I didn't want to leave because I had already gotten adjusted to the school I was attending, but I didn't trip. I said okay, and left it at that. Soon after that conversation, I ended up moving to my grandparents' house the day before school started. As suspected, my parents gave me another lecture about school, my behavior, grades, and listening to my grandparents, so I kept my mouth closed and listened to them as they got everything off their chests.

The summer of '98 was over, and we were now back in the classroom doing it all over again. I was now attending Alice Birney Middle School, just as my parents had said. When school started back, I didn't feel strange or anything, because I was surrounded by loved ones and childhood peers. Although I was surrounded by them, I still got myself acquainted with the teachers, administrators, and new friends. One of my new friends was a female who ultimately became a good friend over the years, due to an unexpected incident that occurred in my life. As I reflect on the olden days at Alice

Birney Middle School, I'm reminded of how this young lady and I became acquainted.

The connection between me and my newfound lady friend stemmed from a conversation about damsels that ultimately led to a wager between me and my partner. Outside of school, my partner and I linked up at his place, where I camped for a weekend. During that stay, however, is when the conversation and wager between my partner and I emerged. The wager we made was more like a competition, versus a bet, because he and I both were competing to see who could collect the most phone numbers, and that included two of the most attractive and popular damsels of the school.

With all things considered, I accepted the challenge, and soon my partner and I arrived back to school, and the competition began. As we competed, I ultimately approached one of the most attractive and popular damsels of the school, which happened to be my newfound lady friend. The instant I approached her I said, "Hey, girl, what yo name is?" She told me her name in response, and then I said, "I can holler at you?" Straightaway, she said, "Can you holler at me?" She then asked, "And what is your name?" As soon as I told her my name, she laughed in my face, then walked off, giggling amongst her peers.

By the end of the day, my partner and I tallied up the numbers that he and I had collected, and I'd gotten the most, but unfortunately, I lost the bet due to a technicality—my inability to collect my newfound lady friend's number. We'd said, "In addition to collecting the most numbers, both components must individually collect the numbers from two of the most attractive and popular damsels of the school in order to win the bet." Because I failed to deliver, I lost.

Within that same week, however, a friend of my newfound lady friend approached me with a paper saying, "Hey, boy, she told me to give you this." What do ya know, I received the golden ticket to the chocolate factory. Although I initially lost the bet, I still say that I am the ultimate winner, simply because my newfound lady friend doubled back and gave me her number.

As I proceeded to adjust to the new environment I was in, everything was going good for me; my behavior was excellent, and my grades were outstanding. I was doing everything that I was supposed to do. I even completed homework assignments, which is something I never did much of throughout my years in school. When I was living with my parents, I would lie about completing my homework assignments, that way I wouldn't have to do them, and would be able to run the streets. However, when I moved in with my grandparents, I did the total opposite; my grandparents had no problems out of me. We got along just fine. Once I'd come home from school, and had done everything I was supposed to do, my grandparents allowed me to go outside.

Whenever I would go outside, I sometimes hung in the community where they lived, or I would hang in other communities. Before I got to my destination, I sometimes made a stop that was along the way. The stop that I made was at Miss Brown's house, which is the mother of my little brother Trey). Trey is my biological sibling I mentioned in the beginning of chapter one along with our youngest sibling Jasmine. Back in 1993, my ole man, who was then separated from my ole lady, fathered my youngest siblings with both my ole lady and Miss Brown, but my eldest sibling and I, who were between the ages of eight and ten, had no clue about the matter. In fact, we weren't informed about having another sibling until 1996 or '97. When we learned about having another younger sibling, neither one of us had an issue with it, especially me, because I always wanted a little brother.

Shortly after breaking the ice, my parents sometimes took me and my eldest sibling to see our brother, but my ole man wasn't too fond of that. The reason my ole man had an issue with it was because he was in denial. He truly believed there was a possibility that our brother wasn't his child. As crazy as this may sound, my ole lady was the one who was there for my little brother—and I'm not going off hearsay, I'm going off what I witnessed. For example, there were times when my ole lady purchased clothing for my little brother and took it to him. Whenever his birthday came around, she always gave him something. My ole lady also gave my little brother money whenever he did good in school academically. Truth be told, there was nothing my little brother couldn't get from my ole lady; she always treated him as if he was one of her own. When I saw my little brother for the first time, I told my ole man right then, "That's my brother. He looks like you, especially when you drunk." In response, my ole man looked at me, then laughed and told me to get out of his face. Being that the genetics between my ole man and little brother were that strong, I told him, "If you take a paternity test, it's going to say you are the father." He proceeded to laugh, and once again, said, "Get out my face."

If you think the information I just gave you is crazy, get a load of this. Aside from my ole man fathering a child with another woman, my two youngest siblings were born in the same year, three to four weeks apart. In fact, my little brother was born in the first week of November, and my little sis was born in the first week of December, so in the words of the Temptations, I guess "Papa was a rolling stone." On the days I stopped to speak with my brother, there was no question that he knew who I was; in fact, he and I always got excited every time we encountered one another. Every time I saw my little brother, who was only four years of age, he always greeted me saying "What's up, punk nigga?" Then he would ask me for a dollar to go to the candy store.

After speaking with him, I would mosey on down the road to a damsel's house and/or the community center where my partners were. Once I was done hanging out with the damsel and/or my peers, I went home for the night to prepare myself for school the following day. During the first quarter of the academic school term, I proceeded to do all that I was required at home, as well as in school, both in terms of academics and my behavior. My grandparents had no trouble out of me at all.

As the end of the year approached, all students got a two-week break for the Christmas holiday. During our break, I traveled back and forth between the homes of my grandparents, parents, and other relatives, enjoying my break until it was over. On the eve of Christmas, I stationed myself at my parents' house to spend Christmas with them and my sisters. Within hours, Christmas Eve turned into Christmas Day, and me and my sisters had gotten a number of items we'd asked for, and were under the tree opening our gifts. Truth be told, every Christmas, my ole lady made sure my sisters and I always got a number of items we asked for, if not all.

As I reflect on the Christmas holidays in my parents' household, there were times when my ole lady said she wouldn't be able to purchase anything for us for Christmas. In fact, she would tell me and my eldest sibling that we had to wait until she got her tax refund because she didn't have the funds. Although my ole lady was pulling the wool over our eyes, she still made ends meet, and I later found out why. The reason my ole lady made sure my sisters and I had a good Christmas is because she knew how it felt to wake up on Christmas morning to nothing. She said the only thing she and her siblings woke up to on Christmas morning was a stocking full of candy and fruit. They never got toys, bikes, or any gifts that children generally get. She said she would carefully cut doll babies out of a magazine and play with them, because that was the closest she could get to a doll. When my ole lady told me that, I felt bad, and I wanted to cry, because as hard as she worked on two jobs to take care of me and my sisters, all I brought was emotional distress and pain, which was something she didn't, and still doesn't, deserve. Although Christmas is about the birth of Christ, I still feel like a child shouldn't have to wake up on Christmas morning to nothing, especially since the world made the Christmas holiday the season of giving.

Like I said, my sisters and I had a good Christmas, and I enjoyed spending time with my family. I also enjoyed spending the New Year with my family, considering that I didn't go back to my grandparents' house immediately after Christmas. As always, me, my ole lady, and my sisters attended watch night service on New Year's Eve to start the year off right. Once the new year, 1999, came in, my ole lady dropped me off at my grandparents' house for school, then she went back home to prepare herself for work.

As time went by, I began falling off in school once we came back from our Christmas break. In fact, I started misbehaving again and doing bad academically. I stopped completing homework assignments and I slowed down on classwork assignments. I also started disrupting the class again by being a talkative class clown. Due to my actions, my grades began to decline, and I started to receive consequences, like in-school suspension, out-of-school suspension, and parent-teacher conferences.

In light of me being under my grandparents' supervision, my parents left it up to them to take action in terms of punishment. All my grandfather did was talk to me, but my grandmother was the one doing the disciplining. In fact, I can recall an incident when my grandmother disciplined me. On the day this incident occurred, I was at school. Due to my disruptiveness, the teacher order that I go to in-school suspension, but I refused to do so. I told the teacher, "Take me to my granny. She work in the cafeteria." As a result, the teacher had the officer escort me to my grandmother since I wasn't cooperating.

When the officer and I got into the cafeteria, he took me and my grandmother into a private room. Once we'd entered, the officer explained to my grandmother what was going on. Within that split second, my grandmother didn't ask me any questions; she turned in my direction and pimp-slapped me three times. After my grandmother slapped me three times, she then turned towards the officer and said, "And you ain't see shit." In response, the officer said, "Oh no, ma'am. No, ma'am." Then she turned back towards me and said, "You better take your shittin' ass back in the classroom, and do what those teachers tell you to do. If they have to come and get me again, I'ma tear your ass up in front of the class." Then she turned back to the officer and said, "You can take me to jail. I don't give a shit."

While my grandmother was talking, I didn't say anything, because I was stunned she'd hit me like that. After that slap, the teachers didn't have any more problems out of me for the rest of the day. While I was misbehaving, and not focusing, time flew by. And before I knew it, school was out and I had flunked the seventh grade. When my parents found out, they told me straight up that they weren't paying for summer school, because I had four quarters to get a free education. They also told me that if I didn't get my education in that timeframe, that was on me; I just had to repeat the same grade again until I got it together.

CHAPTER 8

Year-in and year out, I kept myself busy, so much so that my itinerary was always booked, mainly in the summer. As for the summer of 1999, it was the same as the summer of '97 and '98, except for two things: I landed a gig, and the problems in my parents' household got worse. The gig I had, I landed from a longtime friend of the family, Mrs. Dot. Mrs. Dot, my grandmother's best friend, had a soul food shop (kitchen) that was located in the Union Heights community in North Charleston that she independently owned and ran for years. One day as I accompanied my grandmother at work, I sat there observing her, Mrs. Dot, and the other employee work their butts off, and Mrs. Dot asked me, "Lo Mann, how old are you?"

"Thirteen," I said.

"Do you want a job?"

"Yes, ma'am," I replied.

"If you come and wash dishes for me, I'll pay you thirty dollars a day."

"Okay."

So the next day I started working for Mrs. Dot. Because she had customers trafficking in and out like clockwork, I washed dishes from the time I clocked in until the time I clocked out. With Mrs.

Dot serving delightful dinner plates at a convenient location, she had truckers, longshoreman, construction workers, etc. coming in and purchasing more than one meal at a time. Having customers come in like clockwork was an everyday thing for the shop; they never moved slow when I was there. Although I was assigned to a simple task, I had fun, and I appreciated it because it paid my pager bill, kept change in my pocket, and kept me out of trouble for several hours.

Around the time I became employed by Mrs. Dot, the drama at my parents' place proceeded to get worse. Due to my ole man not assisting financially, my family slipped back into hard times, because, again, my ole man gave what he thought was reasonable, if anything at all. Keep in mind that my parents had trailer note, lot rent, car note, car insurance, utilities, and three children. With my ole lady managing everything on her own, it was difficult for her to pay those bills on time, and as a result, several of our services had to be terminated. Our lights and water got shut off. My ole lady made a sound decision to return her car back to the dealership because she could no longer take on the payment. Not only that, my parents were backed up on their trailer note as well, all because my ole man wasn't holding up his end of the bargain. As I recalled, the drama that occurred in our old home was supposed to cease before moving into our new home, which it did, but I guess some things just don't change.

The drama that proceeded to get worse went on throughout the remainder of the summer; it continued around the time school started back. While we are on the subject of school, let's talk about school. Here I am, sitting here talking about my ole man, and how he wasn't holding up his end of the bargain, knowing that I wasn't holding up my end of the bargain either as far as my behavior and academics. During the first quarter of school, I started off misbehaving, so much so that I was not completing classwork or homework assignments. Instead of completing them, I was at the back of the class with my cousin gambling (flipping quarters) with a classmate of ours, disrupting class. And rather than going home and completing my homework assignments, I lied to my grandparents about doing so, so I could run the streets.

In the course of time, however, I began to spiral out of control to the point where my grandparents, parents, and teachers tried everything in their power to keep me out of trouble, but nothing worked. In fact, I can recall this teacher with whom I had a teacher-student relationship, named Miss Ripke, blessing me with an opportunity to come aboard the school hall monitor team, but unfortunately that opportunity was short-lived. After several failed attempts to keep me out of trouble, Alice Birney Middle School suspended me until further notice. Consequently, Alice Birney Middle School contacted my parents to inform them about their decision to put me up for expulsion due to my behavior. In addition, the school told my grandparents and parents that I would have to go in front of the school board for a hearing. They also said that the school board would notify us as to when and where the hearing would be.

When the school board contacted my parents, they scheduled us a morning hearing. Once my grandparents, parents, and I got to the hearing, the school board gave us a rundown on my academics and behavior report. After giving a rundown on my academic and behavior report, the school board made their decision. Instead of putting me out of school for the remainder of the year, they said, "We've decided to transfer Mr. Manigault to Charleston County Discipline School, which is an alternative education program for misbehaving students." Before the school board finalized their decision, they asked my grandparents and parents if they were all in agreeance. They all said yes, so Charleston County Discipline School was where I went.

In the month of January 2000 I began attending the Charleston County Discipline School. Prior to attending, we'd had orientation. In orientation the discipline school staff members explained to students and parents the rules and regulations, the dress code, what the school was about, and what they expected of us, the students. In the discipline school there were teachers, and there were instructors. The thing that separated the instructors from the teachers was their backgrounds. For example, the teachers we had were your everyday academic teachers, but the instructors were men and women who'd served in the armed forces. I'm talking about an ex-Marine, Navy SEAL, etc., so you can imagine how they dealt with us.

On the first day of school, the other recruits and I were assigned to this insane boot camp instructor name Mr. Drayton. Mr. Drayton, who was an ex-Marine, told us that being newcomers, we had to complete two weeks of boot camp with him before starting our academic classes. The two weeks of boot camp consisted of learning rules and regulations, physical training, and introducing ourselves and getting to know one another. Every morning after breakfast, Mr. Drayton had us doing PT, performing push-ups, jumping jacks, and sit-ups. He also had us walking around the school premises carrying heavy logs on our shoulders, two men to a log. Within those two weeks of boot camp, Mr. Drayton taught us how to march, how to do command voice, general principles, and command drill commands. He also taught us to address the teachers and instructors with "Yes, sir" and "Yes, ma'am" at all times.

As I reflect on the lessons Mr. Drayton taught us, I can recall him saying, "All for one, and one for all," meaning each individual should act for the benefit of the group, and the group should act for the benefit of each individual. I can also recall him saying this as well: "Expect the unexpected," meaning to not be surprised by an unusual event, because anything can happen, and probably will. Every time Mr. Drayton made these statements, he had an evil-but-pleasant grin on his face. In light of the lessons he taught us, it's evident that he incorporated the lessons he'd learned in the Marines into our school.

As far as discipline was concerned, Mr. Drayton had many ways of disciplining us. For example, if we did something we weren't supposed to do, Mr. Drayton would order us to perform a certain repetition of his choice of exercises. However, if he felt like having a little fun, he would make us do something we all hated, which was go in the mud pit. On the side of the school, Mr. Drayton had a mud pit that was at least twenty feet in length and ninety-plus inches in width. Any time one of us did something to piss Mr. Drayton off, he made all of us go in the mud pit. In fact, he would call the other students who were there before us to water the pit and get it ready. While watering the pit, the other students laughed and shook their heads at us as they explained what was about to happen based on their personal experiences. Once they were finished watering the pit, it was on. Mr. Drayton held no punches; we all went down, male and female.

In the beginning of suffering this punishment, there were a couple of knuckleheads who didn't want to cooperate, but after several warnings, they got their acts together. The very first thing Mr. Drayton ordered us to do the instant we got in the mud pit, was lie down on our stomachs. Once we were on our stomachs, Mr. Drayton went berserk; he literally had us rolling, crawling, and marching in the mud pit. As we rolled in the mud pit, I can recall Mr. Drayton yelling, laughing, and calling us a bunch of cocksuckers, treating us as if we were in the armed forces. I can also recall one of the other instructors named Mr. Miller coming to the mud pit, laughing as well, like he had room to trip, considering he came to school every-day wearing black army boots that were laced to the top, tight black cargo pants, a tight black T-shirt, black Avatar-style shades, and a dried-up Jheri curl that was slick to the back, looking like a black Ronald McDonald.

Truth be told, Mr. Drayton had us upset with him for tossing us in the mud pit, and the other recruits, including me, found nothing funny about being smothered in mud. Out of all the things Mr. Drayton could have done, he chose to toss us in the mud pit. Then, to add insult to injury, he forced us to walk around the school for the remainder of that day covered in mud. All boot camp recruits, including me, interacted with one another, and rode the bus home, covered in mud. In those two weeks of boot camp Mr. Drayton held no punches; in fact, he warned us beforehand to not get comfortable, but we were the ones who took him for a joke. Shame on us.

Once we'd completed our two weeks of boot camp, all of us were happy and relieved that we'd completed the task; we were also ecstatic about not having to deal with Mr. Drayton anymore—so we thought. "Although you are no longer in boot camp," said Mr. Drayton, "the same rules still apply. If any of you give the teachers, and/or instructors, any problems, I'm going to deal with you person-ally—and you don't want that. Now go learn something and make me proud."

After completing two weeks of boot camp, we immediately start-ed our academic classes. The academic classes we had were the regu-lar math, science, social studies, and language arts subjects, and were taught by teachers named J. Burwell, K. Reddish, L. Berg, and F. Cunningham. However, the special area classes we had were a tad bit different. Unlike the other schools, we didn't have the regular special area classes, such as gym and music. Ours were life skills, character education, carpentry, and horticulture. They were taught by the other instructors, Mrs. Simmons, Mr. Scott, Mr. Washington, and Mr. Miller. There were only two of those classes that everyone, including me, liked the most: workshop and horticulture.

In the workshop class we were taught by Mr. Washington—a.k.a. Donkey Kong—how to cut, carve, and sand wood. He also taught us how to paint and stain our carvings. Once we got the hang of creating hand crafts, we were on our own; Mr. Washington allowed us to create whatever we wanted, as long as we followed his directions.

Aside from workshop, horticulture was the funnest to me, because we were able to do what I knew and liked to do, planting and landscaping. Our horticulture instructor, Mr. Miller, had two gardens, a greenhouse, and a shed in the back of the school. One of the gardens was filled with vegetables, and the other was filled with fruits (watermelon). The greenhouse he had was filled with plants, and the shed was filled with gardening and landscaping tools. When it came to gardening and landscaping, Mr. Miller knew all about it. He taught most of us students how to plant and landscape, although I was already experienced. He taught us how to till the soil, set up the rows, sow the seed, and nourish the plants. I can also remember Mr. Miller kneeling down, teaching us step by step how to plant, as we all stood around eager to learn. After he showed us the steps, he then gave us the opportunity to plant on our own while standing nearby observing just in case we needed his assistance. Mr. Miller taught us well. Allow me to give you an example of how well he taught us.

One of the male students who graduated from the Charleston County Discipline School took what Mr. Miller taught us and started his own garden at home. Instead of the gentlemen planting fruit or flowers of some sort, he chose to plant marijuana. Once the gentleman reaped what he sowed, he took the herb that was grown and started distributing it in school. Unfortunately for the gentleman, one thing led to another, and he got caught. According to the gentleman with whom I attended the Charleston County Discipline School, he put his partner on, and no sooner had he put the friend on, than the friend got caught up and broke the code of silence (omerta). In fact, the gentleman's partner told the authorities about everything, including the garden. Once the authorities did a thorough investigation, and collected all the evidence they needed, they took action on the gentlemen. The school that the gentleman was attending at the time expelled him, then they sent him back to the Charleston County Discipline School the same year that he graduated.

When Mr. Miller saw the gentleman, the first thing he did was grab him by the back of his neck and asked him, "Boy, what were you thinking?" The gentleman didn't respond. Mr. Miller then said, "I didn't show you how to plant so you could grow weed. I showed you how to plant so you can grow fruits and vegetation, something healthy and edible, not something you could get high off of. Now look at you, you are back in here again."

The moment Mr. Miller said that, the gentleman laughed and replied, "I don't care. I wanted to come back. It's fun." Instantaneously, Mr. Miller looked at him like, "Is this nigga serious?" Then he said, "Boy, get back in line."

Now how crazy is that? The gentleman actually took what Mr. Miller taught us about gardening and grew an illegal herb garden; I guess the gentleman said to himself, "If the farmers can grow produce and make a profit, then I can grow herb and make a profit as well."

During our horticulture class, Mr. Miller kept us active by keeping up the maintenance on the lawn, the parking lot, and the mini pond. Aside from that, Mr. Miller and the other instructors also had us assisting Habitat for Humanity building homes in downtown Charleston. Although I said what I said about Mr. Miller and the other instructors, there was no harm intended; in fact, they are some of the most kind-hearted people that I have ever met, who treated us as if we were their own, especially Mr. Drayton, considering he was the sternest instructor of them all.

As I reflect on the instructors being strict with us, I realize that they only wanted what was best for us; their goal was to help us get our acts together, and shape and mold us into young men and women by teaching us discipline, respect, honor, and integrity. Even though I didn't take heed to the wisdom and knowledge that was given to me at that time, I'm thankful, grateful, and appreciative of it. Believe it or not, I'm actually taking what I was taught at that time and now applying it to my everyday life. For the nine months I was attending the Charleston County Discipline School, I always respected the teachers, instructors, and students. As for my grades, I kept them up, and my behavior was good, except for one problem I got suspended for once. The suspension that I received didn't come from me misbehaving, it came from me not wanting to degrade myself, which I'll explain.

On the day I got suspended, several other students and I were standing in the hallway waiting on one of our instructors. Unlike the other students, I was standing in the doorway with both of my hands gripping the hinges. As I stood there gripping the hinges of the door, the principal was walking towards me. When she got closer, she asked, "Young man, what is your name?"

I replied, "Manigault."

"Why are you gripping the hinges of the door?"

"I don't know, ma'am."

"Say, 'Because I'm stupid, ma'am.'"

"I'm not stupid."

"Say, 'Yes, ma'am, I'm stupid.'"

"No, ma'am, if you want to call yourself stupid, be my guest, but I'm not calling myself stupid."

After the principal noticed I wasn't complying, she told me to either say "I'm stupid, ma'am," or take a one-day suspension, so she wrote a referral for a one-day suspension stating that I failed to comply.

Other than that, the Charleston County Discipline School had no problems out of me. I gave them no hassle. I came in the discipline school attending the seventh grade, and I left out promoted to the ninth grade just before Christmas break.

CHAPTER 9

What a wonderful year it was for me in the year 2000. I'd learned some valuable lessons, and gotten promoted to the ninth grade. Another year rolled in—2001, to be exact—and my family and I were no longer living in Trailwood trailer park anymore. My ole man went back to his parents' house, and me, my ole lady, and my siblings relocated to the home where my great-grandfather's offspring put us out of years back. I was now attending R.B. Stall High School with my eldest sibling, in North Charleston. I was fifteen years of age, with a lot of things on my mind. I had a secret that I hid from my ole lady that finally came into the light.

After going months and years without support from my ole man economically, my ole lady decided to let go of our mobile home. Truth be told, I thought our home got repossessed, but that was not the case. My ole lady felt like before she continued to carry the load by her lonesome, she would rather give our home back, and that is what she did. It is not like my ole man was unemployed, because he was not, he just stopped helping out economically. So my ole lady did what she felt was best. With her making a drastic decision such as this, it put my family in a position to relocate. My ole man moved back in with his parents, while we moved in with my grandfather, Robert Tindal, my ole lady's father.

My grandfather lived in the same home we had gotten evicted from years back, which was also the home we relocated to. Upon moving back into that home, there was a lot of renovating to do, but no funds to do it with, so my ole lady fixed the minor problems, which were the floor and electricity, in order to make the home suitable for us to live in. Although the problems were minor, we were still living in a messed-up circumstance; in fact, we spent our summer sitting in a hot house because we did not have the funds for a window unit, or central air and heat. In order to feel the breeze, we had to turn on the fan and open the front door until we got a window unit. Not only that, when the season changed in the winter, we had no heat. In order for us to get warm, we had to go to my grandfather's side of the house, where the pot belly stove was. Just in case you are unfamiliar with a pot belly stove, here it is.

A pot belly stove is a cast-iron wood-burning stove, round with a bulge in the middle. The name is derived from the resemblance of the stove to that of a fat man's pot belly. They were designed to heat large spaces, and were often found in train stations or one-room school houses. The flat top of the fireplace allowed for cooking of food, or the heating of water.

Once we got warm, we went back on our side of the house and bundled up in a bunch of covers to stay warm throughout the night. As for plumbing, we had no running water; in fact, when it came time for us to bathe and use the restroom, I would go and fill up six or more gallons of water from my uncle's pump so we would have water to use. What we did was take the water that I brought from the pump, put it in a pot, and heat it up on the stove. Once we did that, we then poured the water into a basin that my ole lady brought home from work, and that's how we bathed.

Now about the restroom issue—as crazy as this may sound, it is the truth: When it came time for us to use the restroom, whether a bowel movement or urinating, we used the restroom in a bucket. Once we got finished, we took it and dumped it in the woods nearby our home, then we rinsed the bucket out so we could reuse it again. There were times when we bathed, ate, and used the restroom at my grandparents' house. Then there were times when we handled our business at my uncle's house, but for the most part, we did everything within our household.

While living under those conditions, our Christmas break had already passed, and school already begun. The year 2001 was an exciting year for me because I was no longer attending middle school. I began attending high school, R.B. Stall High School, that is. When school started back, it was straight, because my eldest sibling and I were once again attending school together. During my first day attending Stall High School, I was cooling, trying to adapt to the new environment. While trying to adapt, something unexpected happened. I ran across a lady friend I'd met in middle school. Out of everyone I knew in Stall High School, she was the first person I saw.

At the time she and I encountered each other, we were heading to our classes. We never spoke; all we did was eyeball each other as we crossed paths. What makes it crazy is that she and I were the only two in the hallway at that time. Why did it happen like that? I have not a clue. It may have meant something, or it may not have meant anything, who knows. I guess I'll understand by and by. After I began to loosen up, I started talking to teachers and the students getting to know everyone I did not know. As far as my grades are concerned, I managed to keep them up, completing classwork and sometimes homework assignments. To tell the truth, I was on top of my game. I was not cutting class, nor was I cutting school. I was actually doing the right thing. For my parents to have two of their three children attending high school, trying to get an education, they were as happy as they wanted to be, especially my ole lady; it made her feel good.

Not too long after I began attending Stall High School, a secret that I hid from my ole lady finally came out in the open. One night, me, my ole lady, and two female siblings were sitting in the house. The two siblings were in the room; one was on the phone pillow talking, and the other was playing. Next to the bedroom where my two siblings were, my ole lady was sitting at the table, while I was in the living area watching television. As we all sat around doing our own thing, I heard my youngest sibling run to my ole lady and say, "Oh, mama, look. Look what I found."

When my younger sibling said that, I paid it no mind because I thought it was nothing.

My ole lady asked, "What is this? Where did you get this from?"

And she immediately replied, "Out the room."

Without hesitation, my ole lady then called my eldest sibling's name. "Kesia!"

When she came, my ole lady asked, "What is this?"

My eldest sibling played dumb and said, "Mama, I do not know."

Then my ole lady said, "If you know what this is, you need to tell me."

Again, my eldest sibling said, "Mama, I do not know."

That is when my ole lady called me, saying, "Mann, come here." I got up to see what she wanted. As I got closer and saw the reason my name was called, I said to myself, "Oh shit, damn, I done fucked up now."

Once I got to the table, she immediately asked, "Mann, who one is this?"

I said, "It's mine."

Then she asked, "What is it?"

I said, "Mama, you know what that is."

"Is this what you use to smoke a joint?" she asked.

I replied, "Yeah."

Then she asked, "Okay, now what is that?"

"Man, Mama, you know what that is."

"I do not know what that is. That is why I'm asking." Then she said, "I know this is not what I think it is. Please tell me this is not what I think it is."

Before my ole lady could say anything else or do something crazy, I immediately grabbed the dope off the table and told her, "You can have the herb, but I need this."

When I grabbed the dope, my ole lady continued to question me, asking, "What, and who one is it?"

I told her it was dope, and it was mine.

She said, "I know you are not selling drugs."

I said, "Yeah, I am selling it, I am not smoking it."

My ole lady continued to act as if it was a dream. The last thing I said to her was, "Well, now you know," and I left it at that. When she came to grips that I was dealing drugs, she broke out in tears like a newborn baby left in an unfamiliar environment. In fact, she started fussing at me with pain in her heart, saying, "I bust my ass on my job Monday through Friday, trying to make ends meet, and you out here selling drugs. I try my best to take care of y'all, give y'all what y'all need and want, and you selling drugs." She said, "You see how we living. I know it is not the best, but we making it by the grace of

God. Is it me?" she said. "Is it something I'm doing wrong?"—as if she was the problem, when she was not.

While my ole lady was sobbing in tears and fussing, my eldest sibling got emotional and began sobbing as well. She started saying to me, "Mann, why are you hurting my mama? You making her cry. You gotta go. You need to leave."

When my eldest sibling said that, I said to myself, "I cannot believe this shit. Ain't this 'bout a bitch!" I gave my eldest sibling anything she asked of me, and she flipped. While my ole lady and eldest sibling were fussing and sobbing in tears, I took one good look at them both, then I walked out. In that moment, I felt like they were not talking about anything I wanted to hear, so I left. At that time, I did not care about anything. I just did not give a fuck. I didn't care what anyone had to say, not my grandparents, my uncles, my aunts— no one—not even my ole man. In fact, when my ole lady informed my ole man about me selling drugs, he and I spoke briefly about the matter; however, as he and I talked, I was looking at him like "Nigga, you act like you are a just man, who is in right standing with God. Shut the fuck up, please."

That conversation did not last long; it was over before it began. Now that I am older, and I think back on how I have hurt my ole lady, I was wrong, and I regret it. I regret it for many reasons, and one of those reasons is because I broke her heart, which is something I cannot take back. Not to offend the state of New Orleans, but the damage Hurricane Katrina caused them is nothing compared to the emotional damage I caused my ole lady. That is why I regret it, and that is also why I am apologetic about it.

After my ole lady found out about my secret, I no longer hid anything. In fact, I began to get out of control as I promoted myself from being a part-time hustler to a full-time hustler. What I would do was go to school in the morning, then I would go to my job that I forgot to mention, at Cactus Car Wash located in North Charleston off of Rivers Avenue. After I got off from work, I went home, got myself straight, then hit the streets. Either I would post up by myself, or with several peers, sometimes on Stall Road, Midland Park, or Ward Avenue, which is the street I used to live on. I would grind out from evening until four or five o'clock that morning. Making easy money off of my cell phone that I purchased, knowing I had to be to school the following day. I quit the job I had at Cactus because this young lady was playing with my hours, and I felt like why stay, when I make what they give me every week off one phone call? Why? So I walked up to the boss and told him I quit.

Once I quit Cactus, I started dumbin, living life in the limelight. I started purchasing designer clothing, brand name sneakers, and jewelry. When I went to the mall to purchase something for myself or others, there were times when I spent nothing less than $500. I know $500 is not that much, but at that time, to me five hundred bucks was a lot. I purchased two motor vehicles; one was a gray, four-door '87 Pontiac, and the other was a black, four-door Crown Victoria. The Pontiac was my first car I purchased. When I purchased it, I did not drive it for long because it broke down on me. When the car broke down, I never got it fixed; I just left it as is. The Crown Victoria was my second car I purchased. I drove it for a while, then it broke on me. When that car broke down, I fixed it, then it broke down again. When that car broke down the second time, I said, "Forget it, I will purchase another one if I see one for sale."

When the car broke, it did not matter to me, because I was not a licensed driver anyway. Anyone who rode with me I informed them of not having a license or permit. I said, "If the man get behind me, I am hopping out, because I am riding dirty, so if you are not hopping out, you better not ride." As you can see, I was wide open, making money, living the fast life. Some of that money I was making I tried to share with my ole lady, but she did not accept it, saying, "I'm not taking any dirty money from you." I asked her, "When you go to the bank to cash your check do you think that money is clean? That may be dirty money. You don't know that." She said, "You are right, but God knows I work honestly for mine. If I take any money from you knowing you sell drugs, God is going to hold me accountable for that and I'm not going to hell for you."

Since my ole lady wouldn't take any money from me, I made sure my sisters were straight. Whatever they wanted, I gave them, but I did more for my eldest sibling, though, because my ole lady was tripping. As I think back on those days, I can remember my eldest sibling running game on me. For example, any time I told my eldest sibling I was not purchasing her anything, or giving her any funds, which was not often, she would pout and act like a baby. Any time my eldest sibling caught an attitude and started pouting, I would say to her, "Oh well, I do not care." Then I would walk away if I was in her presence. After having a conversation like that with my eldest sibling, I would feel bad.

All of that attitude and pouting, it worked every time. In fact, if my eldest sibling wanted sneakers or something out the mall, I would call and ask her what she wanted, or I would tell her I would give her the money when I got home. Whenever I came home with what my eldest sibling asked for, she would start smiling and say, "I love my brother," then I would reply, "Get out of my face. You ain't getting nuttin else." Now you would think after the first few times I would have stopped, but I did not. I guess I am a sucker; however, do not get it twisted. That only goes for the ones whom I deal with like that. If I do not deal with you like that, it is not going to happen.

When it comes to looking out for my family, peers, or strangers I have no problem with that. In no way am I trying to make myself sound like a kingpin, but to be honest with you, I have looked out for several people throughout my time in the streets, because that is how I am. Everything that I have just said, I have done it, including drinking alcohol, smoking marijuana, and fornicating. Am I proud of how I lived my life? No, I am not, but I am not ashamed of it either. For I confess that I am a man of many sins who was, and still is, lost, trying to find my way through life's journey.

Months after I began wilding out, I had a run-in with the law and I caught my first charge. One Friday, myself and three partners of mine were posted up at the Willow Lake Apartments off of Ward Avenue, which is the street I used to live on, smoking and serving. While we all were posting, a four-door Saturn with dark tint pulled up. When they pulled up, I looked towards the car through the windshield, and I noticed one of the gentlemen's T-shirts had Metro written on it. When I saw that, I said, " Hey yall boy, dat dem people," then I ran. When I ran, there were several officers who ran in pursuit of me; some officers were on foot, while others were in unmarked vehicles coming from both sides of the complex.

As I proceeded to run towards the gate I was going to jump, I stepped into a water puddle that was ahead of me. By me stepping into the water puddle, I was not successful with jumping the gate, so I surrendered. The moment I surrendered, the officers who were chasing me proceeded to grab me, saying, "Get down! Get down! Get on the ground!" Once the officers had me in their custody, they began the searching procedure, but only found two cell phones and a pager.

One of the officers who grabbed me put me in a headlock and began asking, "Where is the dope?"

I told him, "I do not have any dope."

He said, "I know you got some dope. Where is the dope?"

I repeated, "I do not have any dope."

He said, "Well why did you run?"

I replied, "Because I never had a run-in with law enforcement before. I was scared, and I did not know what to do, so I ran."

Once the officers found no dope on me, they walked me back to the front of the complex, where the other officers and my partners were. When we got back to the front of the complex, the other officers had my partners in the arrest position, questioning them, trying to figure out whose dope it was they'd found. When no one answered, one of the officers told one of my partners, since no one wanted to fess up, he was going to charge him. In response, my partner told the officer, "Go ahead, charge me," but before that went any further, I confessed and told the officer that it was my dope.

One of the other officers said, "Young man, what is your name, and how old are you?"

I replied, "Wendell, and I'm 15."

Then he said, "Young man, open your mouth."

As soon as I opened my mouth, the officer said, "You got gold in your mouth. I started to notify your parents and release you into their custody, but since you have gold in your mouth, I'm going to arrest you."

On that beautiful evening, I was arrested and charged with possession of crack cocaine in proximity of a school, and resisting arrest. The day I got locked up, the officer who arrested me took me to the Charleston County Detention Center for juveniles located on Headquarters Road off of Leeds Avenue in North Charleston. When I got to the detention center, there was a correctional officer awaiting my arrival for booking. From what I can remember, the booking procedure was a simple process. For example, the correctional officer recorded my name and the crime I was arrested for, then took mugshots and fingerprints. I then had to go through the searching procedure that is deeply humiliating. The correctional officer conducted a full-body search, which included a pat-down inspection and strip search.

At the start of performing the searching procedure, I was escorted to a private room where the correctional officer asked that I remove my clothing. Then he began to inspect each garment one at a time, running his finger over every seam to make sure nothing was sewn inside. Once completing that step, the search proceeded from top to bottom, and front to back, with the officer giving instructions on what to do. Generally during a searching procedure, the subjects are ordered to run their hands through their own hair to show that there's nothing hidden on their scalp, but considering my low cut, I was exempt from that step, so the correctional officer ordered that I pull my ears forward and turn my head to show that there was nothing behind them. Next I was instructed to tilt back my head to reveal my nostrils, and roll my tongue around in my mouth. I was also asked to lift my arms to show that there was nothing under my armpits. In the following steps, I was asked to lift up my penis and scrotum, then I was told to turn around and bend over with my legs spread. At that point, I was instructed to squat and cough with the aim of dislodging an object that could have been stored in my rectum. Then the search ended with me being asked to show the bottom off my feet.

Once I was escorted to the shower room so I could wash up, I was given a green uniform, orange slippers, and toiletries prior to being escorted to my cell. The cell I was escorted to had limited space with a toilet sink window and a spot to lay. Whenever I and the other inmates wanted to wash our faces, brush our teeth, and use the restroom, we had to do those things within our room in front of our roommates, where there was no privacy. Not only that, when it came time for us to shower up, we had no privacy there either, because we had to wash up in front of one another. While being locked up, they made sure we were fed. In that facility all inmates got three square meals a day. They also gave us peanut butter and jelly sandwiches with a carton of milk for snack at night.

As far as recreation, they gave us an hour of that. With that hour, we were able to use the phone, watch television, and play games. Once that hour was up, all inmates were sent back to their cells. As for visitation, all inmates were given an hour of that as well, on Sundays. Once that hour was up, all inmates were escorted back to their cells until visitation was over. After three days being incarcerated, I had a court date that was set for that following Monday.

When Monday came, the correctional officers who were on duty that day allowed all inmates to shower up before going to court. After showering, all inmates were escorted to the rec area where the other officers were so they could put on us handcuffs and shackles, which are restraint devices designed to secure inmates' wrists and ankles in order to prevent running and effective physical resistance. Once they did that, the officers lined up all inmates in a single-file line and escorted us out of the facilities on to the paddy wagon. After they'd loaded all inmates into the paddy wagon, the driver cranked up, drove off, and took us to the courthouse located in downtown Charleston. When the driver arrived, the officers put all inmates into a holding cell until our names were called to face the judge.

Before facing the judge, there were several public defenders who spoke with all inmates individually concerning our pending charges. When the public defenders spoke with all inmates, they first stated our names and pending charges, then they asked questions like, "How do you plead?" and "Do you want a trial?" Before asking those questions, the public defenders explain to all inmates what the process would be if we asked for a trial. They also explained what the consequences would be if we pled guilty. Truth be told, I was locked up three days too long. I knew I was guilty, and I wanted to go home, so therefore I pled guilty to all charges.

Shortly after speaking with the public defender, my name was called to see the judge. When I walked into the courtroom I saw my grandparents and parents sitting there as I came in with handcuffs and shackles on. Before the judge started the session, she ordered that I speak under oath, swearing to tell the truth, the whole truth, and nothing but the truth, so help me God. After I swore under oath, the court session began. Just like the public defender, the judge stated my name and the charges I had pending against me. Then the judge said, "Mr. Manigault, as I look at your record I notice that you do not have a rap sheet. Other than your current charges and an incident that took place in the early nineties, your record is clean. What happened?" said the judge.

I replied, "I got caught up with the wrong crowd."

She then asked me another question. She said, "Mr. Manigault, do you remember the incident that took place back in the early nineties?"

I replied, "Yes, ma'am."

She then said, "Well, briefly explain to me what happened."

"One day I was outside with a couple of friends throwing rocks over several cars. After throwing a few rocks, I stopped. But my friends continued. When I stopped, I went and sat down on the left side from where I stood drawing in the dirt. Shortly thereafter, I heard the sound of a window breaking, smash, falling foul to an errant stone. When I got up to see what happened, I noticed the car in the middle of the parking lot's window was broken. After the window got broken, my friends immediately began to frame me, saying repeatedly, 'Oh, Lo Mann did that,' while chuckling. I denied those false accusations, and before I knew it, my partners took off and ran."

When I told the judge that story she looked at me with an astonished expression on her face, like "This young man was only seven years of age when this incident occurred. Now here it is, he is fifteen years of age, and still remembers. Wow!" After I told the judge about the incident, she looked at her files and got back to the case. As she looked at my files, she stated, "After completing the cocaine substance test [which is a substance identification test that identifies drugs and drug residue on any surface], the narcotics Mr. Manigault was caught with tested positive for crack cocaine."

When the judge read those results, I immaturely glorified that moment within myself, because in my mind, that was one of the seals of approval to being a dope boy. She asked my public defender, "How does your client plead?"

In response, my public defender replied, "My client has pled guilty to all charges."

Then the judge said, "Is your client in agreeance with the ruling that has been set before him?"

Again, my public defender replied, "Yes, my client has agreed."

The legal consequences that I was issued were one year's probation, drug court, drug class, community service, and a seven-o'clock curfew.

Towards the end of the court session, the judge asked my parents if they were in agreeance with the ruling of the court, and they replied yes. No sooner than the judge spoke to my parents than she'd reached a verdict, saying, "Mr. Manigault is to be released back into the custody of his mother, Mrs. Paulette Manigault, and his release shall be effective immediately." Then the judge said to me, "Mr. Manigault, I do not like to see young men come in my courtroom for drug charges; I do not like to see young people come in my courtroom for any charges. If I see you back in my courtroom again, the next visit won't be pleasant, do you understand?"

"Yes, ma'am," I replied. Then court was adjourned.

When I came home from being locked up, I followed the court order for three days. On the third day, I said fuck it, and I went back to serving dope. Don't get me wrong, I continued to attend drug court and drug class; I also continued reporting to my probation officer, but everything else it stopped. Although I was living the street life, slanging dope, I made it my business to stay in school. Now granted, there were times where I cut class—I won't deny that—but for the most part, I was there. As you already know, after I caught my first charge, I proceeded to distribute narcotics three days after my release from jail. Months after I caught my first charge, I ended up catching a second charge, but this time around, it was in another community.

When I caught my second charge, that arrest took place in the Oak Grove Community, which is also known as Ten Mile, where my grandparents resided. One day I was on my way to pay my pager bill at Elite Pager, located in North Charleston off of Remount Road. On this particular day, I rode bike from my home that was located in North Charleston off of Ward Avenue to a partner of mine's home that was located in the same city off of Rivers Avenue. The reason I stopped by my partner's home was so I could drop off some of the dope I had in my possession. Once I made that stop, I then left, got back on my bike, and rode through Ten Mile.

When I got on Ten Mile, I made no stops. I rode the bike towards the cut where the graveyard was so I could get to my destination. As I rode towards the cut, I saw this white guy driving a sky-blue, four-door Honda on the back street where I was.

When the gentleman got closer to me, he stopped, nodded his head, then rolled down the window and asked me, "You straight?"

I replied, "Yeah, what you want?"

"You got a twenty?"

I said yes, so I broke down the dope and served him. After I rode off from making that transaction, a dark-colored Intrepid whipped the corner, and some dude hopped out and proceeded to chase after me. When I saw them hop out, I immediately ran and jumped over a big ditch that was by the tracks. Once I jumped over the ditch, I started to run. As I was running, I said to myself, "Damn, I served a setup sale." In the process, I was chewing up the small quantity of dope I had in my possession, and looking back to see where the officers were. When I noticed the distance between myself and the officer, I cut to my right where the graveyard was. The moment I ran in the graveyard, the other officers had me cornered in by the church called Bethel AME. When the officers blocked me in, there was no need for me to try to run again because they had me surrounded from all angles.

While I was being searched by one of the officers, there was another officer standing there questioning me, asking, "Do you not know who you just served?" I replied no. Then he said, "You just served cheetah. Everybody know cheetah. Have you ever heard of cheetah?" he said.

I replied, "Yeah, I heard of him, but I have never seen him."

Then the officer said, "Well, I guess today is your lucky day."

Once the officer searched me and found nothing except for two cell phones, a pager, and some money, he told me I was under arrest for four counts of possession with intent to distribute (PWID): PWID crack cocaine, PWID to an undercover officer, PWID in proximity of a school zone, and PWID.

After the officer listed the charges, he then read me my rights, put me in the patrol car, and took me to the community center on Sumner Avenue in North Charleston off of Remount Road. When the officers took me to the community center, I was surprised, because as long as I'd been living in North Charleston, I never knew speed team worked out of that center; I guess that was where their chief of police had stationed them. It had to be, because that is where they did my paperwork, and that is where I saw a couple of familiar faces on the most-wanted board.

While the officer was doing my paperwork, he turned towards me and asked, "Is there a family member I can contact and notify about what is going on?"

I replied, "Yeah, my ole lady."

Then the officer said, "What is her name?"

I told him Paulette, then he said, "And her last name?"

I replied, "Manigault."

Again, the officer asked, "Does she have a home phone or cell where I can contact her?"

I replied, "Yeah," then gave him the number.

When the officer got in touch with my ole lady, he said, "Yes, I'm trying to contact Mrs. Manigault. Mrs. Manigault, I'm officer [so-and-so] of the North Charleston Police Department. I was just calling to let you know that we have your son here, Mr. Manigault, with us."

When she asked what happened, he told her, "We sent one of our undercover agents out on a drug operation. Mr. Manigault sold the undercover officer some drugs, and we arrested him."

She said, "Well, he just been through this recently, so he knows the routine. Is it possible that I could speak with him?"

"Yes, ma'am, he is standing right here. You are on speaker."

"Hello," I said.

"You got yourself in trouble again, huh?" she said to me.

"Yeah, them boy got me."

"God is trying to tell you something. You need to leave them streets alone, and get yourself together."

"All right, Mama, I'll call you when I get a chance."

"All right, do the officer want to talk back to me?"

"No, ma'am, I'm done, unless you have any questions."

"No, I don't have any questions. Thank you for calling me."

"No problem," he replied. "I was just doing my job."

As you can see, I cut that conversation with my lady short real quick-like, because she was about to lecture me, and I really did not want to hear that. Once the officer got finished filing my paperwork, he put me back into the patrol car and transported me to the detention center for juveniles on Headquarters Road off of Leeds Avenue in North Charleston.

When I arrived, everything was still the same in terms of the booking procedure, searching procedure, and the rules and regulations. However, as far as my court session is concerned, I really don't remember much about what happened; I don't even remember what day I went to court. In fact, all I remember is the judge ordering me to spend thirty days at Midlands Evaluation Center in Columbia, South Carolina.

After the judge gave his order, they wasted no time shipping me. Within that same week, I was transported to Midlands Evaluation Center, along with several inmates. The day I arrived at Midlands, I immediately noticed that there wasn't much of a difference between that facility and ours back home in terms of their booking procedure searching procedure, the size of their cells, etc. The only difference that separated the two was Midlands updated facility, their three square meals, and the inmates' privacy in terms of using the restroom and bathing. With me having to spend thirty days at Midlands, I looked at it as if it was nothing, because being locked up as juvenile is like being under punishment at home, in my opinion.

While I was locked up at Midlands, my time flew by faster than Dale Earnhardt Jr. Because it was being occupied by attending school Monday through Friday, considering that it was in session around the time I got arrested. Not only that, it was also being occupied by writing letters, and recreational time that was given to all inmates. The day that I stepped foot in Midlands facility, I was in the mind-state of laying down and doing my time. As a matter of fact, before I got to the facility, knowing the time I was facing, I told my ole lady straight up, "Mama, don't waste your gas to come visit me. All I have is thirty days. I'll see y'all once I touch down." But she still didn't listen.

Before I knew it, my time at Midlands Evaluation Center was served. In fact, the correctional officer informed me about going home the night before. And just as he said, I was back home first thing that morning. Once I arrived back in Charleston at the detention center, I had to attend court days after my arrival in order to be released. The day that I attended court, the judge didn't enforced stricter consequences; all the judge did was keep me on probation,

and order me to continue attending drug court, drug class, and reporting to my probation officer.

When I came home after being released, I obeyed the orders
given to me by the judge, but I continued to sell drugs. Weeks after
my release, I stopped obeying the orders of the judge because I was
tired of it. What happened was, one day I was sitting by my lonesome without being under the influence of any controlled substance
or alcoholic beverages. As I sat there, I began thinking, thinking and
thinking, as I thought those thoughts, I said to myself, "Fuck this
shit. I'm not attending anything, or reporting to anyone anymore. If
they want me, they better come catch me. Fuck it. That's what they
get paid for." The moment I said that was the moment I went on the
run, but it wasn't for long, because they caught up with me within
two weeks—LOL.

The morning the law caught up with me, I was astonished because I thought they'd never find my place of residence that fast.
The reason I said that is because my loved ones and I lived across the
tracks in a wooded area where our home was surrounded by trees.
If you never rode across those tracks, you wouldn't have known two
homes were back there. Instead of me attending school that morning, I stayed home for the hell of it. As I laid in my bed watching television, I heard a knock at the front door. When I heard that knock, I
said to myself, "Who the fuck is this knocking at my door this time
of morning?" So I got up and peeped through the blinds to see who
it was.

I immediately noticed it was an officer by his shirt. When the officer saw me looking through the blinds, he said to me, "You might as
well come out." After the officer said that, I immediately went back
to my room, put on basketball shorts, a T-shirt, and two different
shoes. Once I did that, I went on the other side of the house where

my grandfather was, and asked him to answer the door because the man was outside. As my grandfather went to answer the door, I fled out the back door with no hesitation, ran across my uncle's field, and hopped the fence where the trucking companies were.

After I jumped the fence behind my house, I continued to run. I ran from my house all the way to the other entrance off of the tracks, which is a pretty good distance, might I add. As I was approaching the other entrance, the officer was riding down Ward Avenue, slowly patrolling, looking for me. When the officers spotted me out, he whipped his patrol car in front of me real quick-like, and stopped. When the officer and I stood face up, he began searching and asking for identification. Instead of me giving the officer my real identification, I gave him false identification to see if he would bite, but he didn't buy it.

After the officer searched me, he put me in his patrol car and asked me where I lived. I gave him false information again, and told him that I lived on Austin Avenue, which was the street that he and I both stood in front of off of Ward Avenue. As the officer drove off, he stopped this dude who was walking down the street, not knowing that it was a relative of mine, and asked him if he knew me. As he asked that question, I shook my head at my cousin to tell him no, then he replied no. After that, the officer asked him if I lived in that area, and my cousin replied, "I don't know." Then the officer said thank you, and rode off.

When the officer rode off, he said to me, "I'll find out who you are." After the officer said that, he went straight to my house. When the officer pulled up in my yard, my grandfather and another cousin of mine were both standing outside. When the officer got out the car, he asked them if my name was Wendell Manigault. My cousin and grandfather both stood there and said nothing at first, then my cousin said, "Yes, that's him." After the officer found out that was me, he told my family where he'd caught me, and that he was about to transport me to the juvenile detention center. As far as my cousin telling the officer who I was, I wasn't upset with her or anything like that, reason being, she had a lot going on for herself. She was in the military, and she was in school to become a dentist. I did not want her to jeopardize that.

Now the officer, he was cool, because although I gave him a run for his money, he gave me no hassle. In fact, he was generous the whole time. When I got arrested I was locked up several days prior to attending court. While I was sitting in my cell, I was thinking to myself, *What is it I can do to get myself out of this situation?* Because I didn't want to be in jail. As I was thinking, *ding!* A light bulb! I had an idea, and my idea was to turn Hollywood. When I say "Hollywood," I mean turn into an actor, or tap into character, for lack of a better term. For instance, my plan was to go into the courtroom, apologize to the judge, their staff, and my ole lady for putting them through all that nonsense by being on the run. I told them I had a lot on my mind; that was why I stopped everything and ran.

Not only did I follow through with my plan to apologize, I shed a few tears as well to make it look as though I was sincere and it worked. The apology that I gave the judge and the staff moved everyone so much to the point where the judge ordered that I be released without facing consequences. However, I still had to attend drug court, drug class and report to my probation officer, but that was it.

After being released from jail for the third time, nothing changed. When I got released, I continued to sling dope; in fact, throughout the months of October, November, and December, I slung dope. For example, Halloween, I slung dope. Thanksgiving, I slung dope. Christmas Eve and Day, I slung dope, so you can imagine what I did

New Year's Eve and Day—I slung dope. And that's the truth, the whole truth, and nothing but the truth, so help me God. While I was steady slanging dope to my family members, peers, and strangers, my ole lady cut no slack on me; she fussed and lectured me every chance she got, which was every day. She would say things like, "Nothing good is gonna come out of you selling drugs"; "The only thing that is going to happen is you're gonna end up dead, or in jail"; and "God is not pleased with what you're doing. You need to stop selling drugs, get yourself together, stay in school, and make something out of yourself."

In all honesty, I thought my ole lady would never stop fussing and lecturing me, but she did. As a matter of fact, she stopped fussing and lecturing me on the month and date of February 11, 2002. Not to say that she was happy about the incident that took place on that day, but it seemed as though she was at peace.

CHAPTER 10

Happy New Year, at least I thought it was. It started off okay, then it became tragic after the first month. On February 11, 2002, I, Wendell M. Manigault Jr., got shot with a .32 revolver by one whom I called a friend. On that day, which was a Monday, I woke up late for school. Once I got up and got myself together, I headed to school. When I arrived at school, I was as excited as all get out; I was very energetic that day, joking around a little more than the norm. Instead of attending all of my classes, that day I attended some, and cut the others. I also told my eldest sibling "I love you" repeatedly throughout that day. Once school was over, I took the bus and rode to my home on Ward Avenue. When I got home I made several phone calls, trying to get a ride downtown because I had to attend drug court. I finally got in touch with a driver. I kindly asked if he would take me downtown to drug court, and he replied, "Yeah, I got you. Meet me outside."

As I opened the front door to head outside, one of my partners mysteriously appeared on the other side of the door. As he and I eyeballed each other, he said, "Lil brah, what's up? And I replied, "Chilling. 'Bout to go to drug court right quick then he said, I've been trying to call you the last couple days, you ain't holla at me or nuttin. In response, I told my partner, "I trying to get dis money, you know how I get down."

Upon my driver's arrival, my partner asked, "How you gettin' to drug court?"

"My nigga coming to get me."

"I'ma ride wit y'all."

"He might not let you ride."

In the process of my partner and I conversating, the driver pulled up. The instant the driver arrived, my partner asked him if he could have ride, and astoundingly he said yeah. When I arrived at the courthouse, I was in there no longer than thirty minutes because it was a simple process. Every Monday at drug court the judge did the same thing, and asked the same questions: How are you doing in school? Are you obeying the orders of your probation? Are you following your curfew?

On top of that, the judge also read the drug test results that all ex-convicts, including me, generally took in drug class the week prior to attending drug court. If any ex-convict drug screen came back negative, we were good, but if it came back positive, the judge would give us weekend detention or some type of punishment. Once the judge got finished with the court process, all ex-convicts were ordered to pay a five-dollar fee, then we were able to leave. The second I stepped out of the court room, I called the driver to ask him if he didn't mind picking me back up to take me home. Five minutes after I hung up, he pulled up, but he wasn't alone. He was still riding with the gentleman who'd come along with him to pick me up and my partner.

Truth be told, I thought my partner would have asked the driver to drop him off somewhere, but as you can see, he didn't. When the driver arrived at my home, my partner got out the car along with me, and went into the house. Once my partner and I entered the house, he and I went into my room. He went to sit at the head of the bed, and I went to sit on the trunk that was placed at the foot of the bed. While he and I sat there, I tried to contact this young lady whom I was associated with to pull up on me, but unfortunately I didn't get an answer, or a call back. At that instant, I looked back and saw my partner gazing at his pistol as he held it towards the floor. As soon as I noticed what my partner was doing, I told him three times to put the pistol up, but he looked at me and said nothing. Being that this was a friend of mine, I thought nothing of it as I proceeded to make that call.

In the process of trying to make that call, I had developed a slight headache, and my body temperature began to get hot. So I stood up from where I was sitting, took my hoodie off, then turned and threw it on the bed to my left. No sooner had I turned and thrown my hoodie on the bed, than—*blam!* The trigger was pulled, and I had been shot. When I got shot I was out no more than fifteen seconds, then my eyes opened. The moment I regained consciousness, I saw myself lying on the floor with my head propped up on the hinges of the door near the dresser. As I continued to look around, I noticed one of the firearms that belonged to me was on the floor where I was. The Glock 9mm was under my legs and the .25 caliber was on one of the nearby beds. Now mind you, I had both of my pistols put up; one was under the dresser, and the other one was on the stand by my stereo. I had no possession of those firearms at the time of the incident, but they were by me when my eyes open.

While I was lying on the floor, my partner was standing over me with his firearm in hand, shivering, shaking, and crying, saying, "I sorry, I sorry, I didn't mean to do it." My partner eventually went into the living area, where my eldest sibling was. And moments later,

I overheard him repeat to my eldest sibling what he'd said to me, "I sorry, I sorry, I didn't mean to do it."

"What? Boy, what you talkin' 'bout?" asked my eldest sibling.

"Brah, brah, Lo. Brah, I shoot Lo, brah."

"Boy, quit playing."

With my eldest sibling on the phone, she didn't pay my partner any attention, because she thought he was joking. Then my partner said, "No, for real, I shoot Lo, brah. He laying on the floor." And that's when she got up to see what was going on.

When she saw me lying on the floor, she lost it; she began yelling, screaming, and crying, saying, "Mann, Mann, Lo Mann, oh Lord, my brother! What you did to my brother?! Why you shoot my brother?!"

As she was kneeling on the floor where I was crying, my partner continued to apologize repeatedly, saying that he was sorry, and he hadn't meant to do it. As my partner was apologizing, my eldest sibling yelled at him out of anger, telling him to call the police. While my eldest sibling was crying, my grandfather and uncle, Robert Tindal Sr. and Jr., came on the other side of the house where we were. Once my grandfather and uncle saw what the ruckus was about, both gentlemen paused, looking puzzled, not knowing what to think, say, or do. They got teary-eyed the instant they saw what was going on. After collecting his thoughts, my uncle then called my name to see if I was conscious as my grandfather stood in silence.

While my uncle and eldest sibling were talking to me, trying to keep me awake, I overheard my partner on the phone speaking with the dispatcher, telling them that he'd shot his friend. From what my partner was saying to the dispatcher, I gathered that the dispatcher was asking exactly what happened because of my partner's response: "Me and my friend was playing with guns, and I missed, and shot him." Minutes after, he went outside. According to what my ole lady told me as she pulled up from work, my partner came running to her car, apologizing, saying, "Mrs. Paulette, I sorry, I sorry, Mrs. Paulette. I didn't mean to do it. I sorry, Mrs. Paulette."

My ole lady replied, "What? What you talkin' 'bout? You sorry for what?"

" I shoot Lo, brah. Mrs. Paulette, I sorry. Mrs. Paulette, I didn't mean to do it. Please forgive me."

The moment my partner told my ole lady that he'd shot me, she said she didn't stop the car and put it in park, or anything, all she did was grab my youngest sibling and cousin (both under the age of seven) out of the car, and ran into the house where I was. Once she entered the house, the first thing she said to me was, "Mann, this Mama. Baby, can you hear me?"

In response, I nodded my head. "Yeah."

"You all right?" she asked.

I again replied by nodding my head. "Yeah."

"Hold on, baby, the ambulance is on the way."

She then went and kneeled down by my left foot, and with a distraught look on her face, blurted out, "Oh Lord, my boy, please protect my boy." She said to me, "Son, I done pray for you all your life. Ain't no more I can do. It's out of my hands now; it's in God's hands. You gotta pray for yourself."

When my ole lady told me I needed to pray for myself, I immediately began thinking about what this minister had told me while I was locked up at Midlands Evaluation Center. He'd said to me and the other inmates, "If you ever have a chance to ask God for forgiveness before you die, say the Our Father's prayer, because in that one prayer, you are asking for many things. That includes forgiveness of your sins, in addition to anyone who may have sinned against you, and in doing so, you may make it into heaven."

After I thought and prayed that prayer, I said to God, "Lord, if you want me here, keep me. If not, take me away." Truth be told, I don't know if I was thinking out loud or what, but it sounded like I heard someone say, "Maintain your breath until the paramedics come. When they come, relax, I got you."

As I was lying on the floor trying to stay conscious, the paramedics arrived. Once they arrived, there was only one paramedic who walked in the house at that time. When he came in, he questioned my ole lady first, asking my name. Then he began questioning me.

"Wendell, can you hear me?" he asked.

I nodded my head. "Yeah."

"How many fingers am I holding up?"

"Two."

"Are you having any trouble breathing?" he asked. "Are you in any pain?"

I shook my head no.

"Do you know who shot you? Was it a friend?"

I shook my head yes.

"What is your friend's name?"

In a very low voice, I told him my partner's name.

After being questioned by the first paramedic, the second paramedic came in and asked, "Is he conscious?"

"Yeah, he's alert," the first paramedic replied.

"Where is the gunshot wound?"

"The blood is running from his left side, but I can't tell where it's coming from. Let's get his shirt off."

When the paramedics cut my shirt off, they noticed the gunshot wound was on the left side of my neck. After they saw that, they told me they were bringing in the stretcher to put me on the EMS truck and transport me to the ER. Once I got on the EMS truck, the paramedics placed an oxygen mask on my face. I twitched my mouth a few times to make sure it was on, then I was out. The next time my eyes opened, I woke up to find myself lying in the intensive care unit at the Medical University of South Carolina, the same night of my injury.

As my eyes began to crack open, I saw a lot of my schoolmates, family members, and childhood peers standing in the hallway at the foot of my bed, as my ole lady sat at the head of my bed on the right side. Out of everyone standing at the foot of my bed that night, that wasn't half of the visitors who were there, from what my ole lady told me. She said I had visitors coming in like clockwork, who wouldn't leave, and the waiting area was overcrowded with visitors, inside and out, so MUSC was generous enough to open up their conference room and allow my visitors to sit in there.

After five minutes of eyeballing everything, I was out like a light once again. When I woke up the next morning, I started moving my eyeballs around because I was in an environment that was unfamiliar to me. As I began to check out my surroundings, I noticed I was lying in a bed that was literally turning left to right, called a Hill-Rom bed. I also noticed I was connected to all types of machines and IV tubes, like a solu-drip, IV fluids, and a tube for airway management while I was intubated. I even had a cervical collar (neck brace) placed around my neck, as well as having had a feeding tube inserted into my stomach. The more I began to look around and check out my surroundings, I saw no one, nor did I heard a single voice. I proceeded to call out for help. As I was calling for help, I noticed that I was not able to speak. I did not know why; I just could not. The minute I found out I could not speak, I started clicking my teeth like a bird to get someone's attention. I heard nurse one say, "What is that noise?"

"What noise?" the second nurse asked.

"That clicking noise. Sounds like something is clicking. Do you hear it?"

"No, I don't hear anything."

The reason nurse two did not hear anything was because I stopped clicking; my jaw was beginning to hurt. When I started clicking again, nurse one said, "Do you hear it now?"

"Yes, where is it coming from?" nurse two replied.

"Let's find out."

As nurse one and two were trying to figure out where the clicking was coming from, I continued to click louder and harder. Once nurse one came down the hallway where I was, I started clicking faster. When nurse one recognized that it was me clicking, she began questioning me.

As nurse one turned left and walked towards me, she asked, "Is that you clicking?"

While nurse one was in my cubicle, nurse two called out to nurse one, "Where are you?" as she walked down the hall.

"I'm in here with the new patient."

As nurse one and two stood in my cubicle , they were apologetic about me not having a way to call them, considering my circumstances. They said to me, "We apologize, we were not expecting you to wake up so soon." Then nurse one and two asked me, "How are you feeling? Are you okay?"

I replied by nodding my head.

Then the nurses said, "I know you are wondering why you are unable to speak."

I again replied by nodding my head.

WENDELL M. MANIGAULT JR.

"The reason you are unable to speak," said nurse two, "is because you have a tracheostomy in your throat that the doctor surgically implanted."

After she filled me in with that information, they asked if I wanted my mother, so I nodded my head, and they went to get her. When my ole lady came in my cubicle, she and the nurses questioned me, making sure that I was straight, while checking my vitals.

While my ole lady and I were in my cubicle, the doctor came in. He said, "Mr. Manigault, you are awake. Is it okay if I sit on your bed?"

I replied by nodding my head.

The doctor sat on my bed, then stated his name and let me know he was the doctor who'd dealt with me when I came in the night of my injury. He asked me, "How are you feeling? Are you okay? Are you feeling any pain or discomfort?" Then he said, "I have some good news, and some bad news. Which one do you want to hear first? The good news?"

I nodded my head yes.

"Well, the good news is, you still have your life, but the bad news is, you are paralyzed from the neck down, and you will never be able to walk again. When you got shot, the bullet went into the left side of your neck, did a horseshoe-like turn, and fractured your spinal cord at level C5, which left you paralyzed. Now as far as the bullet is concerned, it is still in your neck, but it is now on the right side. I could have surgically removed it, but I did not, because I did not want to cause any more damages."

My ole lady asked, "Will the bullet ever move?"

"No, ma'am, the bullet is lodged in an area where it won't move, so you don't have to worry about that."

"I just wanted to make sure," she said, "because we don't need any more damage."

"I understand. I totally understand, and you should be. If it was my child or family member, I would be. Now you do have the option of removing the bullet. It is your right, but it is in your best interest to leave it be."

So that's what we did, let it be.

Once the doctor got finished explaining to me why I was paralyzed, he said that out of all the years he'd been a physician, he'd never seen a situation such as this. He told me, "Due to the severity of your injury, you weren't supposed to make it." He said it was mind-blowing to know I'd gotten shot in my neck, and still had my life. Then he said, "I don't know who you are connected to, but whoever it is, stay connected to them."

"God," I responded. "Because he is the one who spared my life. I know I didn't do it, because I don't have the power to do so. If I had the power to spare my life, then I would have raised myself up from this bed of affliction when I got shot. That's why I say if it had not been for the Lord, and the prayers of others, I would have been dead, lying in the pits of hell a long time ago."

Once the doctor had finish speaking with us, he went his way, while my ole lady and I stayed in the cubicle.

While I was in the intensive care unit, I still had my schoolmates, childhood peers, family members, church members, and members from Mount Moriah Baptist Church, visiting me like crazy; I'm talking about as soon as one group left, the next group came in. On top of the visitors I had coming in and out, I had a physical therapist coming in as well, to perform range of motion exercises on my upper and lower extremities in order to keep my muscles from contracting.

While the therapist was exercising my upper and lower extremities, she said to me, "Try bending your elbows," so I did. As I tried bending my elbow, the therapist got excited, then asked me, "Did you feel that?"

My response to her question was no, because I wasn't paying any attention while trying to bend my elbow.

"I just felt the tension of your muscles as you tried to bend your elbow. Try bending your elbow again. Do you feel it now? Look at your arm. You can see it as well. Do you see it now?"

"Yeah."

"Mom, do you see it now?" the therapist asked her. "Wow! Are you guys sure he is disabled from his neck down?"

"Although our trust and belief is in God, that's what the doctor said," my ole lady responded.

"Well, you guys saw it yourselves. He was trying to bend his elbow. I'm amazed!"

After the therapist finished with me, she left, and my ole lady said to me, "Do you see that? The doctor said one thing, but God says another. God can raise you up from this condition, but you have to turn your life over to him. Once you begin doing what he wants you to do, then he will move. He didn't spared your life for nothing. He spared your life for a reason, but until you do what he wants you to do, your situation won't change. God isn't going to make you do something you don't want to do; you have to be willing."

While I was still in the intensive care unit, one of my aunts, whom I love dearly, brought us some devastating news. When my aunt visited, she kissed my forehead as usual, then asked my ole lady for an update on me. My ole lady informed my aunt about what was going on, and then my aunt broke the news.

"He's gone," she said. My aunt rubbed my hand, while she and my ole lady made direct eye contact.

My ole lady replied, "Who?"

Then my aunt said, "Mr. Manigault."

When my aunt told us about the death of my grandfather, my ole lady's eyes instantaneously popped open as her jaw dropped. Once she collected her thoughts, she and my aunt proceeded to talk about my grandfather's character; how he conducted himself, and what he had endured throughout that process, how he was better off in the afterlife, considering all that he'd endured.

Sometime before I got shot, my grandfather was diagnosed with cancer, and throughout his stages of cancer, the doctor ordered him to undergo chemotherapy. During chemotherapy, my grandfather's health began to decline, to the point where he had to be admitted at the Medical University of South Carolina weeks prior to my injury. Being that my grandfather's health was declining, he was placed on life support because he was declared brain dead, and as a result, he ultimately passed away.

During their conversation, my aunt and my ole lady thought I was asleep from the medication I was on, but I was wide awake, playing possum. Finding out about my grandfather's death didn't affect me at all, because I'd visited him the week prior to my injury. However, I couldn't begin to imagine what my family was going through, considering there had been two tragic accidents within the same week. After spending two weeks in the intensive care unit, the doctor transferred me to the seventh floor because they felt I was doing good.

When I got on the seventh floor, everything was pretty much the same as it was in the ICU; the only difference was that an incident occurred while I was on the seventh floor, and I was no longer lying on a Hill-Rom bed, or connected to most of those machines anymore. The incident that occurred was crazy, but it is something to think about. As I was lying in bed, there were two male visitors that I know came to visit me while my ole lady was in the restroom.

When my visitors came in, I was ecstatic to see them, because I hadn't seen them since I'd gotten injured. From what I was told, those visitors had come to the hospital before, along with the gentleman who'd shot me, but they were not able to see me because the medical staff wasn't allowing any visitors in at the time.

As my visitors walked towards my bedside, they said, "Lo Mann, what's up?" One sat on the left side of my bed, and the other on the right. They began asking me, "How are you doing?"; "What did the doctor say?"; "Will you ever walk again?"

My response to them was, "I'm paralyzed from my neck down, and the doctor said I'll never walk again."

One of them asked, "What did you want to do with the gentleman who shot you?"

"Nothing," I responded. "Leave him alone, because it was my beef."

He then said, "Since the doctor said you will never walk again, let me get yo phone."

I replied, "No, I can't do dat."

"Lo Mann, you know you got all da sales on yo phone."

"I know, dat's why I said I can't do dat," I replied with a smile on my face.

After visitor one and two noticed that I wasn't giving in, we all began reminiscing about what we'd done in the streets. While we talked, my ole lady finally came out of the bathroom from taking a shower. When she noticed I had visitors, and recognized who they were, she began conversing with them; How were they doing? How were their families doing?

Once they finished their conversation, my visitors told me that they were about to leave. Their last words were, "The next time we pay you a visit, we're going to bring movies for you to watch."

After my visitors had left, my ole lady walked over and stood to my left side. With a discombobulated expression on her face, she said to me, "Mann, let me ask you a question. I don't know whether I was hearing things or what. I don't think I was, but did they tell you to give them your cell phone since you'll never walk again?"

"Yeah."

"What do they want with your phone?"

"I have a lot of sales on my phone."

"Oh, so y'all use y'all phone to deal drugs," she said.

"Yeah."

"They don't have their phones?"

"Yeah."

"Oh, so you making more money?" she asked.

"No, I just got a lot of sales on my phone," I replied.

"Okay, but what I don't understand is, why would they ask you something like that at a time like this? Do they not see you laying in this bed?"

"Ain't nuttin' like dat. Dem boy straight."

"They might be, but something doesn't sound right. It may not be anything; it's probably me. I'm not saying that they had something to do with what happened to you, but it just doesn't sit well with my spirit."

When my ole lady approached me with that question, I was shocked because I didn't know she'd heard them. Not only that, with my ole lady asking me that question, I knew for sure she and I were thinking the same thoughts, because if we weren't, she wouldn't have asked me that question. If you pay attention to our conversation, you will notice that I was trying to throw her off as she was questioning me, considering that she already had a lot on her plate with what happened to me. Isn't it ironic how my visitors told me they would come back to visit, but never did? Have I spoken with them since then? Yeah, we spoke a few times, I just hadn't seen them. In fact, as of January 22, 2011, nine years after my injury, I still hadn't seen them, Selah. (Pause, and calmly think about that.)

What I have just shared with you are events that occurred throughout my stay at the Medical University of South Carolina. There is one event that constantly occurred, though, and that was prayer. In the course of my stay there, spiritual leaders and members from my church, lovely Mountain Missionary Baptist Church, and Mount Moriah Missionary Baptist Church, came to visit me frequently. During those visits, the spiritual leaders and members from both churches always asked if it was okay for them to say a word of prayer. Being that it was a devastating time of my life, I always accepted prayers. Once I gave the spiritual leaders and members permission to say a prayer, everyone bowed their heads, closed their eyes, and prayed. At the end of prayer, the spiritual leaders and members always said, "God is still in the healing business, but you must believe and have faith, for if you have faith the size of a mustard seed, you can speak to the mountain and tell it to move, and you shall have whatsoever you say."

After nine days of being on the seventh floor of the Medical University of South Carolina, they were ready to discharge me because I was doing good, and they felt like they had done all they could do. From the information my ole lady gave me, MUSC wanted to transfer me to a rehab facility in Florence, South Caroline for fifteen to thirty days. After my ole lady spoke with Miss Linda Collins, a coworker, however, I was admitted to Roper Rehabilitation Hospital on the eighth floor, where my ole lady worked, the same day I was discharged from MUSC, March 5, 2002.

When I got to the eighth floor at Roper Rehabilitation Hospital, I had round-the-clock care like never before. Because of God's grace and mercy, and my ole lady being a well-known, sweet employee and coworker, I had a great support team. I had just about every nurse, doctor, and therapist from the eighth floor and other floors taking care of me, and my ole lady as well; I even had janitors checking on me. Don't get me wrong, although I had a great support team at Roper Rehab, I'm thankful and appreciative for the help that MUSC gave me, because they did a marvelous job. It's just that when I got to Roper, I had even more help coming from everywhere.

As I was getting myself adjusted to my new temporary home, Roper Rehab, I was given daily activities to rehabilitate myself and stay active while I was there. The daily activities included therapy, where I was assigned to have different therapists who dealt with me individually. I was assigned to two physical therapists, a recreational therapist, and a speech therapist, who were all females. I also was assigned to a male psychiatric doctor and a couple of male wheelchair specialists.

The two physical therapists I had were wonderful, whose names were Robin and Sonja. Although Robin and Sonja were both physical therapists, they each had wonderful, different personalities. Robin cut jokes, laughed, and had a good-time type of personality, while Sonja had more of a sweet, soft, and laid-back personality. Any time Robin and I got together, it was always a comical moment. Robin and I would always tell jokes about anything and anyone. She and I sometimes laughed and told jokes about ourselves. With all the comical moments Robin and I had, there are two memorable moments that I will never forget.

One evening as I was lying in my bed watching television, there was a knock at my door, and someone entered. As I looked towards my left to see who it was, I saw that it was Robin.

When Robin entered my room, she walked towards the right of my bedside, talking to me, saying, "I just came in to sit and chat before clocking out." During our conversation, she said to me, "Let's find names for ourselves, names that we can call one another. It'll be our thing."

"All right," I said.

As we brainstormed, trying to find names for ourselves, Robin said to me, "I know what I will call you, I'll call you Batman."

"Why Batman?" I responded.

"That was the first name that popped up."

"Well, I guess you Robin."

"Well, duh," she said. "I guess so, since my birth name is Robin." She laughed, then said, "Batman and Robin, it is."

While Robin and I were sitting around chatting, the social worker who brought me over from MUSC to Roper Rehab, Miss Linda Collins, walked in the room. When Miss Linda came in the room, the first question she asked Robin and I was, "What are you guys up to?"

"Nothing," Robin replied.

"Well, I know it's not Wendell who is up to something. Robin, it's you," said Miss Linda.

"Me? Why me? Why am I the bad guy?" asked Robin.

"Because you are always the bad guy," Miss Linda replied.

Robin told me, "Don't believe her, she's lying." Then she said to Miss Linda, "I'm just kidding, Batman and I were just chatting."

"Why are you calling him Batman?" Miss Linda asked her.

"That's our new thing," Robin answered. "He's Batman, and I'm Robin."

"I want to be a part of that," said Miss Linda. "Who am I going to be?"

Robin looked at both me and Miss Linda several times, then replied, "Penguin."

The second Robin called Miss Linda "Penguin," all I could do was laugh, because it was hilarious. With all due respect, Miss Linda was a beautiful person, but she really did fit the description because of her height and walk.

The other comical moment Robin and I had wasn't anything major; it was something simple. One morning Robin had me at the gym performing range of motion exercises on my upper and lower extremities.

Twenty minutes in, she said to me, "Batman, I'm supposed to be giving you a workout, but you are working me. You got me sweating bullets, boy. You know I'm a big girl."

Of course, I laughed when Robin said that, because she was crazy. Although I know Robin liked to joke around, I wasn't expecting that from her; she caught me off guard with that one. While Robin was talking about herself, she stopped and took a break, saying she needed a breather because I was putting her to work. When you are dealing with a person as crazy as Robin, it's best that you expect the unexpected, because if you don't, they'll get you every time.

Now that I have shared with you a couple of comical moments I had with Robin, let's talk about Sonja. Whenever Sonja and I got together, it was always a personal moment between us. Sonja and I would always converse about some of our personal life experiences, or life in general. If I was in my power chair, I sometimes drove to the gym were Sonja was for physical therapy, or she would come to my room. Once Sonja got finished performing range of motion exercises on my upper and lower extremities, she would have me tilt my power chair back completely to massage my shoulders and neck. As Sonja began to massage my shoulders and neck, either one of us would spark a conversation.

One of the conversations I can remember Sonja and I having was about my injury, and life before. While I was relaxing and enjoying my massage that only my wonderful therapists Sonja could have given, she asked me, "Do you mind talking about what happened to you? Or does it bother you to do so?"

"No, I don't mind," I responded, because it didn't bother me to talk about it, and it still doesn't.

"Well, what happened?" she asked.

As I began explaining to Sonja how I got injured, and who was behind it, she was in awe.

"Was it an accident?" she asked.

"No, it wasn't an accident. He knew the gun was loaded; it was his gun."

"Why would your friend do something like that? You did say he's your friend right?"

"Yeah."

"Why would he do something like that, especially if you guys are friends?"

"I don't know."

"Did you guys have an altercation?"

"Nah, that's the thing," I said, "we never got into it."

"He did get arrested, didn't he?"

"Yeah," I said, and left it at that.

Although me being a drug dealer didn't have anything to do with me getting shot (meaning, it wasn't gang related, nor did it have anything to do with a drug deal gone bad), I never Told Sonja, or any of my ole lady's coworkers, I dealt drugs. Not that I was ashamed of being a drug dealer, because I wasn't, I just didn't want my ole lady's coworkers to treat her different because of my stupidity.

After explaining to Sonja how I got shot, she proceeded to question me. "How was life before your injury? Do I have any children?"

As far as telling Sonja about my life, I did that. I also told her I didn't have any children; I just didn't tell her I dealt drugs. Once I finished answering her questions, I asked if she was married. "Do you have any children?"

Sonjas response to my question was, "Yes, I have one child, a son, but currently divorced."

That was only one of many conversations Sonja and I had. Like I said before, whenever Sonja and I got together, it was always a personal moment; she and I would conversate about anything. Out of all the conversations Sonja and I had, I later found out that she was attracted to black men; yes, black men. When Sonja told me that, I said, "Huh?" because I couldn't believe it. Then I said, "You? Black men?"

"Yes, is there something wrong with that?"

"No, ain't nuttin' wrong wit dat, as long as the person you are dealing with loves you unconditionally, and treat you as a woman should be treated."

After I told Sonja how I felt about her dating someone from a different cultural background, I said to myself, "That explains why she feels comfortable around me." If Sonja never told me that she was attracted to black men, I would have never known; in fact, my ole lady told me that Sonja ended up marrying a black man years after my injury. Congratulations, Sonja! One thing I'll say about Sonja, although she and I had a personal relationship and conversated about many things, she never got out of line; she always kept it professional.

The other two therapists I had, whose names were Barbara and Kim, were the recreational therapist and speech therapist. They were cool, and it was a pleasure working with them both. Barbara, the speech therapist, did an excellent job with me. When I came in to work with Barbara, she stated her name as all professionals do, then began explaining what her job consisted of, and the techniques she was going to use to help strengthen my voice. While Barbara was explaining the techniques, I said to myself, "I wanna see dis happen." Not that I didn't believe they would work, I just wanted to see how something simple could have an effect on something as major as my voice. In the first session I had with Miss Barbara, starting off, she had me inhale, taking deep breaths, then exhale. As I began using the techniques Miss Barbara taught me, she began explaining their purpose.

"As you know, you had a tracheostomy placed in your throat," she told me, which was needed for me to breathe after my accident. "Because of that tracheostomy, and your injury being at the C5 level, your diaphragm was affected. The diaphragm is a muscle responsible for inhaling and exhaling air, which also helps a person produce a strong cough to clear the lungs or throat of material, like mucus, food, liquid, or medication, for you to produce a louder voice. For more functional communication, you must work on increasing your pulmonary hygiene and respiratory support by using exercises like these because your respiratory system is weak."

After Miss Barbara finished explaining the purpose behind the inhale/exhale technique, she went on to say that in order for me to produce an audible voice, I had to use the inhale/exhale technique not only in sessions with her, but every day, throughout the day. Once I performed that first technique, Miss Barbara had me to practice the word pronunciation technique. When she saw there was room for improvement with the second technique she had me to perform, she told me that was one of the techniques she'd have me practice while I was there as well. As far as the reason behind the second technique, there was no difference; it all served the same purpose. Although there were times when Miss Barbara and I laughed and joke around, she always made sure we did what we were supposed to do, and that's one of the things I liked about her most.

As a patient at Roper Rehabilitation Hospital, I enjoyed my therapy sessions, but out of all sessions, there was one session I always looked forward to attending the most: recreational therapy. In my recreational session, Kim, the recreational therapist, reminded me of the fun I used to have before I went astray as I got older. Whenever Kim and I got together, she always had a game set up, such as Connect Four or Uno, for us to play. While Kim and I played whatever game she had set up, we at times had conversations with each other. One of the conversations I can recall us having was about my extracurricular activities. Kim asked me if I'd played any games or sports.

The other conversation I can remember us having was about my future plans.

She asked, "Prior to your injury, what did you want to do once you graduated from high school?"

"I wanted to be a truck driver. Truck driving is something I had a passion for since I was five years of age," I said. "And due to my uncle having years of experience as a long-distance and local truck driver, he gave me the opportunity to experience that any time our school district was on break."

In fact, he'd taught me how to connect and disconnect the cables from the cab of the truck to the chassis/container; how to lock and unlock the fifth wheel; how to secure or unlock the container; and how to lock and unlock the doors of the container, and seal it with zip ties if need be.

After explaining to kim why I wanted to be a truck driver, she asked me another question. "What are your plans now that you are in this condition?"

The only response I could have given her was "I don't know."

Not to disrespect Kim, but how was I to know what my plans were a month after my injury, when I never knew I was going to end up disabled? To be honest with you, the only thing I was thinking about at the time was walking. I wasn't thinking about my schooling, career, or anything of that nature; all I wanted to do was walk again.

Seconds after my reply, Kim closed out by telling me, "Life for you doesn't have to stop here because of your condition. No, you may not be able to do what you want, but there are some things you *can* do; you just have to find out what you like."

"Not to discourage you or anything," she said, "but this is something you need to think about, because you don't want to waste your life expecting for something to happen that may not."

Later that evening, I took what Kim had said into consideration. Did I act upon it at that time? No, but I always kept it in mind. Having Kim as my recreational therapist was fun; there was never a dull moment. As you can see, Kim was a fun, joyful, outgoing person, whose goal was to bring life back into the lives of her patients through dedicating her time, and through fun activities. Although I didn't look at the activities Kim had me do at that time as therapeutic; they were including an outing she took me on to Applebee's, along with my ole lady and anonymous lady friend.

Now that I've talked about my wonderful therapists, and shared with you some of my memorable moments, let's talk about the caregivers and my daily routine with them. The caregivers I had were Joel, Amy, Lynn, Alfreda, Ronnie, Elizabeth, Richard, and Lavinia, and they were hardworking nurses who took good care of me. Another caregiver I had then and now is my ole lady; she is also a hardworking nurse, and continues to take care of me on a day-to-day basis. My caregivers always made sure I was comfortable, and had what I needed, therefore I wanted for nothing.

Waking up every morning at Roper Rehabilitation Hospital was an adventure every time; I had my work cut out for me. When I woke up in the morning, the nurses performed my activities of daily living (ADLs), which included bathing, clothing, transferring me into my power chair, and feeding me, although I didn't have much of an appetite. Once I got squared away, I would attend my first therapy sessions. During the day, in between breaks from therapy sessions, my caregivers checked my vitals signs (blood pressure, temperature, etc), bladder, and tracheostomy.

Due to me being a quadriplegic, I was unable to do things on my own, such as urinate. Because I was unable to urinate on my own, my caregivers had to check my bladder frequently throughout the day to make sure everything was going properly by using an ultrasound machine, or by pressing on my bladder. If my bladder didn't empty out completely on its own, the nurses would have to catheterize me by placing a tube in my penis, then apply pressure to my bladder and allow the urine to discharge. After emptying my bladder, the nurses placed a condom catheter onto my penis with a leg bag attached to catch the urine.

The nurses then made sure my tracheostomy was clear of secretion (mucus) by suctioning it out with a vacuum-like tube because my diaphragm wasn't strong enough to cough up mucus. What they would do was pull the cap out of my tracheostomy, insert a tube inside my trachea, and vacuum out the mucus so that I could have a clear airway to breathe. Once that procedure was performed, they recapped my tracheostomy, and that was the end of that.

Another thing the nurses did was check my rear end periodically throughout the day to make sure I didn't have a bowel movement, because I was incontinent. Often I would become impacted, and in order for me to have a bowel movement, the nurses had to insert an enema into my anus to stimulate to help my bowels move. Once the enema was inserted, it did not completely do the job, so the nurses had to insert a finger in my anus to remove the bowels, and once they were finished, I was bathed and left alone.

With my injury being at the C5 level in my spine, I was told spinal cord injury patients were prone to getting sores if not positioned correctly, or if they were left in any one position too long. Being that I'm in a power wheelchair and cannot move, I had to tilt my power chair up and down every thirty minutes for thirty seconds to prevent from getting a pressure sore. In order to prevent getting a pressure sore while lying in bed, I had to be turned every two hours from side to side to help alleviate the pressure from my body. Turning me was something my nurses did in the evening once I got back in bed, and throughout the night as I rested. To have someone turn you every two hours was annoying, but it was either that or bed sores.

The nurses I just named were only a few of the many I had. Out of every nurse who took care of me, there was one nurse I'll never forget, whose name was Mary Lou—the nurse from hell who meant well. Mary Lou was the nurse who was hardest on me, versus the others, including my doctors, who were more lenient. When it came down to me eating, drinking lots of fluids (water), getting bolus through my peg tube, taking meds, and doing pressure reliefs, Mrs. Mary Lou rode my back like a drill sergeant.

As I begin to think back, I can hear and see Mrs. Mary Lou walking in my room saying, "Knock, knock! Guess who!" Whenever Mrs. Mary Lou entered my room like that, I would roll my eyes and sigh, because I knew she was going to make me do something I didn't want to do. One of the things Mary Lou always forced me to do was drink lots of water. Being that spinal cord injury patients were prone to having different health issues, drinking water was something that could help prevent some of the issues, such as urinary tract infections. Every fifteen to thirty minutes Mrs. Mary Lou came into my room and asked if I was thirsty. If I said yes, she gave me something to drink; if I said no, she still gave me something to drink. Either way it went, she gave me something to drink. As I would begin drinking, I can remember Mary Lou saying, "I know you are tired of me forcing you to drink, but this is something you must do, because you don't want to get a UTI, or have kidney failure."

At that time, I understood Mary Lou's concern, but I could have cared less at that point because I was tired of drinking water. Although Mary Lou had other patients she was tending to, she made it her business to keep me hydrated; if she couldn't, she had one of the other nurses make sure of it. Mary Lou was so adamant about me drinking fluids to the point where she asked my visitors to make sure I drank. She would say to them, "I know you are here to visit, but while you are visiting, will you please make sure he drinks? He knows he needs to drink, and he knows why. Aren't I right, Wendell?"

"Yes, ma'am," I'd say, as I smiled and nodded my head, considering that my voice was still weak.

Then she said to my visitors, "He has a pitcher of water, and a cup over there. I'll be back in a few minutes. If he doesn't drink, let me know. Thank you."

What did I tell you? The lady had gone beserk, crazy, cuckoo, I tell ya—cuckoo.

As you know, I had a tracheostomy implanted in my throat, and because of the tracheostomy, the doctors ordered me to not eat solid food by mouth. Because I couldn't eat through my mouth, I had to get my nutrition supplements through a peg tube, which, over time, completely left me with no appetite. Prior to coming to Roper Rehab, the nurses and doctors were well aware of me being unable to eat, and that I didn't have an appetite. Before I was able to eat solid food by mouth, the doctors had to run several swallowing tests to make sure I didn't have any trouble swallowing. Once they saw that I didn't have any trouble swallowing, I was allowed to eat.

From not having used my swallowing glands in such a long time, they'd become resistant; instead of it pushing the food down, it forced it back up, causing me to gag or vomit every time I ate. Mary Lou had me ate a small portion of my meals (breakfast, lunch, and dinner), rather than the whole meal, so I could work my muscles, and get them used to swallowing again. After I ate the small portions of meals, Mary Lou gave me bolus through my peg tube to substitute for the portions I didn't eat. With Mary Lou's knowledge and experience with spinal cord injury patients, all she was doing was making sure I was straight, which I appreciated.

If you noticed, as I was talking about Mary Lou—"the nurse from hell"—and the other nurses who were lenient on me, I mentioned my doctors, who were lenient as well. Dr. Elizabeth Rittenberg and Dr. James Warmoth were excellent doctors, who made sure my needs were met; they also were loving doctors, who allowed me to have my way. In the hospital, when the doctors wanted to run tests on their patients, they sometimes ordered for them to be "nothing by mouth" (NPO). NPO is when patients are unable to eat or drink anything after a certain time.

With my doctors wanting to run tests on me they ordered for me to be NPO until the tests were run and the results were in. For some reason, I always got hungry and thirsty every time I was ordered to be NPO. On one occasion when I had to be NPO, I got real thirsty. The more I thought about me being unable to drink, the more I wanted to drink. As I lay in bed, desiring something to quench my thirst, I asked my ole lady, who stood on my right side, if she would give me something to drink. She replied no, and explained why, as if I didn't know. Being the determined young man I am, I continued to ask my ole lady for a drink, but she refused to cooperate. Minutes after practically begging her to give me something to drink, I asked her politely if she would go and get my doctor. She said to me, "Boy, I ain't going to get no doctor. All she gonna do is tell you the same thing I just said." Just so happened as my ole lady and I were having that conversation, both my doctors, Rittenberg and Warmoth, walked into my room. As soon as they entered, one of them spoke, saying, "We just came to check on you. Are you okay? Do you need anything?"

"Yeah, I thirsty," I said with a sad face.

Dr. Rittenberg said, "Are you? I'm sorry, but until the tests are ran you won't be able to drink or eat anything."

"I know, but I thirsty, real thirsty. Can I please have just a lil bit?" I asked with a sad face.

Dr. Rittenberg looked at me and said, "He's giving me the sad face and those beautiful puppy dog eyes." Then she looked at Dr. Warmoth and my ole lady, and said, "He's giving me the sad face, with those puppy dog eyes. Paulette, what do you do when he does this?" But my ole lady stood speechless.

The more I begged Dr. Rittenberg, like James Brown, for something to drink, she ultimately gave in. She asked me what I wanted to drink.

"A Capri Sun juice," I said.

Dr. Rittenberg replied, "I'm going to give you something to drink, but you have to take one swallow."

If you are asking yourself whether I took one swallow, the answer is yes, I did—but after I took three big sips before that one swallow. As far as the test was concerned, the results came back good. In fact, those three sips and one swallow didn't interfere with it at all.

Seconds after both doctors exited my room, my ole lady looked at me and said, "Mmm, mmm, boy, you something else. I can't believe you did that."

I smiled. Now do you see why I call my doctors, excellent doctors, doctors who allowed me to have my way? What more could I have asked for? Both of my doctors were like a dynamic duo on the eighth floor. If you saw one, you saw the other. They were the type of doctors who never made a decision without each other. Although I only spoke about my doctors allowing me to have my way, they really did make sure all my needs were met.

Days after being admitted to Roper Rehab, there were two wheelchair specialists named Rick and George who came to see me about my power chair. The day Rick and George paid me a visit, we made a decision about getting me a power chair that was equipped with special adaptations for me to operate independently on my own. During our discussion, it was understood that it wouldn't make any sense for me to have a joystick, since I'm disabled from my neck down. The idea Rick and George had in mind was this device called the Sip-and-Puff. Sip-and-Puff is a straw like device that you must blow into or Puff a certain number of times in order to operate the power chair. Being that this was my only way to independently operate the power chair, I agreed to the decision Rick and George made. Once finalizing the decision, Rick and George told me to give them a few days to get everything together, and they would be back.

Before I go any further, let me describe to you the type of men Rick and George are. Rick ("Slick Rick") is a slim, well-dressed guy who likes to impersonate me whenever I call their office. George is a fit bodybuilder, who comes to my home any time I have a problem with my power chair. Although they are both different, both gentlemen are family oriented men, who make sure I have what I need as far as my power chair is concerned.

Just as Rick and George said, they came back. As both gentleman entered my room, they brought in a candy-apple-red power chair, with the Sip-and-Puff device attached. Everyone who was in my room at that time, including both wheelchair specialists were all estatic, asking if I was ready to get in the power chair and try it out. After replying yes, Rick and George took the power chair they loaned me out of my room into the hallway, as my nurses put me on the Hoyer lift and transferred me from the bed to my new power chair.

The second step after getting transferred is positioning. Getting positioned is a simple process that doesn't take much work at all. All the nurses did to possession me was slide me completely up in my power chair, then shift my hips to the center of the power chair to make sure I was positioned comfortably and correctly. Once completing step two, we moved on to the third and final step, which was operating the power chair. For days I'd been eager to learn how to operate the Sip-and-Puff device on my new power chair, only to find out that the gentlemen who'd brought my power chair didn't know how to operate it either. Finding out Rick and George didn't know how to operate the Sip-and-Puff device was hilarious to us all, even they laughed at the fact they didn't know how to operate the device. On top of everyone not knowing how to operate it, there were no instructions that came along with it either. Without instructions, Rick and George left it up to me, the genius, to figure out how this thing worked.

Before trying to operate the Sip-and-Puff device, Rick adjusted the straw-like device that was mounted on the back of my power chair so it was closer to my mouth. He then adjusted the screen that was mounted on my left arm rest so I could see the menu as well. Once doing that, I gave it a shot. As soon as I put forth an effort, I got the chair to tilt. I don't know how, all I know is that the chair tilted. Everyone in my room stood in shock and asked, "What did you do? How did you get the chair to tilt?"

Since I didn't know how I'd gotten my power chair to tilt, I played with the device for a couple of minutes until I figured it out. As I played with the device, I immediately noticed the menu settings changing every time I puffed the straw. The settings on the menu included tilt mode, drive mode, etc. Since I discovered how to change the settings, I went back to the mode setting to examine exactly how I'd gotten the chair to tilt. By me switching the settings back to tilt mode, I quickly learned how I had done it. In order for me to tilt the chair up or down, I had to puff or blow into the device, holding it until the chair tilted at the level I wanted it. Once I got the hang of tilting, Rick and George told me to put the setting in drive mode and try driving.

Changing the setting from tilt mode to drive mode was simple; all I had to do was change the speed rate once in drive mode. The moment I switched the setting to drive mode, I put the speed rate on low, because I didn't know how to steer the chair. As the chair began to move like a turtle, I noticed it was veering off to the right slowly. When I saw the chair veering off to the right, I immediately began puffing the device to see which direction it would go, and it began turning left. With the chair automatically turning to the right on its own, puffing the device instinctively showed me instantly how to steer in any direction (left, right, or straight). Gaining the knowledge of how to operate this device gave me the confidence and motivation I needed to test drive.

Before test driving, I had to learn how to stop the chair if need be, because I didn't want to run anyone over. I knew blowing into the device would increase the speed rate, and common sense told me puffing the device would stop it, and it did. Once I learned how to stop the chair, it was on; I increased the speed again, and begin driving. Putting the chair back in drive mode left everyone standing in awe, saying, "Wow!" For me to have operated a device I'd never seen before within minutes, without any instructions, really was amazing, but I refused to take credit for it, because that belongs to God.

After driving around the rehabilitation floor several times, Rick and George said to me, "I guess you don't need us anymore. Looks like you have everything under control." Then they said, "Since you are doing such a great job, we are going to leave, but we will be back in a few days just to check on things."

Ever since I gained the confidence to test drive, I never stopped; I continued. From that day forward, I drove to all of my therapy sessions independently; I even drove to my psychiatric sessions with Dr. Barton (which I didn't talk about). Allow me to elaborate on Dr. Barton a little. The first time I saw Dr. Barton, I thought he was a descendant of President Abraham Lincoln, because that's who he resembled. Speaking to a psychiatrist was a first-time experience for me. I had never spoken to a psychiatrist before in my life. With this being a first-time experience for me, I didn't know what to expect, so I kept quiet. Coming into my psychiatric session, Dr. Barton greeted me, then stated his name. As I sat there, Dr. Barton began asking me questions like, "What is your name?"; "How old are you?"; "Do you know what month, day, and year it is?"

The more I answered Dr. Barton's questions, the more he asked; there was no stopping in him. I said to myself, "You got to be kidding me. Here it is, I got shot in my neck, and he's speaking to me as if I have a brain injury." Instead of me saying what was on my mind—which was "Let's rap this session up, and not have another one"—I continued to cooperate. He then asked me the ultimate question: "What happened?" As I began to explain how I'd gotten injured, he was astounded; his eyes popped open as if he had seen a ghost. Unlike others, Dr. Barton waited until I got finished sharing my story with him before he responded.

"Wow! I can't believe you remember that," he said, sounding like Ben Stein from the Clear Eyes commercial.

I told him, "Whether you believe it or not, that's what happened."

Sharing my story with Dr. Barton left him convinced, but he was more so amazed at the fact I remembered what happened, especially after all I'd endured. With God allowing me to keep my sanity, Dr. Barton saw me twice after our first visit to do other evaluation, then he discontinued our sessions. Dr. Barton was a gentleman who took his job seriously; he was also a person who had a willing spirit to assist his patients in any way possible. As for the other sessions, Dr. Barton evaluated me by having me recite over ten numbers he showed me on a piece of paper for a split second, from front to back, and vice versa. The other way he evaluated me was by flashing those

Rorschach test cards that determine whether you are sane or insane. Although I wasn't enthusiastic about attending my psychiatric sessions with Dr. Barton, I still have a great amount of respect for him and his profession.

After a long day of attending those different sessions, I would drive back to my room for a little quiet time. Around the time I drove back to my room with intentions to relax, I had visitors come in minutes after I entered. Some of the visitors who paid me a visit included my eldest sibling, a good lady friend of mine and her cousin, other schoolmates, and relatives. Every day between the time of two thirty and a quarter to three, my visitors began to roll in. The set of visitors who always came to see me first at that specific time was my eldest sibling, my good lady friend and her cousin, and a partner of mine. Any time those four came to see me, we would always have fun.

Thinking back on my days at Roper Rehab, I can remember my eldest sibling and good lady friend speaking in a language that only those two understood. Whenever they spoke in their language, her cousin and I would look at one another with a confused expressions because neither one of us knew what they were saying.

They noticed our expressions and asked, "Y'all wanna know what we talkin' 'bout, innit?"

We said, "Yeah," because we really wanted to know.

"No, that's between me and Kesia. That's our thing."

Although I was entitled to know what my eldest sibling and good lady friend were talking about, I left it alone, because I knew they would do it again. Soon after my eldest sibling and good lady friend stopped speaking in their secretive language, they did it again. The second time, I told them both to kiss my ass. That didn't change anything; in fact, they laughed at me and said, "You can't get mad because we are not telling you what we are talking about."

Despite giving my eldest sibling and good lady friend a legitimate reasons as to why I should have known what they were talking about, they still didn't give in. Since I couldn't convince them to tell us what they were saying, I tried to kick them out, just like Martin Lawrence did his visitors, but that didn't work either.

The whole time I was going at it with them, the cousin agreed with me, until my good lady friend threatened her, saying, "Remember, I'm your ride back home."

Without hesitation, the cousin stopped and said to me, "Mann, I love you, but I need a ride home."

Moments like that are examples of the fun I had with my visitors, especially my eldest sibling, good lady friend, and the cousin. Even though I only shared with you one story about how my visitors and I had fun, there were other things we did, such as watch movies, reminisce on life before my injury, and talk about some of my visitors. If my eldest sibling and the cousin didn't come to visit me along with my good lady friend, she would come alone.

The time she and I spent together alone was in dead silence; all you heard was the television. As I think back, I can remember her saying to me, "Why aren't you talking? You run your mouth any other time. What's the matter? Are you scared? Cat's got your tongue." Any time she asked me that question, I would smile as I replied, "Nothing." To tell the truth, I don't know why I was silent, but I do know I was trying to figure out why she kept coming to visit me on a day-to-day basis, especially since she and I were no longer dating. I got used to her visiting me on a day-to-day basis, staying past visiting hours; in fact, if she didn't arrive at the time she generally came, it dimmed my spirit. Although she visited me more than the other young ladies I'd dealt with, the young lady whom I was in a relationship with visited me as well, but I saw her more at the Medical University of South Carolina. The other visitors who came to see me weren't as outspoken as my good lady friend, however they did speak, but they were nervous.

As you can see, I was being visited by a lot of my schoolmates, but what I didn't mention is the visit from my language arts teacher, Mrs. Windham. The times Mrs. Windham visited me brightened my day, because I wasn't expecting any of my teachers to visit me. Out of every visit I got from Mrs. Windham, there is one visit that meant a lot to me. One day when Mrs. Windham came to see me, we talked as usual, and she asked how my day was, etc. Then she said, "I have a surprise for you!"

When Mrs. Windham told me she had a surprise, I replied, "Yeah?"

Before Mrs. Windham told me what the surprise was, she asked me, "Did the students tell you about the surprise?"

Then I replied no.

Once we got that squared away, Mrs. Windham showed me the surprise. The surprise she'd brought me was a banner that read We Miss You, Wendell, with a lot of signatures on it. As I started to read the banner, Mrs. Windham began explaining how the idea came about. Being that I was going through a trying time in my life, Mrs. Windham and the students wanted to do something for me to show their love and support. The more I began to read the signatures and notes, Mrs. Windham went on to say how she was nervous about the whole thing, because she thought the students would have let me in on the secret. Once Mrs. Windham showed me the banner and I read it, she hung it up on the wall under the TV, then left. At that time other than saying thank you, I didn't express how I felt, but the thought and effort of it all truly did mean a lot.

While being visited by family, friends, and schoolmates during the weekdays, other family members of mine visited me on the weekend. The family members who came to visit me were my ole man, sisters, grandparents, aunts, uncles, and cousins. Just like the other visitors, any time my family visited me they brought get well soon cards, balloons, or something beneficial. As I jog down memory lane, I am reminded of the visit when my family treated me the same, despite my injury. During our visits my family and I always had conversations with one another about anything. Some of the things my family and I talked about were new movies, the young ladies who visited me, and the beautiful caregivers who took care of me.

Around the time I was at Roper Rehab, one of my aunts and her family came to see me. As my aunt was visiting with me. she asked, "Have you seen *Hollow Man* and *Rush Hour*?" Since I replied no, my aunt began explaining what both movies were about, and how interesting they were. After sharing details about both movies, my aunt then said, "I have to purchase those movies for you when they come out on VHS," and she did.

Other visits I'm reminded of are those with my ole man, youngest sibling, and cousins. Any time they visited me, they would conversate with me as usual, but behind those conversations came a question. "May I have a snack?" Being the nice guy that I am—and yes, I did say nice guy—I told them yeah. Once I gave them the okay, they would grab what they wanted, get comfortable, and proceed to conversate with me, or watch television as if they were the patient. At that time I thought nothing of it, but now that I think about it, it seemed as though they only visited me for my snacks.

Despite my injury, my family visits showed me I had something that money couldn't buy—their love and support. In all honesty, I enjoyed every visit, but there is one visit I will always remember. One evening as I was lying in bed, I had an unannounced visitor who came to see me.

When the visitor entered my room, he greeted everyone, then stated that he was a member of Mount Moriah Missionary Baptist Church. He said, "I heard about what happened, so I came to show my support." After he greeted everyone, he asked my ole lady if it was okay for him to speak with me. Once she gave him the okay, he said to me, "Hey, Wendell, how are you?"

"I straight."

He asked, "Do you know who I am?"

"Nah," I replied.

Then he said, "Take a good look. You still don't know who I am?"

"Nah."

"How old are you?" said the gentleman.

"Sixteen."

"What year were you born?"

"In 1985."

Then he said, "That explains why."

Once we came to the conclusion as to why I didn't know who the gentleman was, he stated his name. The person who paid me a visit that evening was NFL All-Pro Wide Receiver, Number Eighty-Seven of the Washington Redskins, Charlie Brown. When Charlie Brown stated who he was, I said to myself, "Oh shit," as my cousin visiting me responded with such excitement, stating that Charlie Brown was the reason he picked the number eight-seven jersey while playing recreational football. For me to have had an NFL superstar standing in my room amongst my family and I, it was truly a privilege and an honor.

After all of the excitement, Charlie Brown stuck around to chat with us for a while, then he left. Before leaving, Charlie Brown gave me two autographed pictures signed by him personally. To say I'm a Washington Redskins fan, it was sad that I didn't know who Charlie Brown was, but I know now. Interacting with everyone at the hospital helped me out a lot; the laughter, the trash-talking to one another, and the love that was shown, it all kept me from stressing about my injury. As for the prayers that were prayed from day one, they never stopped. Everyone, including my ole lady's supervisor, Mrs. Kathy Therell, prayed continuously at Roper Rehab as well.

After having to spend days and nights at Roper, my discharge date drew near. Before getting discharged, my case manager Miss Linda Collins had set me up with home health services. The home health services Miss Linda Collins set me up with was one of South Carolina's in-home care providers that provided me with dependable certified nursing assistance, Monday through Friday, from eight in the morning to four in the afternoon.

In addition to that, Miss Linda Collins set me up with a company called Pharmaceutical Healthcare. PHC was dedicated to providing the highest quality healthcare and other related services that included home medical equipment and supplies, custom wheelchairs and mobility equipment, occupational, physical, and speech therapies, and skilled nursing.

Along with the home health services, Miss Linda Collins set me up with, she assigned me to another case manager name Peggy Repole, who was once employed with HASCI Waiver-SC DDSN, which is a company that provides services for people with traumatic brain injuries and/or spinal cord injuries and similar disabilities.

The other thing that was done before I got discharged was the removal of my tracheostomy. After having a discussion about this removal, my doctors came to an agreement to have the tracheostomy removed. In fact, my doctors said, "Since you are doing well with breathing on your own, there's no need for you to keep the tracheostomy in your throat any longer." Once the tracheostomy was removed, the doctors told me to give it two to three days, and the hole would close on its own completely.

Before leaving, my speech therapist told me to keep using the same techniques that she had me practice to continue to strengthen my voice and breathing, considering that the tracheostomy was no longer in. Throughout my time spent at both the Medical University of South Carolina and Roper Rehabilitation Hospital, my ole lady never left my side. The only time my ole lady went home was to check on my sisters; other than that, she was at the hospital with me. Having my ole lady by my side isn't something that started when I got injured; this has been going on since the beginning of time; I guess that's why I'm a spoiled mama's boy.

Finally, I left the hospital and went home. Instead of me getting transported to the home where I lived, I was transported to my grandparents' home on Ten Mile in North Charleston, because the house where my family and I lived wasn't suitable. Upon my arrival, Pharmaceutical Healthcare had already delivered my medical equipment and supplies. As the paramedics transported me off the EMS truck into the house, my grandmother, ole man, and sisters welcomed me with open arms. Since my power chair wasn't delivered until the next day, the paramedics transferred me to the bed.

After being transferred to the bed, my family did whatever it took to make me comfortable. Hours into being home, one of PHC's employees came out to show my family and I how to operate the equipment. Within that same day, PHC sent out a skilled nurse to check out my peg site and skin for breakdowns. As the day went on, my new case manager, Peggy Repole, met with me and my family for the first time to make sure the home health services were on post, and to talk about the services being provided. During that conversation with Miss Peggy Repole, my ole man and grandmother were present, but my ole lady did the talking.

After explaining how everything worked, the last thing Miss Peggy repole said was, "I'll be calling and stopping by to make sure you all are satisfied with the services, and to do an annual checkup, but if you guys need anything, feel free to call."

Aside from the services that HASCI provided, my ole lady had a longtime friend of the family come out and build me a ramp for my power chair. Later that evening, a few of my family members and friends visited me once they got word that I was home. The friends who visited me were childhood peers from my grandmother's community. Being that this group of friends didn't have any means of transportation to visit me at either hospital, they wasted no time visiting me at home. As the first visitor walked in, I immediately noticed that he was in shock from his facial expression. Seeing that he was in shock, I spoke with him as I generally would to help him loosen up when he greeted me. Shortly after realizing that I couldn't change the thought of what he saw, I fell back and proceeded to watch BET.

After visiting with me for a brief moment, my visitor left. The other friends who visited me did no different than the first visitor; they were all in shock, not saying much, and only stayed for a brief moment. Recognizing and seeing the reaction of my peers didn't surprise me, because I dealt with that at both hospitals. After such a busy day, my ole lady gave me my meds, set up my feeding pump, turned me on my side, and I went to sleep. Periodically throughout the night, my ole lady turned me from side to side just like they did at both hospitals.

Early that next morning, the nursing agency I was provided with sent me an aid for the day. and As I lay in bed asleep, I woke up to my ole lady saying, "Mann, wake up, baby. Your aid is here. Wake up for Mama, baby."

As I woke up, my ole lady went to get a hot washcloth for my face. The moment I opened my eyes completely, there stood my ole lady alongside the aid as she introduced herself. Soon after, she then asked me and my ole lady about our daily routine. Being that I'd just come home, my ole lady and I kept up our activities of daily living as was in the hospital.

Immediately after giving the aid a rundown of our daily routine, she and my ole lady began to get me squared away. Once completing my activities of daily living, I stayed in bed because my power chair still hadn't arrived. Around noon, Rick and George from PHC finally delivered my power chair. As soon as they brought it in, both of my parents transferred me into it using the Hoyer lift. During the process of transferring me, I would get dizzy, and sometimes pass out. Because I was getting dizzy, one of my parents always tilted the power chair completely back to regulate my blood pressure. After getting my blood pressure regulated, I would gradually tilt the power chair up completely. After sitting in my power chair for a couple of hours, both of my parents transferred me back in bed. Frequently throughout the day, and days after, my loved ones and my aid check on me.

As time went by, both of my sisters came home from school, and more visitors arrived. Due to my eldest sibling being employed at Chick-fil-A, and the youngest sibling having homework to complete, conversations with them after school were brief. Surviving all that I had endured, and my grandfather losing his life, as well as my partner getting shot and killed the same month I got shot, you would think nothing else could happen—but it did.

On Saturday, April 13, 2002, my eldest sibling woke me up, saying, " Mann, Mann, wake up. Cee dead. Somebody killed Cee. Wake up."

Hearing what I heard, I woke up immediately and asked, "What happened?"

When she said she didn't have any information about the incident, I then asked her, "Who told you he was dead?"

According to the information she gave me, a mutual friend of ours, who was related to my partner, called her with the news, but she didn't know exactly what happened either. During the conversation, she turned the TV on local news, and there it was, the coroner carrying my partner on a stretcher off of Stall Road, where he was shot and killed. When I saw my partner being carried away on a stretcher, all I could think about was him visiting me that Friday evening prior to his murder. Before my partner had come to see me, he called asking if I wanted anything. "Yeah, Applebee's," I told him.

My partner told me that he was going to pick up my eldest sibling, and was going to let her ride along with him, so I should tell her what I wanted. As they arrived back from the restaurant, my partner talked about putting me in his car and taking me for a ride in the hood once I got better. Being that it was a Friday, my partner didn't stay long, but before he left his last words to me were, "I just stopped by to holler at you before I go."

As I reflect on that moment, it didn't dawn on me that my partner was giving his final farewell. In fact, reality didn't set in until I was informed about his death and homegoing service that I was

120

unable to attend. With all things considered, the death of my partner didn't affect me right away, because it seemed surreal, but I did get emotional months later as he appeared to me in a vision.

On the evening of this vision, I can recall myself lying in bed as my partner appeared to me on a pillar of cloud. No sooner had my partner appeared, than he and I began conversing and greeting each other, then instantaneously, I asked him, "Brah, why you leave?" In response, my partner said he had some work to do, but he was back now. Due to my partner's absence, I began expressing to him how much I missed his presence, then I began sobbing, and said, "I need you, brah. I out here by myself. Ain't nobody riding wit me."

During my vision, while I was conversing with my partner, my ole lady entered my room, and asked who I was speaking to. I replied, "Cee. He's standing right here. You don't see him?" Being that I had taken prescribed medication prior to that vision, my ole lady thought I was hallucinating, so I tried to convince her that my partner was standing right there as she cradled me in her arms, trying to soothe me. Soon after, my partner said, "Brah, I 'bout to leave. I just came to check on you." As my partner began to fade away on the pillar of cloud, I began to call his name repeatedly. "Cee!" Then I asked him one last question: "Do you think I will ever walk again?" In response, my partner said, "I don't know. You have to take that up with God." Then he vanished.

Around the time of my partner's death, I was in the process of getting a new aid. The aid assigned to me when I arrived home from the hospital was a cool and quiet nurse, but unfortunately her time with me was short-lived due to her pregnancy. Without delay, a new aid was sent to my home the day after the agency gave someone else my case. The next aid who was sent to my house was a black nurse in her early thirties. With my ole lady and I having a set routine, all she did was give the aid a rundown, and assisted her from that day forward, just like she'd done with the other aid.

One day while sitting in my power chair, a couple of unexpected visitors (detectives) came to see me. As the detectives approached me, they stated who they were and let me know that they'd come to talk about the incident that occurred on the evening of my injury. Seconds after introducing themselves, the detectives asked me what happened that evening. With no hesitation, I cooperated with them, and began explaining what happened. After I'd finished, they shared with me the story given to them by the gentleman who shot me.

The story he gave them was that he and I were aiming guns at each other's heads, saying that was what we were going to do if someone ever approached us, and in the process, his gun accidentally went off and shot me. As soon as the detectives shared this with me, I said, "If he and I were aiming guns at each other's heads, how come I have a bullet in my neck, rather than my head?" When I made that valuable point, one of the detectives said, "We need to give you our badges." Then he asked if I wanted to press charges. I said no.

The reason I didn't press charges was because I knew being incarcerated, or becoming a victim of a violent crime, came along with that territory. In addition to that, I was in the mindstate of retaliation. Although the detectives came by unexpected, I appreciated their concern. However, it's crazy how I almost lost my life, and all they offered was a year or two probation if I pressed charges—so much for justice being served.

Days after working alongside the new aide, my ole lady felt comfortable enough to start back working. She'd informed me of it beforehand, which left me distraught. In light of her decision, I quickly put myself in the mindstate of getting used to her not being around. The first few weeks of not having my ole lady around, assisting me and the aid, went well. The only difference was my ole man took the place of my ole lady, and began helping out, considering he was unemployed.

Before the night of my injury, my ole man had been locked up in the Al Cannon Detention Center, serving time for old charges. While locked up in county, a childhood peer asked my ole man if he and I had the same name. My ole man replied, "Yeah," then the childhood peer asked him if I lived on Midland Park, and again he replied, "Yeah." Immediately after my ole man answered those questions, the childhood peer said, "Your son just got shot, and he's paralyzed." According to the information my ole man gave me, he immediately went into his cell and shut down after receiving that devastating news. The more I questioned my ole man, he began to explain how he'd felt the night of my injury, but I quickly cut the phone conversation short because I got emotional.

Several days after I got shot, my ole man was released from county days before his father's death. Ever since my ole man had gotten released from county, he and my ole lady made an agreement for him to stay home with my sisters and care for them, more so my youngest sibling. They also agreed for him to stay home with me while my ole lady was working, considering that the home health services were new. Between hours of the day, my ole lady called to check on things, since she was no longer there physically.

In just a few weeks of her being back at work, I picked up on my ole lady calling a little more than the norm. Every time my ole lady called, she would ask to speak with me once she'd spoken to my ole man or the aid. The phone conversations she and I had were basically about my day, and the aid's work ethic. Generally after we finished conversating, she would clear the line, but then she started asking to speak with my ole man or the aid before hanging up. The first few times my ole lady asked to speak back to one of them, she was able to, because they were nearby. Even though she was able to speak with him or the aid, she still did something that neither one of us expected—she popped up.

As soon as my ole lady walked through the back door, the first thing she saw was the aid sitting in my grandmother's room, along with my ole man. The first day the aid started working with me, she was specifically told to sit in the living area, or at the kitchen table, but instead she sat in a room that was off limits. (Strike one.) When my ole lady entered the house, the aid quickly jumped up and followed her to my room. My ole lady acted as if she'd come to check on me, and the aid asked her if she'd gotten off early. "No," my ole lady replied, "I just came to check on my boy."

After she'd peeped out the scene, my ole lady left and went back to work. One week later, she called to speak with me, as she generally did. At the end of our conversation, my ole lady asked to speak with my ole man; however, in the process of me calling him, I looked towards the kitchen and my grandmother's room to see if anyone was sitting there. As I called out for my ole man, I didn't get a response from anyone, so my ole lady told me to call the aid. Needless to say, I called out for the aid, but I got no response from her either. After calling my ole man and the aid for ten or fifteen minutes, my ole lady told me she was going to call back.

Ten minutes after I got off the phone with my ole lady, my ole man came to hang the phone up. Not too long after he hung up the phone, it rang again, and it was my ole lady. The conversation my parents had was about no one being around to answer my call. When my ole lady questioned my ole man about no one being around, he defended himself by saying that he'd stepped outside for a moment.

Once my parents got off the phone with each other, my ole man went back outside.

Fifteen minutes after my ole lady got off the phone, I heard her voice as she walked through the door, saying, "Y'all supposed to be taking care of my damn son, and y'all outside bullshittin' around." (Strike two.) The moment my ole lady walked in the house unexpectedly again, I said to myself, "Oh shit, it's on now." As my ole lady entered my room hotter than a fiery furnace, she asked if I was all right, then went back outside to my ole man and aid.

When she went back outside, I don't know what words were exchanged; all I know is the aid came back in the house, grabbed her belongings, and left. Prior to that incident with the aid, I was scheduled for a follow-up appointment, in addition to getting prepared for a major event. The follow-up appointment that had been scheduled was an appointment for my neck imagery. At the beginning of that follow-up, the doctor had me drive my power chair to the X-ray machine as close as I could possibly get. Then the doctor asked me if I could hold my head up on my own without the support of my headrest. I replied, "I don't know, but I will try."

As I put forth the effort to lift my head on my own, I was able to. During this process, the doctor told me to move it completely backward and forward as he snapped the imagery. Once the doctor got finished taking the imagery, he came back to where my ole lady and I were. Seeing that I was able to hold my head up on my own successfully, the doctor was amazed. I was amazed as well, because I'd never tried it before.

Because I was able to hold my head up on my own, the doctor removed the cervical collar for good. After leaving the X-ray room, my ole lady and I went to sit in the lobby and wait for public transportation (Tel-A-Ride), since we didn't have a personal van that was wheelchair accessible.

As we sat in the lobby, a familiar face and I spotted each other from a distance. It was the mother of the gentleman who shot me. Before she walked in our direction, my ole lady noticed his mother staring at me, and asked if I knew who she was, and I said I did. Then she asked if that was the mother of the gentleman who'd shot me, and again, I replied, "Yeah." Then my ole lady went further, saying, "I wonder if she has the decency to stop and speak, because I know she see you."

Astoundingly, after my ole lady said that, the gentleman's mother walked up to me, along with her two youngest daughters, and spoke. "How are you doing? Do you remember me?"

I replied, "Yes, ma'am," and then she introduced herself to my ole lady.

After staring at me for a couple of minutes, the gentleman's mother told me that she was going to tell her son she'd seen me, and walked off. As soon as the mother left, my ole lady asked if I was okay, then said, "It was nice of her to stop and speak."

The major event I was getting myself prepared for was a prom hosted by the administrators of R.B. Stall High School. During my stay at Roper Rehab, the young lady I was courting at the time called and asked my ole lady if she would let her escort me to her senior prom. My ole lady replied, "Baby, I don't mind. Let me put him on the phone so you can ask him." I replied, "Yeah."

Weeks after being discharged from Roper Rehab, the prom date came up. On the evening of the prom, I was well-dressed in a black tux, with a white collared shirt and no tie. In addition to that, I had on my gold jewelry and had a fresh cut, looking debonair. As my ole lady and I awaited transportation (Tel-A-Ride) to pick us up and transport us to the hotel where the prom was held, she began taking pics like paparazzi. Once Tel-A-Ride came to pick us up, the driver transported us to the prom, where I met up with my prom date. The moment we arrived at the hotel, I got nervous, because I wasn't used to being in the public eye with a significant other.

As the driver lowered me off the lift of the bus, there stood my prom date, looking beautiful as ever, wearing a black dress with silver trimmings, silver diamond accessories, and an updo hairstyle. Once I got off the bus, my prom date greeted me with a smile, kiss, and hug. After greeting each other, my prom date and I entered the building along with my ole lady, eldest sibling, and others. Prior to entering the actual room where the prom was, everyone who attended had to show their tickets to the teachers and administrators who stood at the door. The teachers and administrators standing at the door greeted me along with everyone else, saying, "How are you doing? It's nice to see you. Enjoy your evening."

As soon as everyone entered the room, we immediately looked for a spot to sit. Shortly after finding a spot, my ole lady suggested that my prom date and I take pictures before the line got long. Taking prom pictures was a simple process. All my prom date and I did was stand where the photographer asked us to, and pose for the camera. Once the photographer had taken several shots of me and my prom date, we exited the photo booth. As we went back to our seats, I began socializing with people I'd both seen and hadn't seen since my injury. Over time, the crowd grew larger, and the DJ began playing hit records, such as "Hot in Herre," written and produced by Nelly and Pharrell. Prior to that moment, my ole lady had tried to convince my eldest sibling and peers to get on the dance floor, but they'd refused to do so. Seconds after, the DJ played "Hot in Herre." My ole lady is a fan of that song, and she lost it. She grabbed my eldest sibling's prom date, dragged him on the dance floor involuntary, and forced him to dance with her, saying, "Y'all ain't wanna dance. Let me show y'all how to party, since y'all ain't know what to do."

Everyone who was in our circle was in awe, because we hadn't expected my ole lady to do that. In fact, my ole lady hadn't expected for that to take place either, but it did. The whole time she was on the dance floor with my eldest sibling's prom date, everyone laughed continuously, saying, "Y'all mama crazy." As my ole lady continued to dance, my prom date walked on the other side of the room to speak with a friend. After my prom date walked away, a young lady whom I spoke to from time to time at school came over a couple of times to ask for a dance, but I replied no.

While she and I were having our conversation, my prom date came out of nowhere, asking the young lady, "Is there a problem?"

"No, I was just hailing him," the young lady said, then left.

My prom date said to me, "You think you slick? I've been watching you the whole time. Let another one of your little girlfriend come over here."

After that incident, and dancing to a couple of songs, my ole lady and eldest sibling's prom date finally got off the dance floor. Watching my ole lady put on a show was hilarious, but it was even funnier to see my eldest sibling's prom date stand there like a bump on a log to every song. Shortly after the two of them left the dance floor , the administrators announced the prom king and queen, and gave them the spotlight before the last call. Time went by, and the prom ceremony ultimately ended, and everyone left. Prior to parting ways, everyone who stood in our circle gave their goodbyes, then went elsewhere to enjoy the rest of the evening, but as for me, I had to turn in.

What an evening, what a wonderful and memorable evening. As I reflect on it, I'm reminded of the enjoyment I had spending the evening with my prom date, watching my ole lady be herself, and being amongst my eldest sibling and our peers. And if I had the opportunity to trade that evening for anything, I wouldn't.

Days after the prom ceremony, my prom date brought our prom pictures to my grandmother's house, and it was our last encounter. I tried contacting her, but she didn't answer or return any of my calls or pages, so I took it as a loss.

Due to the incident that occurred with the second aid, the agency told my ole lady to give them a couple of days and they would send another aid. On one of the days I didn't have an aid, my ole lady left my ole man in charge to tend to my needs. During that day, he made sure I was squared away, but later on, he went somewhere. Minutes after my ole man stepped out, my grandmother came to check on me and asked if I needed anything, but I replied no. In the process of checking on me, my grandmother closed the door to see if I'd had an accident (had a bowel movement, or urinated). As she pulled the sheet and gown back, she said, "Oh shit." Then she yelled out my cousin's name, who was present at the time. "Chris!" Suddenly, my cousin got up and said, "Granny, what's wrong?" Our grandmother told him to come in the room.

As soon as my cousin came in, our grandmother uncovered me and said, "Look! Ain't he got a rod on him." The moment I realized why my grandmother had called my cousin, I couldn't believe it. Here. It. Is. I thought she was in pain, and needed assistance turning me, but much to my surprise, she wanted to expose my private area.

When my cousin saw why she'd called him, he immediately exited the room, saying, "No, Granny, I ain't wanna see dat."

As our grandmother laughed, she told my cousin, "I didn't know he was holding like that."

"Granny, he's a Manigault," my cousin replied. "What you expect?"

In all honesty, it was embarrassing to have my grandmother and cousin see me in the nude, but it also was hilarious. The last thing my grandmother said to me as she covered my nakedness was that I'd scared the shit out of her, and the Lord had sure blessed me.

According to the information my ole lady gave me, my grandmother called her at work, sounding hysterical, and asked, "Why didn't you tell me about Wendell?" My grandmother also called several of our family members and told them as well. Although that was an embarrassing moment, I appreciate the compliment my grandmother gave me. Thanks, Granny. Once the agency found a new aid, they sent her to my home. The new aid was a twenty-five-year-old black nurse. Considering what had happened with the second aid, my ole lady stayed home that morning to meet and greet her.

When the third aid arrived, my ole lady spoke with her privately before escorting her to my room. Once my ole lady spoke with the aid, she brought her in my room so we could meet each other, then left for work.

Working with the third aid turned out great. She followed the schedule routine that was set prior to her arrival, and we got along just fine. Ever since the new aid had come, I'd gotten back in the swing of things, such as getting up in my power chair and going outside. Being that I trusted no one other than my ole lady to transfer me by themselves, I'd stopped getting in my power chair the day she'd gone back to work, but after demonstrating to two or more people how to transfer me using the draw sheet, I began getting up again. The first step in transferring a patient using a draw sheet is to get them positioned toward the power chair close to the bedside. One lifter must be at the head of the bed, and the other at the foot of it. The lifters must grip both ends of the sheet, as well as the patient's upper and lower extremities. Then, on the count of three, the patient can be transferred.

On the days I went outside to enjoy the spring weather, I would sit on the porch with the aid, my family, peers, or by my lonesome. Another thing I would do while sitting on the porch is help my youngest sibling with her homework. Every day my youngest sibling came home from school, she would ask one of our parents to assist her with her homework, but they started sending her to me for assistance. Being the obedient son I am, I did exactly what my parents asked me to do—*help*.

As I began helping my youngest sibling with her homework, she did fairly good, but there were some problems with which she needed assistance. Seeing this, I tried helping her by using our parents' method, but since that wasn't working, I tried my way, which was the total opposite of how our parents would help. Our parents would guide them step by step on how to solve a problem, but I assisted by giving answers to the problem. As soon as I gave my youngest sibling the answers to those few problems, she jotted them down so fast, to the point her pencil ignited in flames.

When she finished jotting down the answers, I said to her, "Hey, don't tell Mama and dem I gave you the answers"—and she never did. Giving those answers to her was the best thing I could have done for us both at that time, because she was able to play with her friends before the street light came on, and I didn't have to spend all evening helping her with homework. People who are big on kids getting an education would say I made a poor decision by just giving her the answers. In fact, my youngest sibling at times told me it was, but

I say I did an excellent job, considering she's graduated high school on May 30, 2012. Congratulations, lil sis.

Besides those two events, there are other things I did while sitting outside, such as drive my power chair to the corner where a few of my partners stood. I also sat in my grandmother's backyard to do something I hadn't done since I'd gotten shot. One evening as I sat on the front porch with my eldest sibling, good lady friend, and cousin, my cousin said to me, "Lo, brah, I 'bout to roll dis blunt. You burnin'?" and I replied, "Yeah." In response, he laughed at me and said, "You ain't burnin' nuttin', brah." My cousin wouldn't take me seriously, so I tried convincing him by repeatedly saying, "Yeah, I burnin'," but he still didn't believe me. The whole time I was trying to convince him I was going to smoke, my eldest sibling and good lady friend were in disbelief as well. Since no one took me seriously, I did the only thing I knew to do, which was drive my power chair down the ramp and to the backyard. When my cousin and I got in the backyard, he rolled the blunt, lit it, and we began our smoke session. As my cousin and I were getting high, my eldest siblings and good lady friend looked back at us from the front porch and said, "He smokin' for real. I can't believe he's smokin'."

Truth be told, I don't know what there was to be shocked about, especially when I'd blatantly told them I was going to smoke. During our smoke session, my ole man came out the back door to where my cousin and I were, and said, "Zeke, what y'all doin'?" and I replied, "Burnin a lil herb." My ole man didn't want my ole lady, grandmother, or Aid to find out, so he told me and my cousin to hurry up and put out the blunt. My cousin and I took a couple more pulls, then put out the blunt.

The next day, I woke up with a migraine, which indicated to me that something was wrong with my physical body. Generally, when I get a migraine, it comes from my bladder not emptying completely, which means I have a urinary tract infection. In light of the activity I'd partaken in the day before, I lied to both my ole lady and the doctor, telling them I'd drunk lots of soda instead of water. In all honesty, lying is something I shouldn't have done, but I didn't know how my ole lady would have reacted to finding out that I was smoking. I didn't want my parents to be held accountable for my stupidity. Having the sweet doctor I had, she didn't take a urine specimen from me. In fact, she took my word for it, and wrote an order for antibiotics. Was that a close call or what? Although physicians and nurses suggested that I smoke a joint since I didn't have an appetite, I felt I could have gotten my parents in a lot of heat because of that.

Ever since I smoked that homecoming blunt, I fell back from smoking for a while. As the days went by, my eldest sibling graduated R.B. Stall High School in June 2002, which was around the time school ended for summer break. During that short period of time I was home from the hospital, PHC sent a physical therapist to my home, but that didn't last long, because I wasn't up for that. On top of having a therapist come to my home, my teachers Mrs. Windham, Mrs. Bond, and Mr. Doctor came out as well to do homeschooling. The only thing my teachers asked of me was to watch a Shakespeare's film, and complete several worksheets, but because I failed to complete those assignments, that didn't last long either.

Unlike others, who enjoyed their summer break going to the pool and/or beach, I enjoyed my summer break going to the mall and/or visiting with loved ones or peers. My aunt through marriage always visited me, along with my two cousins. Every time my aunt visited, she would always give me a facial. As she started the facial procedure, she and I conversated about anything, as my cousin stood nearby grumbling.

I also had another aunt through marriage who came to visit me a lot with her family of four. Any time this group of family members visited me, we would always joke around, although my aunt and I bumped heads several times in a funny way. What caused it was some information my cousins (her sons) had given me. According to what my cousins told me, my aunt would say to young ladies who asked about me, "What you want wit him? He ain't got time for no girlfriends."

When my cousin's gave me that information in front of my aunt, she said, "Yeah, I said it, and I'll say it again."

"Oh no! You can't be doin' dat," I told her. "You killin' da set."

She replied, "Boy, shut up. You ain't got time for no fast tail girls."

Question: Who died and made my aunt queen? Don't get me wrong, my aunt was right about what she said, but as Bobby Brown would say, it was my prerogative. As much as I want to tell you that this is a joke, it wasn't. In fact, this incident took place more times than I can count. If she hadn't been my aunt, I would have said some ungodly things, but since I have the Lord in my life, I laughed, because it was funny.

What a wonderful feeling it is to have your loved ones' and peers' support. Every visit I got, I appreciated. I enjoyed going to the mall with my ole lady and cock-blocking aunt, who, by the way, purchased me a solid gold chain while we were there. Sometime during the summer, my family was blessed to move out of my grandmother's home and relocate to a home that our church owned off of Midland Park Road. Moving into this home was a major relief for me and my loved ones, considering our living conditions. The living conditions in my grandmother's three-bedroom home weren't bad at all; the only thing was that my family of five had to share two rooms amongst one another.

With my family making this move, my grandmother was able to retrieve her privacy, and my family and I were able to do the same. While in the process of moving, my family and I hadn't forgotten about the third aid. In fact, we brought her along with us to resume care. This home, which my church was generous enough to let me and my family live in, had three bedrooms, one-and-a-half baths, and a nice view of the lake. Getting settled in this new home didn't take much, considering we had our personal space.

Once word got out that my family and I had moved back in the area, more visitors whom I hadn't seen since I got injured came flocking like birds. In the weeks since we'd moved out of my grandmother's home, my seventeenth birthday, Thanksgiving, and Christmas had all arrived. On the evening of my birthday, November 15, 2002, my ole lady tried convincing me to get up in my power chair. Being that I was in my lazy mode, I refused to get up. Seconds after, my aunt entered my room and tried to convince me too, but I told her no as well. As soon as my aunt left my room, she came back, along with my ole lady, with a cake and other visitors I didn't know was there, who were singing, "Happy birthday to ya!"

The moment my family entered the room singing, I began smiling, because I wasn't expecting a surprise party. When they finished singing, they said to me, "This is why we were asking you to get up, but since you were being stubborn, we came in here to you." In all honesty I don't remember what I told my loved ones, but knowing me, I probably said, "Y'all should have said something."

Once my family gave their birthday wishes, the party started. Celebrating my seventeenth birthday with the party planners and attendees really meant a lot to me, especially when I almost hadn't lived to see it. In the near future, if someone wants to surprise me with something, please inform me beforehand so I can cooperate the next time.

CHAPTER 11

What a crazy year 2002 had been for me, considering the situation I'd gotten myself into, and for the first time it was a situation I was unable to get myself out of. In fact, the only way I would be able to make it through, in, and out of this situation was by the grace and mercy of God. Due to God allowing me to survive that deadly gunshot wound, I felt it was in my best interest to start the new year off right. Instead of shooting fireworks before the clock struck midnight, I chose to do what my ole lady instilled in me and my two siblings as children, which was attend watch night service.

If I may be allowed to briefly educate you on the history of watch night service: According to Ann Brock it is a tradition that has been traced long before you or I were a thought. The watch night service in black communities celebrated today can be traced back to gatherings on December 31, 1862, also known as "Freedom's Eve." On that night, Americans of African descent came together in churches, gathering places, and private homes throughout the nation, and anxiously awaited the news that the Emancipation Proclamation had become law. Then at the stroke of midnight, it was January 1, 1863, and according to Lincoln's promise, all slaves in the Confederate states were legally free. People remained in churches and other gathering places, eagerly awaiting word that emancipation has been declared. When the actual news of freedom was received later that day, there were prayers, shouts, and songs of joy as people fell to their knees and thanked God. Black folks in North America have gathered annually on New Year's Eve since the earliest days, praising God for safely bringing us through another year and praying for the future. Certainly those traditional gatherings were made even more poignant by the events of 1863, which brought freedom to the slaves and the year of Jubilee. Many generations have passed since, and most of us were never taught the African American history of watch night. Yet our tradition and our faith still brings us together at the end of the year to celebrate once again "how we got over."

On New Year's Eve, me, my ole lady, and my two siblings were getting dressed to attend watch night service that started at nine o'clock. Once my family and I got ourselves squared away, my ole lady transferred me from the manual wheelchair into her car, then we headed to church. On our way to church, I was under the influence of an alcoholic beverage called Paul Masson, thinking to myself, *Wow, it is New Year's Eve, and I'm still here.* During that thought process, my ole lady pulled up to the church, which was only five minutes from where we lived.

The second my ole lady stepped out of the car to transfer me to my manual chair, some of our church members offered their assistance, but she had everything under control. Once my ole lady got me squared away, we entered the church for service, which had just begun. As my family and I sat in the congregation, spiritual leaders, musicians, and the congregation members were singing, having a good time in the name of the Lord. The further we got into the service, the tithes and offerings were taken up, the floor was open for testimonies, and the pastor preached his sermon. Then the lights got shut off fifteen minutes before midnight.

Shutting off the lights didn't have anything to do with a power outage. In fact it is a tradition that has been taken place for years in Baptist churches, so members and visitors can pray, praise and worship God as he ushers us into a new year. Deacons would stand on post as watchman's of the north, south, east, and west harmonized, singing, "Brother watchman of the east, could you please tell me the time?" In response to the first watchman's question, the next watchman would say, "The time is now ten minutes till the hour." Having received the time, the congregation would make a joyful sound by praising, worshipping, and thanking God, because we understood that the hour was near for a new beginning.

Once the clock struck midnight, the watchmen then informed the congregation that it was a new year. Being that the congregation was already praising, worshipping, and thanking God, we continued to give him our crazy praise as we embraced one another for the new year. Unlike the other members and visitors of the church, I did not give God the crazy praise that he deserved, but I did thank him for sparing my life yet another year.

After watch night service is over, African American families generally go home and eat a dish that the older generation says brings you good luck and money, Hoppin' John and collard greens. With all due respect, I love the older generation—Lord knows I do—but y'all need to cut that superstition jazz out about Hoppin' John and collard greens, because all my life I have been eating Hoppin' John and collard greens, and I'm still broke with no good luck.

In the beginning of the year 2003, I proceeded to carry on with my life. The aid that my family and I brought along with us continued to do an excellent job working with me; she and I also got used to each other over time. As scheduled Pharmaceutical Healthcare continued to deliver my monthly medical supplies, as well as send a wound care nurse to my home for their weekly visit, three times a week at that time.

Later in the evening, once I'd completed my activities of daily living, more visitors whom I had seen and had not seen since I'd gotten injured continued to come. The visitors who came to see me were family and strangers; they were also visitors whom I mentioned towards the end of the last chapter, but didn't elaborate on. Being that I was already used to the shocked reactions from past as well as present visitors, I got myself prepared for this new group of visitors. Just as I expected. this group of visitors, including the strangers, were in shock like everyone else.

As I began visiting with them, they started asking me the same questions everyone else generally asked: "How are you doing?" and "What did the doctor say?"

Once I answered their questions, some of them were courageous enough to ask what happened. The people who generally asked that question were doctors, nurses, and therapists, but since this group of visitors decided to ask, I told them. At the end of my explanation, my visitors began telling me the stories they'd heard. They heard I'd gotten shot due to a gambling debt that I owed the gentlemen. They'd also heard the gentleman and I were playing with guns, and his accidentally went off and shot me.

Listening to those stories didn't affect me at all, considering that I knew the truth, but like I told everyone, this was one of the reasons God spared my life—so the story could be told. Once those family members, friends, and strangers found out what really occurred, some of them contemplated murder, but for various reasons, the spirit man inside of me told them to leave it be.

Months into the new year, I decided to follow through with a decision I'd contemplated for months after my injury: baptism. Being that God had spared my life on the evening I got shot, I felt it was only right to give him my life back in return. Instead of me waiting to announce the good news in church that following Sunday, I decided to contact my pastor and inform him about my decision. When I broke the news to my pastor, he immediately spoke out of excitement, then began telling me the steps I had to take prior to getting baptized.

Once I'd spoken with my pastor, he and I took the first step by announcing my candidacy for baptism in church that following Sunday. From that point on, everything was set in motion. Before being baptized, I also had to attend and complete baptism class, which I'll explain.

Baptism class are sessions where spiritual leaders educate candidates of baptism on the true meaning of baptism, so for those of you who are not educated about the true meaning of baptism, here it is. The true meaning of baptism is basically symbolic to the death, burial, and resurrection of Jesus Christ (the anointed one). In the beginning of time, man gained the knowledge of good and evil by eating of that tree which God forbid them to eat. Consequently, God cursed the deceiving serpent (Satan) above all animals. He also multiplied the grief and suffering of woman in pregnancy, then he cursed the ground of man because of their sin. Over time, God sent special messengers, such as Moses, to deliver his people from bearing (sin), and to have them acknowledge and serve him as the true and living God he is. God also destroyed mankind and beast by flooding the earth due to the wickedness of man. In doing that, man still failed to acknowledge and serve God as they should; in fact, man continued to sin, as well as serve other gods that don't exist, but "for God so loved the world that he gave his only begotten son, that whosoever believes in him should not perish, but have everlasting life" (John 3:16).

The day God gave His only begotten son Jesus Christ (the Messiah), you must understand that he offered him up as a perfect sacrifice to die for our sins. You must also understand that when he arose from the dead on the third day, we became free from sin, so realize that when you are submerged underwater, you died the same death as Christ did, and when you are raised up from that water, you are resurrected just as Christ was, and freed from sin; "therefore, if any man be in Christ, he is a new creature; old things are passed away; behold, all things are become new" (2 Corinthians 5:17). In other words, you are no longer a slave to sin, but a part of the body of Christ through baptism.

Now whatever you do, please don't get baptism and salvation misconstrued, because those are two different things. According to Romans 10:9, salvation (getting saved, deliverance) is simply you confessing with your mouth, and believing in your heart, that Christ is Lord, and that God raised him from the dead.

For example, in the book of Luke, Chapter 23, one of the criminals that was suspended alongside Christ on the cross received salvation. I know this because in so many words of verse forty through forty-two, the criminal confesses with his mouth, and believes in his heart, that Christ is Lord. In response to his confession and beliefs, Christ said unto him in verse 43, "Verily I say unto thee, today shalt thou be with me in Paradise." Always remember that baptism is symbolic of the death, burial, and Resurrection of Christ, and salvation is simply you confessing with your mouth, and believing in your heart, Romans 10:9.

Due to spiritual leaders briefing me on the true meaning of baptism a couple of days prior to getting baptized, I didn't get the teaching you just received, but I still followed through with my baptism. On April 11, 2003, I got baptized early that morning in an unusual way. Two days prior to getting baptized, spiritual leaders of my church were brainstorming on how they were going to baptize me, considering my physical disability. They came up with one idea, which was for them to transfer me out of my power chair into the baptism pool, quickly baptize me, then transfer me back into my power chair. As they pitched their ideas to me, I immediately looked at them like they were fools, and said, "Who? Y'all better find another way."

They all laughed at my reaction, and one of the spiritual leaders sarcastically said, "You don't trust us? We're not going to drop you on purpose."

As we all laughed at one another, they kept trying to convince me to let them transfer me into the baptism pool by saying they would have a good grip on me, as well as have my ole lady stand by. To be honest with you, if those spiritual leaders had told me, "Wendell, we're going to have Jesus Christ himself stand in the baptism pool as we transfer you into it," I still wouldn't have allowed them to transfer me—that's how much I didn't trust it. Once they noticed I wasn't changing my mind, they found an alternative, which was to poor a basin of water over my face. Now, how brilliant was that thirty minutes of brainstorming that lead to a safe idea that finally made sense. Good job, guys. Considering this was an offer that I couldn't refuse, I immediately took them up on it.

Early the morning of the baptism, my pastor called me to the altar to start the baptism ceremony. On my way to the altar, the spiritual leaders were lying clear plastic on the floor to catch the water; they also brought in a basin of water for the baptism. Once everyone positioned themselves, the pastor went on with the baptism ceremony, baptizing me in the name of the father, the son, and the Holy Spirit. Truth be told, I don't know if my spiritual leaders thought I was that same guy in the book of John, Chapter 5, who lied at the gate, called beautiful when they came up with that insane idea, but they quickly found out I wasn't.

After the baptism ceremony, my pastor proceeded to follow through with our normal church service. When I got baptized, I honestly didn't feel different, but I felt like I did something I was supposed to do. Once church was over, the spiritual leaders and members congratulated me, then we all went on with our lives.

Shortly after being freed from the power of sin through baptism, I once again became a slave of sin by yielding to its cravings, and being subject to its lust and evil passion. One of the cravings I yielded to was alcohol. Years prior to getting injured, drinking alcohol, such as Paul Masson, Seagram's Gin, and Hennessy, was something I did in my leisure time, but ever since I'd gotten shot, I hadn't drunk anything for the first six or seven months after my injury.

As I continued to receive visits from everybody, there were two visitors who came every Friday after work. Every time they came around, they brought alcohol for themselves to have while visiting me, but I didn't drink any of it. Being that I'd once lived and conducted myself in the passion of the flesh, I eventually obeyed the desires of my flesh and the thoughts of my mind, by drinking. In a situation like this, the youth are sometimes pressured by their peers, but in my case, I drank of my own free will. Once I took that first swig, I fell in the routine of drinking along with my partners throughout the week.

Yielding to the cravings of alcohol isn't the only craving I yielded to. I became subject to the lustful desire of sex—yes, sex. Even though I was a newly spinal-cord-injured patient, I was still hitting homers like Babe Ruth, or better yet, I was still taking it to the hole like Wilt Chamberlain. With everything I had going on, sex shouldn't have been on my mind, but how could it not have been when temptation arose and stood in front of my face?

One of the young ladies who I had sexual intercourse with was someone I'd met after my injury through a family member of mine; she is also the young lady who has my disabled virginity. The thing that attracted her to me was three-way phone conversations between me and her, as well as my cousin. Periodically throughout the week, my cousin and the young lady called me once he came home from school. What started off as every-other-day phone conversations turned into everyday conversations, which led to one-on-one conversation, as well as visits between me and her.

During one of our visits, probably the second or third visit, something normal but crazy happened. (I had an erection.). Being that I was well aware of this happening everyday for no apparent reason, I would usually place a pillow over my midsection whenever company came around, but this time I forgot. The second I noticed the midsection of my sheet rising, I said to myself, "Oh shit," as I laughed within. I glanced towards the left in a slick way to see if the young lady had noticed me having an erection, but her eyes were glued to the television. I continued to play it cool, hoping that my soldier would stand down.

Later that night, once the young lady had gotten home and settled, she gave me a call. She said to me, "Hey, ain't you say you paralyzed from the neck down?"

I replied, "Yeah."

"Well how come you still can get an erection?"

Before I replied, I laughed, because I'd thought she hadn't noticed, then I told her, "Your guess is just as good as mine."

Out of curiosity, she asked me if I was still able to feel anything in my midsection.

I replied, "Yeah."

Then she said, "So I guess that means you can have sex?"

And I replied, "Yeah."

She came to my house the next morning, and made me a happy man! In all honesty, I really am unable to feel anything from the neck down, but being that I'm a man with pride and desires, it was hard for me to resist temptation. One of the other young ladies I had sexual intercourse with was someone I knew from childhood. The thing that led to us having sex was a phone call I received.

One night while lying in bed, my phone rang, and it was the young lady. As soon as I answered, she asked me if I was busy, and I replied no. She then boldly blurted out, "Mann, I wanna fuck you."

I replied, "Huh?" then repeated what she said. Being that I was clueless as to how this young lady's desire had come about, I tried picking her, saying, "Ain't nuttin happening."

Surprisingly, the young lady fell for my strategize plan and it began to work. She told me I was lying, and there wasn't anything I could say or do to make her believe otherwise. The more I tried to convince this young lady that my tool was no longer in service, the more she wasn't buying it; in fact, she went on by sharing personal information with me about my physical body.

I immediately asked her where she'd gotten her info, but she refused to answer my question until I answered hers. Once I did, she then gave me the 411. Apparently, a home health nurse who took care of me told her the information about my physical body. Receiving that information from the young lady did not upset me at all, because the nurse put me in the game—but I now know what some nurses do when they deal with certain clients.

Within that same week, if not the next day, the young lady came to my home, and she, too, made me happy! Man. Prior to having sexual intercourse with her, there was a problem: She was afraid to put a condom on me. I didn't want to pass up this opportunity, so I told the young lady to get my ole man. When my ole man entered the room, I asked him if he would put the condom on me. At first my ole man said, "Zeke, you hear what you just asked me?" But after I begged him, he put it on. Once my ole man made that move for me, the young lady came back in and took care of business. Before, during, and after having sex with her, my mind went back to when I was five years old.

Ever since I'd been five years of age, I'd followed this young lady around the community I came up in, asking her to be my girlfriend, but she denied my request. In fact, she would walk me back home and tell my ole man I kept following her. Around the time I was trying to get at the young lady, she and her family moved to another community, which put a halt to my pursuit. Years later, I ran across her in church. The moment I saw her sitting in the fellowship hall, I figured I should try my luck once again.

As soon as I approached her, she said, "Mann, you still trying to holla at me? You been trying to holla at me since you been a little boy."

I told her, "I grown now," but still, she denied my request.

One year and some months after my injury, I received an unexpected visit from her and her nephew. Before she entered my room, her nephew came in first, saying, "I brought a surprise for you." When I saw who the surprise was, I couldn't believe it; in fact, I thought I was hallucinating. As I kept my composure, she said, "I heard you got shot, but it didn't dawn on me that it was you until my nephew said he was going to visit his homeboy." In the midst of our conversation, I began undressing her with my eyes, but I didn't try my luck that time due to my physical disability. Once we'd ended our conversation, her nephew spoke briefly, then they left.

Prior to my visitors leaving, the young lady surprisingly asked me for my number, and I gave it to her. Even though the nurse violated my privacy, that visit was the beginning of our sex scandal. Temptation, temptation, what do you do when you are suddenly faced with temptation? My advice to you who are faced with temptation is to ask God to lead you not into temptation, then make efforts to resist temptation.

Besides yielding to these cravings, I started back attending family gatherings, be it cookouts, birthday parties, etc. These events were thrown by two aunts of mine, one who's the eldest sibling of my ole lady, and the other, the wife of my uncle. Every year, throughout the year, my aunts would host such events and invite family members as well as friends of the family to come out and have a good time. With my aunts taking my situation into consideration, they would invite me as well.

Gatherings with my family were like an episode of Soul Train, with the exception of alcohol beverages and soul food. At the beginning of these events, everyone would listen to the music and socialize with one another as the food was being prepared. Once the food was finished, everyone would grab a plate to eat, then the party began. One of the most memorable moments of these events that comes to mind is everyone dancing to R. Kelly hit single "Step in the Name of Love." The second my cousins spinned that record, everybody and their momma got on the dance floor; in fact, those who complained about being in pain, jumped out of the their seats.

As I sat there watching everyone have a good time, I began to laugh, because I noticed everyone stepping—but not in the name of love. Initially, when you do this dance, you're supposed to step, twist, and turn a certain way, but because everyone didn't know what they were doing, they added their own twist. Once that song went off, everyone went back to their seats and started complaining about pain again, while the rest of us spoke about getting ready for church the next day. Although some of them didn't know what they were doing, I must say they all were on beat.

Another memorable moment of those events that comes to mind is my ole lady and cousins dancing to the hit single "I Smoke, I Drank" that was recorded by the Body Head Bangerz. I witnessed my ole lady, who was in her mid-thirties at the time, on the dance floor, dancing with my generation. As soon as that particular record was played, I thought I was in the club, because all I saw was my generation on the dance floor, a town stomping and two-stepping with Styrofoam cups in their hands. While my generation was having the time of their lives, there came my ole lady out of nowhere, doing those very same dances. It wasn't a surprise to me, however, it was to everyone else who hadn't witnessed it. With this being the first time everyone had witnessed my ole lady performing that act, they were laughing their butts off, saying, "Oh, look at Paulette"; "Paulette crazy"; "Mann, what wrong wit yo mama?"

I told them, "I don't know, because the things my ole lady do is unexpected."

As that record continued to play out, everyone was still laughing because my ole lady continued to dance like a youngster, saying, "Oh, oh" with her right hand in the air. Once that song ended, my ole lady came to me and said, "You see yo mama? Ain't dat how y'all do 'em?"

Even though everyone was laughing at the act my ole lady performed, my generation embraced it by dancing with her because they got a kick out of it. What did I tell you? Events with my family really are like episodes of Soul Train, but if you don't believe me, come to one of our events, and you will see exactly what I'm talking about.

The other events that were thrown weren't as live as those. They were much calmer, because they were Christmas events, however my family and I still enjoyed ourselves. By the time I got back in full gear, engaging myself in past activities, summer had quickly approached. During the summer my family and I were fortunate enough to receive a week-long visit from loved ones who resided in Sacramento, California, my ole lady's eldest sister and her family. They were generous enough to visit me and my family on their summer break.

Back in the late eighties and early nineties, four of my ole lady's eldest siblings left the state of South Carolina and migrated to two different areas of California state. Around the time my ole lady's siblings left South Carolina, I was either non-existent, or seven years of age. Being that I was so young at the time of their departure, I have no memories of the first two siblings who left; in fact, I have no memories of the third sibling who left, but I do remember the third sibling's firstborn child, and the fourth sibling who departed. I had never met the third sibling's husband, nor had I met their four youngest children prior to that visit.

As I anticipated the arrival of my family, something unfortunate happened: I was admitted to the hospital to be treated for a urinary tract infection. Before I got admitted, I tried convincing my doctor to write a prescription for antibiotic tablets, but due to me catching

UTIs frequently, the doctor decided to treat me with IV antibiotics. In a situation like that, I generally don't get upset, but that time I did, because I wanted to be home amongst my loved ones, who I had no memories of, and had never met.

Since I had no choice as to how and where I was going to be treated for that UTI, my ole lady took me to the hospital. While being treated for that urinary tract infection, she finally brought our loved ones to visit me two days after their arrival. The day my ole lady brought them to visit me, I was ecstatic; in fact, we all were, because that was the moment we'd been waiting for.

At the beginning of that visit, everyone started off by introducing themselves, then they began explaining why it took them so long to come visit me. The reason was because everyone was trying to get in their visits, which is understandable, considering that my aunt hadn't been home for years. They sat and visited for a while, then left. One or two days after they visited me, the doctors were generous enough to discharge me with prescribed medication, so I could be with my family. Being that I was discharged prior to the original date, that gave me and my loved ones enough time to bond before their departure.

The moments that I have and appreciate most about my family's stay are them checking on me periodically, and keeping me company. For instance, one of my cousins, the son of my aunt and uncle, sat in my room everyday, asking me every question that came to his mind. He asked how I got injured, and where the gunshot wound was. As I began sharing my testimony, I can distinctly remember my little cousin giving me his undivided attention. I didn't realize what was happening until that moment; but it blew my mind to witness a person of his age give me their undivided attention.

Once I'd finished sharing my testimony with my little cousin, he then began asking more questions concerning my physical body, and about the person who shot me. As I continued to answer my little cousin's questions, in came my aunt to check on me, not knowing that her son had already beat her to the punch. The first thing my aunt said as she entered my room was, "Tell Mooch he's in here with Mann." Then she asked my little cousin and me, "What are you guys up to?"

Just before I could tell my aunt what my little cousin and I were doing, in came my uncle, holding their baby boy, asking the same question. He'd been able to hear what I was doing with my little cousin. Initially, my aunt didn't want my little cousin to question me about the incident, but once I told her it was okay, she was cool with it. Immediately after sharing my testimony, both my aunt and uncle gave their input as I expected, then everyone parted ways.

The other memory I have of my family's stay is my aunt and uncle's two youngest daughters and their baby boy. Bonding with my little cousins was like spending time with my sisters because of how they interacted with me. As I collect my thoughts, I'm reminded of my aunt and uncle's two youngest daughters entering my room to chat. In fact, I can recall the two sisters bombarding my room the first day I arrived home from the hospital. When they came to my room, I was lying in bed with my eyes glued to the tube. The two sisters unexpectedly appeared in my doorway and asked, "Are you asleep?" In response, I told the sisters, "No, uh uh." Then straightaway, the two bombarded me with a boatload of questions. What were my likes and dislikes? How old was I? Did my friends visit? What was that machine for? Did I have a girlfriend?

Just as the questioning was getting steamy, both sisters began bickering about whose turn it was to ask a question, considering that

IF IT HAD NOT BEEN FOR THE LORD

one had already asked a number of questions. In efforts to diffuse the dispute between the two, I began to ask the sisters questions quite similar to what I'd been asked. Consequently, me and my aunt, who caught the tail end of the dispute, were able to safely reel both sisters back to shore before the rip current took them under.

I can also recall spending time with both sisters separately. On those separate occasions, I had the opportunity of getting to know both sisters on a personal level. In the process of bonding with my cousins, both sisters opened up about things that they generally wouldn't speak about amongst themselves or others. However, due to those conversations being had in confidence, I am not permitted to disclose that information, but for you, I'll go out on a limb and leave you with this one little secret.

One day as I sat in my room alone, one of the sisters came to chat with me as they generally did, and she informed me of some very interesting news that I was unaware of. Much to my surprise, a conversation that occurred years later between me and another relative confirmed that it was true. In addition to bonding with my aunt and uncle, two youngest daughters and son, I also had the privilege of chatting with their two eldest daughters who were unable to make the trip. We chatted periodically throughout and after our family's stay, but I did the majority of talking due to their fascination of this Gullah Geechee dialect I possess.

The last tale I have to tell is about my aunt and uncle's youngest offspring, "Noonie," the baby boy. If I had to give a description of Noonie, it would be that he was a quiet, light-complected toddler, who had long silky hair that was generally in two plaits. For the most part, Noonie stayed to himself if he wasn't in the arms of my aunt, uncle, or his siblings. In order to get a peep out of Noonie, you had to confiscate his most prized possession.

153

As I record this tale, I can recall an immediate relative confiscating Noonie's most prized possession. The instant it was taken, Noonie had a fit; you would have thought a stranger had mysteriously appeared and abducted him by how he was wailing. In Noonie's defense, my aunt and uncle tried to retrieve his most prized possession, but the immediate relative refused to hand it over. After a while, things quieted down tremendously, and as a result, the immediate relative decided to check on Noonie and see how he was coming along without his most prized possession. Instead of the immediate relative going to physically check on Noonie, they confidently yelled out to my aunt and uncle for their report. Much to their surprise, he was sitting there quiet as kept, as he possessed a spare of his most prized possession. Instantaneously, the immediate relative and my aunt began feuding about Noonie and his most prized possession.

During that dispute, the immediate relative (my ole lady) implied that Noonie was too old to possess his most prized possession (a pacifier), but my aunt, on the other hand, agreed to disagree.

As the two fought, my ole lady asked my aunt, "Well, where he get dis one from?" implying that the second most prized possession wasn't identical to the first one she confiscated.

In response, my aunt told her, "He didn't get it from me, if that's what you're thinking."

"Well, if you didn't give it to him, who did?"

"He got it himself. I don't have to tell him where it's at; he knows where to get it."

According to my aunt, Noonie was known for catching temper tantrums if he misplaced his most prized possession, so any time their family traveled, in or out of town, they packed extras he was aware of, to avoid the headache. In spite of my aunt and uncle expressing their experiences with Noonie's temper tantrums, my ole lady confiscated his most prized possession for the second time. She confiscated the one in his mouth, and the other extras that were packed. Needless to say, Noonie caught another temper tantrum, but ultimately my aunt was able to get him to simmer down. If memory serves me correctly, I believe Noonie went without possessing his most prized possession throughout the rest of their trip, but don't quote me on that. With all things considered, Noonie was a great kid, who was well-behaved as long as he had his most prized possession, and although he was a toddler of few words, his only request was that you stay clear of his belongings.

At the beginning of the year, tragedy struck my family once again. On January 7, 2004, my grandfather Robert Tindal Sr., my ole lady's father, passed away. Prior to his death, he took sick, and had to be admitted into the ER. During my grandfather's visit at the ER, the doctor collected blood cultures and ran several tests to find the cause of his illness. Once the test results came back, the doctor informed my ole lady. According to the doctor's report, my grandfather suffered from stage four cancer ,which led to his illness. The doctor gave him the option to undergo chemotherapy, or ride it out. Being that my ole lady had knowledge about the history of cancer, my grandfather consulted her first, then he made his decision.

After my grandfather decided to ride it out, he was able to come home, where my ole lady and two uncle took turns caring for him. In the weeks since my grandfather arrived home, my ole lady decided to put him in a nursing home because it was becoming a bit much for her to take care of both me and him. Within the third week of my grandfather's stay at the nursing home, he passed away in front of my ole lady. Hours before he passed, one of the administrators at the nursing home contacted my ole lady and told her to come down because things weren't looking good.

Upon my ole lady's arrival, one of my grandfather's siblings was standing outside; however, instead of entering the building right away, he and my ole lady decided to walk around the facility together to gather themselves. Once my ole lady and uncle got themselves together, they went to my grandfather's room, where the other siblings were. With my family understanding that my grandfather was near death, they sat with him for as long as they could, because they knew it would be the last visit.

My ole lady told me that she sang the gospel single "I'll Make It" as they visited. While she sang, a shadow came over my grandfather, she said. Then he passed away. The day my grandfather passed away, left us all emotional, but we were able to persevere. Being that my ole lady had power of attorney over my grandfather, she contacted everyone, including her four siblings located in California, to inform them about his death, then she immediately began setting up funeral arrangements.

By the time my ole lady had set up my grandfather's funeral arrangements, my aunts and uncle flew in from California, and within the first or second week of my grandfather's death, our family went forward with the memorial service. Soon after, I received some exciting news in the mail, the results from a test I'd taken for my high school diploma. Prior to my grandfather's death I was informed about the opportunity to receive my high school diploma from an anonymous school. The person who informed me about this opportunity was an aid who took on my case a couple months before the end of 2003.

At the end of 2003, I had a conversation with the aid who took on my case about school. She asked, "Were you able to finish school?" And I replied no. Then I said, "I did partake in homeschooling, but that didn't last long." She then informed me about an anonymous school located out of town. This anonymous school that she spoke of was a ministry designed to help people acquire their high school diploma. In order to get the process started, said the aid, you had to contact the school, express your interest, and they would send an enrollment application with their requirements. Once the enrollment application was filled out, and you'd met their requirements and re-sent the packet, the school would then send a test packet with all five subjects for you to complete at your own pace.

Being that I really wanted my high school diploma, I took down the anonymous schools number and contacted them personally for more information. Within that week, I contacted the anonymous school inquiring about their program, and the administrator I spoke to gave me the same information that I received from the aid. In ad-dition, the administrator sent an enrollment application, along with brochures, to my mailing address for me to look over. Before I hung up with the administrator, I asked her if I would be able to enroll in college with their diploma. She said, "Yeah," but she also told me to check with the community colleges in my area before I followed through with my decision, because some colleges didn't accept the school's diploma.

Needless to say, I took the young lady's advice and checked with a popular community college in my area to ask whether they accepted them. Once I got the green light, I proceeded to follow through with my decision. The day I received the anonymous school's test packet, I immediately began testing, working at my own pace. After I com-pleted all five parts of the test, I sent it back to the anonymous school some weeks later. Shortly thereafter, I received a letter by mail.

Dear Wendell M. Manigault Jr.,

CONGRATULATIONS, GRADUATE! We have just completed the grading of your tests, and we are very proud to announce that you have passed all of the exams. We knew that you could accomplish your goal once you set your mind to it. Listed below, you will find your scores for each subject that you completed. We are happy for you and your progress. Enclosed, you will find your high school diploma, evidence of a job well done. Again, we say congratulations to our newest graduate.

TEST	SCORES
Language Arts:	86
Writing skills:	84
Social Studies:	89
Science:	91
Mathematics:	86

Opening that envelope and reading that letter, in addition to the test scores, brought joy to my heart, because despite the adversity that I'd faced, I was able to achieve the goal of becoming a high school grad.

As we got further into the new year, summer mysteriously appeared once again. During the summer of 2004, I had the privilege of lodging at the Vocational Rehabilitation Development Center in Columbia, South Caorlina. Voc Rehab Center is a residential facility for clients with physical disabilities in West Columbia, that assists clients in the Midlands and the Lowcountry with discovering their potential, and helps them develop their vocational strengths and abilities. The person who presented me with this opportunity was Kim Aquino, the recreational therapist at Roper St. Francis, located in downtown Charleston.

One day while working, Kim brought the idea to my ole lady. Then, once my ole lady arrived home, she brought the idea to me. Being that I was eager to learn more about the facility, I decided to contact Kim personally. As Kim began informing me about the facility, I thought it was a great opportunity, so I decided to go. Kim got me registered immediately, and just like that, I was on my way. Prior to leaving for Voc Rehab, my ole lady made sure I had all the necessities, then I had a going away party with immediate family and friends.

On the morning of my departure (Sunday), I did not attend church service as I normally would have, but me, my ole lady, and the driver still went and had the pastor come out to say a quick prayer. After the pastor blessed us with a prayer, we started our journey. Being that the facility was no more than ninety minutes away, we got there in no time. As soon as we arrived at the facility, my ole lady went into the building to check and make sure we were at the right location. Once she gave us the green light, she and the driver began unloading the vehicle.

The moment I entered the facility, the administrators immediately checked me in and escorted me to my room. Before my ole lady unpacked anything, she began questioning the administrators about some concerns she had. One of her main concerns was my diet; she wanted to know if they would continue the dieting regimen we'd been doing at home, or if they would change anything. The dieting regimen I had at home worked fine; the administrators didn't change anything. The other concern my ole lady had was about a call bell system; she wanted to know how I would be able to call the nurses station if I needed assistance. Due to the facility not having a call bell, they had me swap rooms with a resident lodged in front of the nurses station.

Once the administrators answered my ole lady's questions, and had taken care of one of her main concerns, she unpacked my belongings and got me settled before she left. As all of us new residents were getting adjusted to the facility, the nurses began telling us about the activities that the administrators would have us do throughout the day. The nurses briefed us on the activities of daily living, and we went to bed at a reasonable time so we'd be prepared for the following day.

Early that morning (Monday), the nurses completed our activities of daily living, then we went to the cafeteria for breakfast. Once we all ate breakfast, other staff members came out to meet and greet us newcomers, and they explained what the sessions they taught were about. After the administrators gave us an idea of what to expect, it was time to attend our first session. Being that there were a number of sessions, I don't remember them all; however, I do have memories about the other sessions that I enjoyed, therapy and computers. The reason I have memories about those two sessions is because of a discovery I made.

One of the things I discovered was the mobility of my upper extremity. The thing that led to this discovery was a therapist asking, "Have you ever operated a hand cycling exercise equipment before?" And "Do you know what type of mobility you have in your upper extremities?" In response, I told the therapist, "No, I have never operated a hand cycling exercise equipment before, nor do I know the extent of the mobility in my upper extremities, but I'll try." Since I was willing to operate this equipment, the therapist immediately got me set up. After I got set up, I put forth the effort to operate the machine and it was a success. As I witnessed the mobility in my upper extremities, my heart was filled with joy and hope because I was doing something that I was told I would never do again.

The other discovery that was made was my mobility to operate a computer. One day after leaving a schedule session, the staff member who taught the session asked me, "Are you able to operate a computer?" And I replied no. Being that I was unable to operate the computer with my hands, the staff member said, "I have a way, if you are willing to try." Although I wasn't, and am still not a fan of computers, I was curious as to how I would be able to operate it, so I told the staff member, "Let's do it."

Once I told the staff member that I was willing to give it a try, I was immediately escorted to the room where the computers were. As I positioned myself at the computer desk, the staff member went to look for an object designed for spinal cord injury patients to operate a computer with. The object I was presented with was a pencil-like object called a mouth stick. This particular object had a horse-shoe-like mouth piece on one end of it, and on the other end, it had a rubber cap used for typing. As soon as the staff member found the mouth stick, he gave me simple instructions on how to use it before I tested it out. He told me to place the mouth stick in my mouth, get a good grip on it, and type like a woodpecker, using the strength of your neck.

After receiving those instructions, I made an attempt to operate the computer. Just as the staff member and I expected, I was able to successfully operate the computer with no problem. Operating the computer by using a mouth stick was another joyful/hopeful moment for me, because I did something I didn't know I was able to do. While I had the opportunity to use a computer, I continued to operate it until my time was up. After a long day of attending those sessions, all residents were free for the remainder of the day. During my free time, I sat outside on the phone conversating with my loved ones, partners, and lady friends; I also interacted with the nurses and residents, if I wasn't listening to music.

During certain nights of the week, all residents were to report to the cafeteria/rec area for group activities, be it game or movie night. Game and movie night at Voc Rehab were activities orchestrated by the nurses; it was their way of bringing all residents together so we could interact as one. As I reflect on game night, I can recall partaking in a few games of Bingo along with the group. Prior to starting the game, I was paired with a resident who assisted me with the Bingo cards and chips, due to my physical disability. Once all residents were set and ready to play, the game began. In the beginning of our group activity, all residents, including me, were quiet and attentive to the numbers being called. Further into the game, you heard a little whisper, got laughter, and a "false alarm" Bingo caller. As the game went on, there were a couple of residents who got close to hitting bingo, but we were a few games in, and there were still no winners.

Several games later, a resident finally struck gold, and who else could it have been other than yours truly? Bingo! Truth be told, I thought no one would become a winner, but after doubling up on the Bingo cards, the dynamic of the game created winners. After playing a few more games of Bingo, the nurses wrapped things up, and all residents retired for the night.

I can recall partaking in movie nights as well. As I reflect on movie night, I can recall one of the nurses and residents installing the DVD player to the television. By the time all residents reported to the cafeteria/rec area, the electronics were installed, but before going any further, the resident who provided the DVDs gave all residents the option to select the film of our choice.

In the process of selecting a film, a resident asked one of the nurses, "Do you have any refreshments?"

In response, the nurse apologetically replied, "No, unfortunately I don't, I'm sorry. If any of you have refreshments that you would like to munch on during the movie, you are more than welcome to go to your rooms and grab them."

Considering that all residents didn't have refreshments, the residents who did have refreshments were generous enough to disperse them amongst the group. Once selecting the DVD of our choice and dispersing refreshments, the lights were dimmed and the film began rolling. The film that all residents selected to watch was the 2004 American crime thriller *Man on Fire*, based on the novel by A. J. Quinnell and Brian Helgeland, starring Denzel Washington and Dakota Fanning. During this movie, we were sitting on the edges of our seats as we tuned into this jaw dropping, riveting film. I can honestly say that it was the film's plot, in addition to the explosive yet brilliant scenes, that had all us on the edges of our seats.

During our stay at Voc Rehab, the nurses and staff members kept all residents active, but my time at the facility was short-lived due to a false alarm. Three weeks into my stay, the nurses entered my room at the crack of dawn, making their rounds as usual. In the process of making their rounds, the nurse woke me up to start the day, but I was a tad bit sluggish. After making a few attempts, the nurses then checked my vital signs, and unfortunately, my blood pressure was low—just my luck.

Immediately after checking my vital signs, the nurse then frantically asked, "Are you okay? Do you feel light-headed?"

I told the nurses that I was okay. I said, "There's nothing to be alarmed about. My blood pressure fluctuates. I promise you, I'm just tired."

As a result, both the medical staff and case manager of Voc Rehab came to me and expressed their concerns about my health; they were deeply considering sending me home as a safety precaution. Despite my plea to stay at the Voc Rehab facility, their staff decided to discharge me, and before I knew it, I was transported back to Charleston, long before the sunset.

Being that the staff at Voc Rehab was concerned about my well-being, I scheduled an appointment to visit my primary care doctor within that week of my arrival. As I suspected, my health was still intact; in fact, my vital signs were normal, and the blood cultures that were collected showed no signs of any bacteria, yeast, or microorganisms in my bloodstream. With regards to Voc Rehab in Columbia, South Carolina, I unfortunately did not return to their facility, but I enjoyed my stay, and I greatly appreciated the assistance that was offered.

Shortly after I returned home from Voc Rehab, and after visiting my primary care doctor, I picked up where I left off, and began engaging in past activities, like drinking alcohol and fornicating, and attending family events like cookouts, birthday bashes, and holiday events. I also reverted to an old force of habit. I can distinctly remember where I was, and what caused me to turn back. The underlying force that led me to turn back was a consumer's demand for a certain product.

One late evening as I lay in bed, a visitor stopped by as they generally did prior to going home. The instant they arrived, they greeted everyone, then made their way to my room.

As soon as they entered my room, they greeted me, then asked, "You straight?"

In response, I told the visitor, "Yeah."

Then they said, "Cut that shit out, dog. You bullshittin', or you for real?"

And I replied, "I for real."

After spending several minutes disputing with this visitor about whether or not I was straight, it all made sense the instant the visitor stuck their hands in their pocket and pulled out a wad of money.

"Well, let me get a fifty," said the visitor.

Truth be told, I thought the visitor was asking about my well being, but the moment I realized they were talking about drugs (crack cocaine), I humorously said, "Dat's what you talkin' 'bout? Man, I thought you was talkin' 'bout my health or something. Man, I ain't got no dope."

Without hesitation, the visitor replied, "You got me all pumped up, and you ain't got shit. Dat's fucked up, dog."

At the end of our dispute, the visitor asked a favor of me that led to another dispute; in fact, the visitor asked that I contact one of my partners to get them straight, but I declined the request. Prior to leaving, the visitor said that I needed to get straight, because unannounced consumers arrived at their home daily in search of purchasing drugs. In light of the opportunity that was presented, I took the visitor's advice, and organized a team. The team consisted of me, the head of operation; my cousin, the supplier; my eldest sibling, the runner; my uncle, the visitor/consumer/booster.

Once the team had been organized, my eldest sibling and I linked up with the supplier to purchase our first package, then she and I made our first run. On that first run, we were in route to my uncle's home, considering he was the gentleman who'd presented me with the opportunity. Once we'd arrived at our destination, we contacted our uncle to come outside, and immediately he came. We all sat in the driveway for a moment shooting the breeze, prior to making any transactions. Within a few minutes, one of my uncle's guests, a well-known friend of the family, came outside in search of my uncle, and said, "Bernie, where you at?" The instant the guest called out my uncle's name, my uncle replied, "I talking to my niece and nephew." Due to the guest's next response, I take it they didn't hear my uncle, because the guest then said, "Bernie, hurry up, we waiting on you." My uncle said, "Goddammit, I told you I talking to my niece and nephew. Either you wait, or get the hell on."

Needless to say, my uncle's guest heard my uncle loud and clear the second time around; in fact, the guest came to the car to hail me and my eldest sibling, and apologize for his misconduct. Immediately after shooting the breeze with my uncle and his guest, my eldest sibling and I took care of those two gentlemen prior to parting ways; then she and I proceeded to make our runs.

At that first location I taught my eldest sibling the ins and outs of being a street pharmacist. I taught her to know what to look for when purchasing a certain quantity of drugs, whether small or large. It wasn't about the quantity, it was about the quality. I taught her how to be discreet when making a transaction; how to bust down the dope in portions, and what those certain portions were—nicks, dimes, twenties, etc.; to count her profit prior to parting ways with the consumer; that once she accumulated a lump sum of cash, to put a large portion of the profit away, then proceed with her runs; and I taught her not to distribute to every consumer who approached her.

Back in route, my eldest sibling and I then made a few stops to areas and consumers with whom I was familiar, but it wasn't a success; the consumers were either out of funds, or MIA (missing in action).

In addition to those runs, my eldest sibling and I pulled up on a few of my partners I hadn't seen prior to that evening. As she and I were shooting the breeze with a few partners of mine, I noticed it was getting late, so I suggested that we head home. Prior to ending the night, my eldest sibling and I had given my uncle a courtesy call to see if he and his guest needed our service, but both gentlemen said they were straight, so my eldest sibling and I retired for the night.

Despite the insignificant funds made on the first night, that old force of habit instantly became a part of my daily life. As I spearheaded this small-time drug operation, the team and I had to take other avenues in order to distribute the product. One of those avenues consisted of my uncle stopping by my place of residence to purchase the product, then from there, he would transport it to its destination, either his place of residence, or another location, where he distributed it amongst himself and acquaintances.

The other avenue we took consisted of my eldest sibling gathering the quantity of the product that was ordered, then transporting it to its destination, either our uncle's place, or another location, where my uncle would again disperse it amongst himself and acquaintances. Once the product sold out, I would give my eldest sibling a percentage of the profit that was made. For example, if I profited thirty bucks, I would give my eldest sibling ten bucks, or if I profited fifty bucks, I would give my eldest sibling twenty bucks. As for my uncle, I didn't give him a percentage of the profits, but considering that he'd presented me with this opportunity to make a few dollars, I did bless him any time he and/or his acquaintances made a purchase.

Apart from orchestrating a two-bit drug operation, I experienced an unexpected transition, which American physicist, historian, and philosopher of science Thomas S. Kuhn called a paradigm shift.

According to Dr. Thomas S. Kuhn, the term "paradigm shift" is a dramatic change in the paradigm of a scientific community, or a change from one scientific paradigm to another.

Below this paragraph is a picture of a duck that Thomas S. Kuhn used to illustrate the concept of a paradigm shift. In this illustration, Dr. Thomas S. Kuhn asked that you look at the picture of the duck, then continue to stare at the picture of the duck. The longer you look at the duck, you'll realize that it's not just a duck, but also a rabbit. By using this illustration, Dr. Kuhn is trying to get you to see that it depends on how you look at something.

"If you look at this picture from the right perspective," said Bishop TD Jakes, "it will speak to you in a different way based on your ability to have transference of perception so strong that you perceive differently the same sketching."

Now that you have been introduced to the term paradigm shift, allow me to explain how it is relative to the unexpected transition that occurred in my life. Within the first two years of being a spinal cord injury patient, 98 percent of my loved ones and peers abandoned me. As a result, I was left broken and confused, having no one to call on in my time of need. In that time of need, I got a dose of reality about my injury. In fact, as I lay in bed trying to move my limbs, both upper and lower extremities, I said to myself repeatedly, "I can't move. I'm paralyzed. I really can't move. Wow."

As I lay there uttering those words to myself, I became regretful about the opportunities that I took for granted. Aside from bettering myself about the poor decisions I made, past memories about me mocking my disabled neighbor as an adolescent flared up. Oftentimes as an adolescent, I assisted my disabled neighbor by opening and/or closing his car door; I also assisted him by unlocking and/or opening his apartment door. I can also recall my ole man and disabled neighbor in each other's company as they both downed a few beers.

As I hung around both gentlemen, I carefully observed my disabled neighbor as he proceeded with his activities of daily living. In doing so, I became aware of my disabled neighbor's adaptation to life despite his disability. Gaining the knowledge that I obtained about my neighbor, I at times give my loved ones a good laugh by impersonating him. For example, I did impersonations about how my neighbor transferred himself from or to his manual wheelchair and car; I also did impersonations about how he cracked open his beer cans. Although I meant no harm by these impersonations, both of my parents said to me, "Despite his disability, he is no different from either one of us." They also said, "You must be respectful, mindful, and of assistance to those with disabilities, because you never know what you may have to come to in life."

As I reflected on those moments, I still couldn't fathom the reality of being paralyzed. In fact, I said to myself, "Me? Lo Mann? Wendell? Nah." Instead of wallowing in self-pity about life's adversities, I perceived the opposition as an opportunity to connect with God, and evolve into the person God predestined me to be. The moment my perception about life changed, I took advantage of that opportunity to seek God and his will for my life through daily prayer, literature, and televised sermons, and in doing so, the unexpected paradigm shift occurred.

In the process of change, I began to acknowledge my faults, accept responsibility for my actions, and make efforts to correct them. I also refrained from drinking alcoholic beverages, smoking marijuana, and fornicating. In fact, I refrained from listening to secular music, but I must admit, that didn't last long. Throughout that process of change, I evolved in more ways than one, and will continue to do so. However, it all begins in your mind, the change, that is. If you do as I did, and perceive your opposition as an opportunity to connect with God, and evolve into the person who God predestined you to be, then you, too, will be able to make that connection, and evolve and thrive like never before.

CHAPTER 12

Around fall of 2004, my family and I moved into a four-bedroom, two-full-bath home, with the addition of an elevator lift for my power chair that was built by Habitat for Humanity in the Rosemont community, located in the neck area of the Charleston Peninsula, just off the King Street Extension. Two years prior to having this home built, a coworker of my ole lady's told her about a meeting that Charleston Habitat for Humanity was having, and suggested that she attend it. My ole lady knew the home we currently resided in wasn't suitable for anyone to live in, so she took her coworker's advice and contacted Charleston Habitat for Humanity for the date, time, and location of their meeting.

According to the information my ole lady gave me, the staff members of Charleston Habitat for Humanity explain to the applicants what the organization is about, and the steps that have to be taken prior to having a home built. Then they had all applicants fill out applications to get a jump start on the process. Once my ole lady filled hers out, the staff members of Charleston Habitat for Humanity told her they would be in touch for the approval of her partnership to build a new home.

For those of you who are uneducated about what Charleston Habitat for Humanity represents, it is an organization that has been on a mission since 1976 to make home ownership a reality for very low-income families across the country. In order for selected partner families to have a home built, there are several requirements that have to be fulfilled prior to determining the start of the construction of their home. They have to complete five hundred hours of sweat equity, complete the homeowners workshop, and pay a $500 down payment.

Being that my ole lady didn't want the enemy blocking her blessing, she informed certain people she believed would support her in the building of her home. Months after Charleston Habitat for Humanity held their board of directors meeting, all selected partner families were asked to attend a mandatory welcome and orientation meeting before given the opportunity to meet the requirements. In that meeting, all selected partner families received a copy of Charleston Habitat for Humanity's partnership agreement, as well as important information regarding what was required of them as a partner family, and what they could expect from the organization as an affiliate. If any of the selected partner families did not attend that meeting, it would signify their lack of willingness to partner with Charleston Habitat for Humanity, and they would have been dismissed from the program.

After attending that mandatory meeting, all selected partner families were able to start the process of Habitat's sweat equity requirements. Once they were clear to start the process, my ole lady once again contacted people she believed would support her to come out and give a helping hand. The welcome and orientation meeting was held on September 10, 2002, in the Rosemont Community Center, and if I'm not mistaken, the partner families started working toward their sweat equity requirements within that same month. With having had the privilege and experience of working with Charleston Habitat for Humanity years back while attending the Charleston County Discipline School, I knew and understood that Charleston Habitat for Humanity was an organization that worked thoroughly Monday through Friday, as well as Saturdays, to build simple, decent, and affordable housing—not dream homes—for qualified and low-income families.

All partner families were free to accumulate their sweat equity hours through the week, but because my ole lady and her supporters had to work Monday through Friday, most of her sweat equity hours were accumulated on Saturdays. The five hundred hours consisted of construction on the homes of other partner families in different communities, and also providing lunch for all workers, staff, family, and volunteers. One of the communities where Charleston Habitat for Humanity held their construction site was the Chicora Cherokee, also known as the Macon. That was where all selected partner families and volunteer helpers were able to dedicate their time and earn sweat equity hours.

Every Saturday morning, my ole lady and her supporters woke up faithfully with that construction site on their agenda to work toward meeting the sweat equity requirements. As I think back, I can remember them contacting one another the night before, and working with Habitat the next morning. The phone calls that took place were basically discussions of parties agreeing to follow through with their plans to work with Habitat. Once all parties agreed to follow through with their initial plan, they all got themselves prepared for that day.

Working with Charleston Habitat for Humanity began with my ole lady completing her ADLs, as well as mine. If I wasn't awake, then she would leave to pick up two of her main supporters from their homes, although they insisted on meeting up at our house as the headquarters. Once my ole lady picked up two of her main supporters, she would sometimes stop at a restaurant for breakfast if they hadn't already eaten, then she would drive straight to their destination. At the construction site stood United staff members, partners, families, and volunteer helpers of different nationalities to help make a low-income family's dream come true.

Prior to starting construction, the staff members of Charleston Habitat for Humanity instructed all selected partner families and the volunteer helpers based on their description of work. Once the Habitat staff members gave the instructions, construction began. As I questioned my ole lady about her experience of working with Charleston Habitat for Humanity she began to share with me information about conversations that took place between all selected partner families while working on the construction site. The conversations were about them having the opportunity to be homeowners; they also talked about the start of construction on their homes, as well as plans they had once they'd moved into them. My ole lady said all the families were saying how appreciative they were of Charleston Habitat for Humanity, and how they couldn't wait to start construction on their homes and move into them.

The more I questioned my ole lady about her experience of working with Charleston Habitat for Humanity, the more information she gave. Another experience my ole lady shared with me concerned the homeownership workshops. Homeownership workshops were scheduled meetings that all selected partners families had to attend in order to be affiliates of Charleston Habitat for Humanity. In these meetings staff members, homeowners, and business executive who are affiliates with Charleston Habitat for Humanity shared their knowledge and experiences of partnering with the organization. The knowledge and experiences included important information concerning the maintenance of their homes, mortgage management, homeowners insurance, and a will for the home.

I wanted to know the exact information that was given in those meetings, so I asked my ole lady to explain in full detail. According to her, the affiliate of Charleston Habitat for Humanity explained how to maintain the maintenance of their homes, and they also talked about the range of their monthly mortgage payments, and proposed different affordable options for home insurance for homeowners. Once she'd shared the full details, I proceeded to further my research study.

As I gathered information to write about concerning the Rosemont community, I ran across some interesting, educational news articles about the community's history. The news articles stated the development of early Rosemont was done on the backs of enslaved Africans. Some of the early names for the area were Silver Hill, Magnolia, Discher Farms, and plantations called San Souci Plantation, the Rat Trap Plantation, and the Pendarvis Plantation sprung up along the Ashley River. Today, with the exception of the San Souci Plantation, they are all a part of Rosemont.

Several of the African-owned areas of land date back as early as the 1700s. The Pendarvis Plantation, owned by John Pendarvis, he bequeathed to his African servant Parthenia, and her seven children that he fathered, their freedom and 175 acres of land, making her the first African land owner in that area. He also granted freedom to two enslaved Africans, Sambo and Phyllis, on the condition they help Parthenia care for his children by her. Records show that in 1756, Judy West, also known as Free Judy, purchased sixty-seven acres near Dorchester Road. Rosemont today is in the midst of a change that makes it one of the last frontiers for development in Charleston. Over forty years ago, the rules of community were split when Interstate 26 was first built, and despite the efforts of some elected officials, the community split again due to the access ramp for Interstate 26 to the Post in North Charleston, that will basically destroy it.

As I proceeded to read that news article in its entirety, I immediately understood why all the residents of that community were opposed to new development of widening Interstate 26, and the economic potential of the area. Fortunately for that community, Senator Robert Ford, who contacted residents in Rosemont, sent a letter to H.B. "Buck" Limehouse Jr., executive director of the South Carolina Department of Transportation, dated May 19, 2007, expressing his concern that it would be premature to consider details of widening until the exact route and design of the port terminal access was finalized. Ford also asked the state's port authority to consider the likelihood of violating pending revised air quality standards.

Learning that I'd once lived on land owned by our enslaved ancestors who later had their freedom granted, brought joy to my heart, because when I think of them being treated like animals, murder isn't the only thought that comes to mind; intelligence, and spiritual and mental strength comes to mind also, so for me to have lived in an area where human beings of their character once lived, made me proud to be an African American, and a resident of such a historical community. As for the development plan of the Rosemont community, I don't know where it stands, but I pray that the state port authority does consider the livelihood of that community, and its ancestral history.

Once all selected partner families completed the requirements in different communities of North Charleston, downtown Charleston, and in the Rosemont community, they were able to start construction on their homes. Before they started, though, Charleston Habitat for Humanity recognized them with certificates that were well deserved. The certificates stated what they had completed and paid, and that they were partners with the organization. It was also signed by a family support committee chair and executive director on June 10, 2004. All selected partner families who received certificates of completion were relieved and excited because they no longer had to worry about accumulating five hundred hours of sweat equity, and they knew their homes were next in line for construction.

Although the families had met their requirements, they were still required to participate in the actual building of their homes. Construction on the homes of all selected partner families was the same as all others. The only difference was their homes were being built in the Rosemont community. With everyone having understood they still were required to participate in the building of their homes, they proceeded to carry on with the scheduled routine set prior to starting construction.

Once construction was completed on the homes of all selected partner families, Charleston Habitat for Humanity allowed us to make that transition of moving into them later that year. As for the volunteer helpers who dedicated their time, they were the family members, friends, and coworkers of all selected partner families, and a great deal of them were strangers to one another.

Prior to moving into our new home, my ole lady asked the head pastor of our church to bless it with a prayer. Blessing a home with a prayer is a tradition that has been going on in families for generations, so when I tell you about this act, don't be alarmed, because as a token of appreciation, we were simply giving back to God what he gave us. Once our home had been blessed with a prayer, my family and I were able to move in.

There were seven homes built by Charleston Habitat for Humanity where we lived, including the home that was across the field from our street. Through the years, my family and I became accustomed to transitioning from one home to another, so when we made that move, it took nothing for us to adjust. As all families were adjusting, our parents proceeded to build on the foundation of their relationship that was laid prior to moving into the Rosemont community. With all selected partner families putting in months of hard work to become homeowners, I could only imagine how rewarding and important it was for them to seize that moment.

Considering the season, all the parents chose to build on the foundation of their relationship indoors, because my folks, black folks, don't like cold weather. Along with talking about how excited they were to finally be in their homes, the parents also talked about their homes' decor, as well as their future plans to sit on their porches and grill out once the season changed. Over the course of winter all of us who were selected partner families managed to knit an inseparable bond amongst ourselves. If we weren't indoors, we spoke to one another as we were passing through, headed to or from completing our activity of daily living.

As time progressed, the season eventually changed, and all the selected partner families began to follow through with their initial plans. At the peak of spring 2005, we all sat on our porches and enjoyed the weather as planned, and made cordial conversation amongst ourselves concerning work, school, etc. One of the conversations I can remember us having was about all the parents taking vacation time. Previously, before that conversation took place, a conversation was had concerning the students being near summer break, which is what led to this conversation. As all parents spoke about taking vacation time, my ole lady and neighbor, Miss Idell, asked our neighbor Mr. Joe if he was considering taking vacation time, and he replied no.

With no hesitation, my ole lady and Miss Idell asked Mr. Joe, "Why not? Your children are all grown and of age to take care of themselves."

The reason Mr. Joe didn't want to take vacation time was because he loved his occupation. He never took vacation time. In fact, if I'm not mistaken, I believe Mr. Joe also said he never took sick leave either. Once Mr. Joe gave his explanation, my ole lady and Miss Idell tried convincing him to take vacation time for himself, being that he was free to do so. Hearing the explanation Mr. Joe gave left me thinking, how would one be able to work an X amount of years on their job and never take vacation time or sick leave if they were ill? At that time, I didn't understand how that could be possible, but now that I think about it, I get it. I finally get it. What I understand is that Mr. Joe, and people from my generation are totally different.

For example, Mr. Joe came from a generation of people who knew that work was mandatory, and didn't mind working to provide for their families. I came from a generation of people who would rather sit on their butts, and have the world handed to them on a silver platter. That was the difference. After having that epiphany, I no longer question how it would be possible to work and never take vacation time or sick leave.

On another occasion, I can remember all of us laughing at our neighbor Mr. Joe as he spoke in his African voice, saying that he was from Africa. During one of Mr. Joe's impersonations, he once kneeled down, plucked the grass, then threw it in the air as he spoke about how different the land back home in Africa was different from

America. He also spoke about going back home to his country. The very first time I witnessed Mr. Joe's impersonation, I didn't take him seriously, because he laughed along with us as he impersonated our fellow African natives.

Once I'd witnessed this impersonation multiple times, I began thinking to myself, *Well, maybe he is one of our enslaved ancestors who was brought to Charleston from Africa back in the early 1700s along with Kunta Kinte, Kizzy, and Chicken George. LOL.*

I was curious about Mr. Joe's roots, so I asked his youngest daughter about it one evening while speaking with her over the phone. She laughed and said, "Boy, my daddy ain't from Africa. Our family from downtown." Then I laughed and said, "Well, shit he *sho* fool me." Her last words to me were, "Boy, don't follow my daddy up. He lying." Now how crazy is it that I allowed one of my neighbors, whom I loved and appreciated dearly, pull a whammy on me? Mmm, mmm, mmm, shame on me. To you who are reading this, here is a tip: Don't believe all that you hear or see, or else you will be hood-winked like I was.

With everyone having their own agenda, many stories were told concerning those topics rather good, bad, boring, or interesting; however those topics—work being mandatory and his African impersonation—are the two that stood out the most. Once we ended our conversation, our neighbors Mr. Joe or Miss Idell brought out their radios and we listened to Star 99.7. As you can see, there was never a dull moment between all of us in the Rosemont community, despite the petty disputes and death that occurred.

Further into the season, we all threw our first cookout as planned. Prior to attending this event, all parents offered their assistance to bring a covered dish, but our neighbor was generous enough to take on the responsibility of providing and preparing all the necessities.

Truth be told, any time we African Americans declined a loved one's offer to bring a covered dish, it's not always an act of generosity; sometimes it's taking safety precautions for various reasons, like the person is a horrible cook, or they're an unsanitary cook. We may be unaware of the person's cooking skills, and would rather not chance it. Past altercations may have led to distrust. The only things you may hear us African Americans ask our loved ones to bring are plastic plates, plastic utensils, beverages, and themselves. To my loved ones who fit one of the descriptions, please stop offering your assistance to bring a covered dish, because we don't want it.

Among the list of great things we all loved about the area was that our homes were built at least six feet high from the foundation, so instead of gathering indoors to attend this event, we gathered outdoors under the home of our wonderful neighbor, Miss Idell, the host. As all the guests gathered under the home of our wonderful neighbor, we socialized with one another as the music played in the background. As I reflect on the evening, I'm remembering a conversation that took place between my ole lady, our neighbor Miss Lavinia, and a friend of the family.

As my neighbor and I drank on a bottle of Armadale vodka I'd supplied, I can recall my ole lady and the friend of our family sharing stories of past incidents that had occurred at an old club called the Dugout, located in North Charleston off of Ward Avenue and Austin Avenue back in the early eighties. I also remember my ole lady sharing stories about her knocking my ole man upside his head with one of her high heel pumps after they left this other club called the Inn Club, located in North Charleston as well, back in the early nineties.

The domestic dispute that took place between my parents stemmed from a little white lie that my ole man told my ole lady. As

181

they were both enjoying themselves at the Inn Club, my ole man was under the impression that my ole lady, who didn't drink at the time, was under the influence of alcohol. He approached my ole lady and said that he was going to take her home, considering she had to work the next morning. He also said he was going home to get some rest once he dropped her off. Being that my ole lady had an uneasy vibe about my ole man, and a young lady who was present in the club as well, she went along with the game he was playing.

Shortly after approaching my ole lady, my ole man took her home almost immediately. Before my ole man could completely leave the premises, my ole lady immediately ran to our uncle and aunt's house who lived directly behind her, and asked our aunt if she could borrow their car. My aunt willingly gave her permission to use their car. As my ole man drove to his destination, my ole lady carefully trailed behind him like a private eye agent. Ultimately, with my ole lady trailing behind, my ole man reached his destination, but it wasn't his place of residence. He pulled up at the other club directly across the street from the Inn Club, called the Riviera.

The instant both of my parents arrived, my ole lady gently stepped out of the car and proceeded to trail behind my ole man on foot. Shortly after entering the club, my ole lady looked around in search of him, and as suspected, he was in the corner, hugged up with another woman. As soon as she spotted him, my ole lady immediately shushed the DJ by pressing her index finger against her lips, then crept quietly but quickly behind my ole man and clocked him upside his head with the heel of her shoe. Given the difficult nature of that situation, my ole man instinctively went into defense mode, but the instant he saw who the assailant was, he refrained. He then followed the gestures of my ole lady's index finger as she exited the building. At the end of that altercation, it wasn't said what transpired between the two once they left the club, but knowing my ole lady, she probably beat the brakes off him like a female Ultimate Fighting flyweight champion.

I'm also reminded of a conversation that took place between me and my neighbor, Miss Lavinia, the following day. On the day of that event, I decided to sit on the porch, as I generally did, to catch a bit of fresh air. As I sat on the porch in a daze, I heard the sound of someone's voice yelling out, "Mann, I ain't messin' wit you no mo!"

In response, I quickly began looking around to see who it was, and immediately I noticed it was my neighbor Miss Lavinia. As she walked out of her driveway, I immediately began smiling, and replied, "Why? What happen?" We engaged in a brief conversation about the night before, and she said instead of going to her destination, she had to go home and sleep off the Armadale vodka that snuck up on her, because she was plastered. In their case, I would have taken the rap, considering that I supplied the alcohol, but due to my neighbor drinking before testing the vodka, I am not at fault for her being plastered.

As time progressed, I gradually got myself acquainted with other residents in the Rosemont community, either by sitting on the porch, or strolling my power chair around the block. I also proceeded to engage in past activities, such as drinking alcohol, smoking marijuana, and fornicating, but also attending church.

Around that time, my eldest sibling had already left the nest, with her first child. In addition, my ole man and youngest sibling went missing in action over the weekends, and my ole lady and I were left home alone. Being that my ole lady and I were left with a lot of time to ourselves, she and I drove around town in her four-door Carolina-blue Chevy station wagon that was no bigger than a Hot

Wheels car; or she and I sat outside of our home for some quality time.

As my ole lady and I drove around town, we went through different communities in the beautiful city of North Charleston. In those communities were family and friends whom I associate myself with prior to getting injured, so I felt it was only right to stay in touch with them. Prior to arriving in any of those communities, I would contact who I was going to visit to make sure they were in the area. During those visits, it was all love; all visitors were excited to see, as well as update, one another on how things were going in our lives. As I sat amongst my family and peers visiting with them, they would update me on how things were going in the street; then I would update them on the progress that I may or may not have made.

In the updating process, I learned who was doing good for themselves, and who wasn't. I learned who remained loyal, and who didn't. I also learned who was incarcerated, and who wasn't. Further into the updating process, I learned about the good girls who had gone bad, and the bad girls who had gotten worse. I also learned about the children—and I do repeat *children*— who'd been created in the process. Although I'm no longer in the streets, it seems as if I am because of the updates I receive. The updates I shared were about the mental and spiritual strength God bestowed upon me to withstand the adversities I was up against; and the physical ability in my upper extremities that God was gradually restoring. Once we finished updating one another, we would part ways until we met again.

Driving around town was something my ole lady and I did on the regular, but that came to an end due to the feeling of being the only one keeping in touch, and the unexpected change in my ole lady's personal life.

On the weekends that my ole lady and I didn't drive around town, she and I sat outside of our home for some quality time, as I mentioned. As I put the pieces of this puzzle together, the pictures of a conversation that took place between me and my ole lady is starting to become clearer. The day this conversation took place was a Saturday, and we spoke about many things I don't remember prior to having this conversation. If I remember correctly, it was dead silence—and I do mean *dead silence*—once we ended our previous conversation.

As my ole lady and I sat in silence, I was battling within myself to spark a conversation that my pride didn't want me to spark. Deep down inside, I knew this was something I wanted and needed to do, but my pride kept trying to talk me out of it. Shortly after my heart and pride played tug of war, I finally built up enough courage, and gave my confession like Usher Raymond.

I had told my ole lady beforehand that I had a confession to make, but I asked her repeatedly not to respond during my confession, or after, for personal reasons. My ole lady surprisingly agreed to keep quiet. Once she agreed, I then took a deep breath, looked into her eyes, and confessed these words: "*I wish I had listened.*" Can you imagine what it took for me to utter such words? Can you? 'Cause if not, I'll tell you it'd be my pleasure to do so now that I have confessed.

Growing up in our household, my parents always preached to my siblings and I about taking heed to the valuable lessons that were being taught to us as children. Oftentimes as our parents preached their sermons, they would quote things like, "I wish Mama and Daddy would hurry up and shut up"; "Y'all better take heed"; and "Y'all gonna say to y'all selves, 'I wish I had listened.'" As our parents preached their sermons, they were right; my siblings and I were saying within ourselves how we wished they would hurry up and shut up; they didn't know what they were talking about; and we would never say that.

Consequently, I had to confess the words of my past, and to utter such words, took the power of God, his only begotten son Jesus, the Christ, the Holy Spirit, and the twelve disciples. Uttering the words "I wish I had listened" left my ole lady in awe. Yep, she was speechless—or should I say, she obeyed my command. LOL! Having said that, I was able to move forward in life once I'd been liberated from that burden.

As time went on, a friend from the past unexpectedly became present in my life once again. In the heat of the day as I sat in the house, I received an incoming call from an unfamiliar number. As I sat there debating whether I should answer the call, I decided to pick up, and to my surprise, it was my anonymous lady friend, contacting me on three-way, with my cousin on the line, who was incarcerated at the time. The instant I answered the phone, the caller and I briefly greeted one another as she introduced herself, then she connected my cousin onto the line. Without my cousin or me having to ask her for some privacy, she respectfully sat the phone down while he and I spoke. Once my cousin and I were about to end our conversation, she "coincidentally" picked up the phone seconds before. Prior to my cousin's call ending, he quickly told my anonymous lady friend, "Hey, keep in touch with Lo, brah." Then he said to me demandingly, "Lo, brah, if she don't keep in touch, I'll handle dat when I touch down."

Much to my surprise, my anonymous lady friend kept in touch. In fact, she and I sat on the phone long after my cousin's call was disconnected. In that conversation, I learned about her place of employment located in the city of North Charleston; I learned about her efforts to attend college out of state, pursuing a career in the medical field; I also learned that she and her male acquaintance were still courting each other years later. At the end of our conversation, she stated that she would call me from time to time. In response, I said, "You know the number."

As promised, my anonymous lady friend kept her word; in fact, girlfriend went beyond that promise by visiting me from time to time as well. During the visits, we spoke about our teenage years as friends, and her coming to my home with my eldest sibling, without my knowledge. At times we also watched different genres of movies, such as *State Property 2*, "You figga deal me."

As I reflect on those moments, there is this one visit that's constantly replaying in my mind, and boy, was that a wild and crazy visit. On this particular day, the sun had already set and I was lying in bed watching television. As she and I engaged in conversation, I politely asked that she give me a swig of Hennessy. "Hmm," she replied, then she immediately denied my request. "Mann, I'm not giving you that." If you saw her facial expression, you would have wet your diaper, because in the words of Bishop Bullwinkle, her eyes said, "Hell nah, to the nah, nah, nah."

Shortly after trying to convince her to give me a swig of Hennessy, I had to bring in my ole lady to assure her that it was okay. Once my ole lady gave the okay, my anonymous lady friend was still hesitant about it, but she came around, and nervously gave it to me. Over the course of sipping on a cup of Hennessy, it gradually started to take effect, and my imagination began to run wild. As I lay in bed, feeling the effects of the Hennessy, I asked my anonymous lady friend to dim the light because the brightness was affecting my vision—step one.

Moments later, I asked my anonymous lady friend to sit beside me because the darkness prohibited me from clearly seeing her—step two. Soon after that, I asked her to give me a bushel, a peck, and a hug around the neck, as my granny would say—step three. Somewhere in those steps, my TV mysteriously shut off, and because I don't recall asking my anonymous lady friend to do so, I'll just place the blame on her, the Prime Suspect. As requested, she did what was asked of her, and boy, did that ignite a flame. Afterward, she went and stood at the left side of my bed and playfully said, "I should . . . " Keep in mind, I was under the influence of an alcohol beverage, and although I remembered what took place, I was not responsible for my actions.

In response to her spontaneous idea, I replied, "You wouldn't," but astoundingly, she did. Prior to her performing that act, I wasn't a believer, but once it was said and done, I believed. Truth be told, nothing out of the ordinary occurred between us; in fact, other than making out during her spontaneous act, nothing else occurred. Shortly after midnight, we ended our private shindig, and neither of us wanted it to end.

As time went by, our friendship gradually came to an end. Prior to that, she and I would contact each other throughout the day to either check in or talk. She also made time to visit me frequently throughout the week; however, over the course of time, I noticed a change in the phone calls we had, and as time progressed, I then noticed a change in our visits. When I noticed those changes, I kept quiet as I observed her, because I didn't want to jump to conclusions. But after a while, I decided to confront her about the issue. In response to my concerns she expressed there was nothing to worry about. She said, "Between working and running personal errands, I don't have time to do much of anything." With all things considered, I gave her the benefit of the doubt, because she wasn't doing anything outrageous to make me believe otherwise.

Subsequently things got better between me and her, but unfortunately the friendship was short-lived once she stopped calling. Before she stopped contacting me, I again noticed a change in our phone calls and visits, but instead of confronting her the second time around, I, too, decided to refrain from contacting her to see how it pan out. She made no effort to contact me through phone calls or text messages. I hadn't received any visits from her either. Although I already knew that the friendship between us was on a downward spiral, I made efforts to contact her not to chat but to make sure I perceived her memo correctly, and as I suspected she deliberately avoided all contact.

Having to part ways with my anonymous lady friend was disappointing, because I thought for sure she would have stuck around and given me the support I needed, but hey, that's life as we know it. Months later, I was told that she had conceived her first offspring, and the news bearer who brought the glad tidings asked if I was aware of her pregnancy. In response, I said no.

Later that evening, I phoned my anonymous lady friend inquiring about her conception, and what do ya know, she surprisingly answered the phone. As soon as she answered the call, I respectfully greeted her, saying, "What's happening? How are you doing?" She did the same in return, then without hesitation, I asked her, "Is there something you wanna tell me?"

She said that she had nothing to tell me. Although she denied she had anything to tell me, I repeatedly asked the same question, but once I noticed that I wasn't getting anywhere, I then said, "I heard that you are with child." In the moment, she played dumb, saying, "Huh? What you talkin' 'bout?" Then she asked, "Who told you that?" Leave it to her, you'd almost never get a straight answer; if anything, she would cross-examine you before giving an answer.

Once she noticed that she wasn't successful with cross-examining me, she then confessed that she was with child. As I processed her confession, it brought clarity as to why she up and left without warning; it also brought back a memory of her regurgitating crabs, which is a favorite for residents in the Low country, including her. The day my anonymous lady friend became ill, I had an inkling about her pregnancy because she had done something I had never witnessed her do. Out of curiosity, I asked her if she was expecting, but she replied no. In light of her illness, I always said to myself, "If it is what I think it is, it will come to light." And boom! The bomb dropped. The Gap Band couldn't have sung those lyrics any better when they said, "You dropped a bomb on me," because that is what she did.

Needless to say I genuinely congratulated her on her pregnancy, because despite how I felt, the gift of life is a blessing. She had to end our call because she was at work, but prior to parting ways again, she and I spoke a couple of times that week. During this time, I got a visit from Rick and George, who were employed with Pharmaceutical Healthcare, concerning my power chair.

Rick and George said, "If we adapted a joystick to your power chair, do you think you would be able to operate it with your hand?"

Then I replied, "I don't know, but I'll try." Due to my willingness to operate the power chair with the usage of my hand, Rick and George asked to see the mobility in my upper extremity. As I demonstrated the mobility in my upper extremity to them, both gentlemen took one look at each other, then looked at me and asking for the second time, "Do you think you can operate the power chair with the usage of your hand?"

As I demonstrated the mobility in my upper extremities to Rick and George, I became aware of strength that I didn't know I possessed, because it was evident that I would be able to, so I confidently replied, "Yeah." After making that exciting discovery, Rick, George, and myself collectively agreed to adapt the control panel to the left side of my power chair. Because of their busy schedule, the power chair was left behind, but it was picked up a day or two later as promised.

On the following week of Rick and George's last visit, both gentlemen brought the power chair back equipped with the control panel that we all discussed. In addition to that, both gentlemen went into detail about the minor adjustments that were made. The minor adjustments consisted of both gentlemen sawing off the left arm rest so that I would be able to access and operate the joystick without any restraint. However, with the assistance of my caretaker, I was transferred into my power chair, and from there I went outside to test drive.

As a first-timer, operating that power chair with the usage of my hand went well, despite the swerving that occurred, but it wasn't until a day or two later that I got the hang of it in an open outdoor area. From then on, I have been independently operating the power chair with the usage of my hand. I was able to operate it without any complications thanks to Jehovah rophe (the Lord who heals). Around that time, I started attending outpatient therapy again at the Medical University of South Carolina OT-PT clinic located on Ashley Avenue in downtown Charleston. At that clinic, I worked alongside an excellent therapist named Vicki, who I'd had the pleasure of working with in the past on the third floor at Medical University main hospital.

Vicki would begin our sessions by her performing range of motion on both my upper and lower extremities, then she would have me independently perform a list of exercises with additional repetitions utilizing my neck, shoulders, and arms. Weeks into attending therapy, Vicki proposed an idea to implement another exercise into our workout regimen, and I accepted the challenge because I was eager to learn about my physical capability.

The exercises included neck workouts and push-ups, so to speak, without the usage of a weighted neck extension or my hands, but elbows. Implementing this exercise into our workout regimen required that I be transferred from my power chair to the clinic's table mat platform, and positioned into a plank position, with my elbows planted directly under my shoulders (slightly closer than shoulder width). Needless to say, Vicki gracefully did what was required, and to our surprise, I was able to independently perform neck workouts and push-ups. Considering the level of my injury, both Vicki and I were blown away by the physical capability in my upper extremities, so much so, that we centered our attention on the workout, rather than discussing it. And from that day on, it has been a part of our workout regimen.

Life has a way of kicking us when we are down, and I say this because just when I thought I was rising above all odds, I got kicked again. Ten-some-odd years ago (2005), both parents of mine informed me about a family matter, some disturbing news concerning my eldest sibling. At that moment, I could not believe my ears, but I knew it was true because it was written all over their faces. In the course of listening, I didn't respond, because again, I was in disbelief.

Shortly thereafter, on another occasion, my eldest sibling then broke the news to me concerning the same issue, as she stood at the foot of my bed sobbing. Even in that moment, I again became bitter. The anger inside of me was brewing like a pot of mash in the backwoods of the Appalachian Mountains as my eldest sibling went into full details. I learned that she had become a victim of criminal domestic violence; she was physically abused on various occasions by the hands of her then male acquaintance who at times tied her up and held her at gunpoint. Her male acquaintance was verbally abusive as well, uttering vulgar language, saying, "You dumb bitch," and "You stupid."

She said he took cheap shots at times by uttering how she had no one, including me, to stand in her defense. He also threatened to take her life, then turn the gun on himself if ever she decided to move on. He threatened to commit arson by burning down their home. Initially, I wanted to reach out and touch her male acquaintance, but a conversation with the Lord and Mama G forced me to refrain, because one poor decision could have cost any one of us, if not all.

In the course of that tainted relationship, my eldest sibling incurred great bodily injury to the face and upper torso that led to typical medical complaints and physical symptoms like headaches, chest pain, facial scrapes, bruises, cuts, or fractures, neck scrapes or bruises, a tooth loose or broken, and body scrapes or bruises. She incurred psychological damage as well that led to many of the common symptoms of abuse—a sense of hopelessness, despair because she believed she would never escape his control, a belief that she deserved the abuse, and was the one responsible for the abuse.

As I gave an ear to my eldest sibling, I had a flashback that entailed several of my peers inquiring about she and her male acquaintance's relationship, implying that they knew things would have been different if I wasn't injured, but it didn't dawn on me until later that my peers were giving me a hint concerning the issue without explicitly stating it. At first, I was infuriated with my peers for withholding that information, but knowing the character of those gentlemen, I then realized, and strongly believe, that they didn't want to ruffle my feathers about the issue, because they felt it was not conducive to my well being, considering my time of adversity.

However, that time around, I responded to the issue calmly, stating that it was best for her to part ways with her male acquaintance, because it was an unhealthy relationship that no man, woman, cat, or dog should have to endure. In response, she expressed how she understood all I stated, then she disclosed how difficult it would be to sever their relationship; she wasn't ready to do so.

As you can see, domestic violence is a serious issue in today's society; in fact, it is the leading cause of injury to women. In order to put a handle on this issue, it is important for victims to be vocal in terms of utilizing their freedom of speech concerning the issue; victims must make efforts to ease their hands out of the lion's mouth and not look back; then the criminal justice system must fulfill their duties to enforce the laws that have been implemented; in addition to developing stricter laws that would protect the victims, and hopefully prevent the suspects from committing the same offence. In closing, instead of acting oblivious to this widespread issue uttering, "It's none of my business," we, the fellow citizens of the victims, should support women and give them the tools that they need to overcome the obstacles they face in today's world, because after all, they are our mothers, daughters, and sisters.

As the years went by, my loved ones and I got an unexpected surprise that neither one of us anticipated. The instant this unexpected surprise surfaced, it not only caught us by surprise, but our other relatives, as well as friends of the family. However, it wasn't just the unexpected surprise that left everyone in awe, it was also the gut-wrenching incident that led to it.

My ole lady was filing for divorce after fifteen years of marriage to my ole man. Prior to the filing process, both of my parents were bickering about their marital issues.

As they were at each other's throats, my ole lady disgustedly blurted out, "I'ma put you out."

In response to that outburst, my ole man, being well aware of the law and his rights, arrogantly stated that he wasn't going anywhere, nor was he signing divorce documents. He said, "Yeah, I do my dirt, but until you can present concrete evidence that prove I'm at fault of any offense pertaining to grounds for divorce or eviction, you don't have legal grounds to do so."

The feud between my parents was about my ole man not fulfilling his duties economically within the household, and his infidelity issues. They had been ongoing issues starting prior to and throughout my existence on this Earth, and quite frankly, my ole lady was sick and tired of being sick and tired. Before long, she was able to obtain tangible evidence that gave her grounds for divorce, and little did my ole man know, it was the evidence that he would live to regret.

Eight years ago, in 2008, my ole lady filed for divorce and submitted the evidence that she obtained to her attorney, then she presented it to my ole man. Just before she did, it was presented to me, and when I tell you my ole lady caught him red-handed, I mean just that. It was footage of my ole man committing adultery with one of his mistresses, but here was the kicker—it was in our household, with a woman who was my permanent caretaker at the time. Initially, I was just as stunned as you are, because I didn't expect my ole man, or the aid, to pull a stunt like that, but more than anything, my heart went out to my ole lady, because I know that was a hard pill to swallow.

To make matters worse, I was present at the house at the time this incident occurred. I was lying in bed asleep as those two engaged themselves in sexual activities. The tip that led to discovering this love affair came from both the adulterer and mistress themselves. It all began, however, with my ole man contacting my ole lady to inform her about the aid coming to pick him up from his place of employment at the time, which was approximately seven miles away from our home. It continued with my aid doing the same thing. It eventually became a habit for both parties. Believe it or not, I was fully aware of the issue because my ole man at times contacted me, asking if I would ask the aid to pick him up from work, but I didn't know that my ole lady was aware of it until she contacted me one day asking if the aid had already left to pick him up.

In response to that unexpected question, I said, "Yeah," then I asked my ole lady, "How do you know the aid went to pick him up?" At that juncture is when my ole lady informed me of the issues, stating how bold my ole man and the aid were, especially the aid, because in addition to her contacting my ole lady, the aid had also left me at home unattended, for their pleasure.

Prior to this love affair emerging, my eldest sibling and I had suspicions about the issue, because the instant she and I entered our home, my ole man and the aid were looking suspicious as they brought their conversation to a screeching halt. However, in light of the issue, we failed to inform each other about our suspicions, but later that day, my eldest sibling told my ole lady that she didn't trust the aid, saying, "My spirit don't agree with her." Little did we all know, my ole lady was ahead of the game. And rather revert to her volatile ways, she stuck to the script, because she had an agenda.

Astoundingly, my ole lady secretly took action by hiring a private investigator in addition to a professional technician to install a video surveillance system in our home. And that, my friend, is how the evidence was obtained. With all things considered, my ole lady did a superb job keeping her agenda under the radar, because no one had a clue; in fact, on the day of the installation, I was under the impression that the technician was there to install a security system, which he did, but as for the investigator, he remained anonymous. According to my ole lady, when she presented the evidence, my ole man was unflappable, inarticulate, not saying boo, considering the squabble between the two months prior to that presentation.

On the next day, my ole man came to me asking if my ole lady had told me what happened, but I lied, replying no. Then he said, "Zeke, I know your mama told you what happened," but again, I denied it.

"I ain't know what you talkin' 'bout," I said. "What are you talkin' 'bout?"

At that present time, my ole man proceeded to explain what had taken place, and I immediately said, "Huh?" Then sarcastically, I said, "Not you! Not Mr. I-Ain't-Goin-in-Nowhere, 'you ain't got nuttin on me.' You always said nothing catches a fish but its mouth, I never knew what it meant then," I told him, "but I know what it mean now."

Shortly thereafter, the petition the court ordered put my ole man out of the marital home, but the court wasn't able to issue the divorce decree until a year later, because in the state of South Carolina, spouses are first required to be separated for a year's time without cohabitation. As for the caregiver, and the agency in which she was employed, my ole lady informed the case manager who was handling my case at the time, and then the case manager contacted the agency immediately terminating the service.

After a year's time and a couple of court hearings, both parents of mine collectively agreed that my ole lady would keep the marital property, and keep living in the marital home; neither spouse would pay alimony; and neither spouse would pay child support. My ole lady was to keep child custody, while my ole man had visitation rights. Then the court signed the decree to finalize the divorce due to the legally sufficient evidence that my ole lady had presented. If you are seeking a divorce or annulment from a marriage, you must be informed about grounds for divorce and the process in your state or country, then file the petition.

Life, has its way of coming back full circle, doesn't it? I say this because soon after my parents were subpoenaed to legally separate, an old friend of mine came back around. In the peace of the afternoon, the silence was suddenly broken as the upbeat sound of my cell phone rang. I immediately gazed at the screen of my phone to see who the incoming caller was. The instant I looked at my phone, I saw that it was an unfamiliar number, so I sat there contemplating whether I should answer the phone or not. As I sat in my power chair staring at the phone, I decided to answer the incoming call three rings in.

"Hello?" I said.

"Hi, Mann!" said the caller.

"What's happening?"

"Nothing. How are you?"

"I straight," I said.

"That's good. What are you doing?"

"Shit, chillin'."

"Chillin', you always chillin'." I laughed, then the caller said, "So how have you been?"

"I been doing good, just taking it one day at a time, dat's all."

"That's great—hold up—do you know who you are speaking to?"

"Nah, who dis?"

Unhesitatingly, the caller drilled me about having a conversation with them, not knowing who they were. The caller asked me if I was trying to catch onto their voice, then implied that I must have had a lot of women calling me. In response, I initially burst out with laughter, then said, "Nah, ain't like dat. I know who you is."

"Yeah, whatever."

Being that the caller didn't believe that I knew who they were, they asked for me to state their name in order to proceed with our conversation, so I said, "This is my anonymous lady friend."

After confirming that I knew who she was, she and I proceeded with our conversation. I learned that she had celebrated her child's first birthday a week or two prior to contacting me. I also learned that she worked nearby where I lived at the time. In response to her updates, I sarcastically made a statement about not receiving an invite to her child's first birthday bash, then I asked her to stop by since she worked nearby, but she had already left the area. Due to her demanding job, she had to end our conversation, but she astoundingly gave me a call back at her convenience. Prior to revitalizing our friendship, she and I initially reconnected through phone conversations.

I'm reminded of a phone call that I received from her one afternoon as she was on an outing with her child at Chuck E. Cheese's. As I reflect on that conversation, I can recall her bickering about me not taking the initiative to call her. "It didn't dawn on me until I checked my call log and noticed that I hadn't received a call from you all day, or any time prior to today," she said. "I understand your disability prevents you from dialing out," she said, "but you do have people like your mother, sisters, or nurse who could assist you with that."

I couldn't agree more with her statements. In fact, I made that clear to her, but what I didn't disclose was that my decision to not contact her was an act of caution, considering that I was unaware whether or not she was going to stick around. Once clearing the air, she stated how long she was going to be on the outing with her child. She said that she was leaving at a specific time, and if I didn't contact her at that specific time, that would be the last time I heard from her. Despite not knowing if she would stick around, I obeyed her command and contacted her.

As soon as she answered the phone, she grumbled a bit because I'd contacted her a few minutes after the specific time that was given.

She said, "Yes? You're late. What do you want?"

"I ain't late. True indeed, you did say call back at such-and-such time, but you didn't specify whether to contact in the morning or the evening, so technically I'm not late."

In response she said, "Ooh, you little . . . You make me sick. Funny."

Due to that technicality, I wasn't disqualified, but I did say she needed to be more detailed in the near future when giving an order.

Within a matter of time, the friendship between us had been rebuilt, and as a result she began visiting me again. In the beginning stages of this reconnection, she visited me between breaks at my home, indoors or outdoors. Within a matter of weeks, however, those visits between breaks led to her visiting me after work, then the after-work visits ultimately led to her visiting me more often, at her convenience or mine. Over the course of time, she and I began to explore new adventures that consisted of dinner and movie dates. As I reflect on those new adventures, I can recall us dining out at a restaurant that was special to us both. Beforehand, we'd talked about exploring new adventures, and as the conversation progressed, she suggested that we go on a dinner date.

I told her that I would be honored to accompany her to a dinner date at a restaurant of her choice. At that juncture, she began brainstorming about the restaurant of her choice, and much to my surprise she said, "Let's go to our spot." Truth be told, I wasn't thinking about that dinner date we'd gone on during my stay at Roper Rehab back in 2002, but the moment she brought it to my attention, it made me want to accompany her all the more.

As anticipated, we went on our dinner date at our spot, where the service was great and the dishes were delightful. On the evening of this rendezvous, it began with us meeting up at our spot, and then it carried into the restaurant's waiting area and the booth where the waitress seated us both. Once we'd sat down, the waitress left us with a couple of menus, then told us to holler when we were ready to place our orders. In the process of browsing through the menu, we expressed to one another how flabbergasted we both were to be on a dinner date for two.

She kidded about who was going to assist me with eating, considering that I only allowed a selected few to feed me. She said, "You better call Mrs. Paulette, or Jazz, to feed you, because I am not feeding you, brah." Initially, I gave her a straight-faced expression as I refrained from laughing, but as she went on with her silly antics, I couldn't hold the laughter in any longer. As we were kidding around, the waitress came back to take down our order, and I allowed my anonymous lady friend to place her order first, then I placed mine.

Needless to say, the orders that my anonymous lady friend and I placed were properly prepared, courtesy of the cook. And thanks to the courteous waitress, our dishes were served within the time-frame she'd given us. As the waitress placed our orders on the table, my anonymous lady friend and I expressed our gratitude, then we immediately began to chow down. As we indulged in our meals, my anonymous lady friend asked if I wanted to take a bite of her dish, but I replied no with a disgusted expression. In response, she said, "Why the disgusted look? You haven't even tried it yet. You should try it. Here, try some. It's good." But again, I replied no. After harassing me about taking a bite of her dish, I ultimately gave in and took a bite. I must say, it was tasty. After taking a bite of that dish, she and I proceeded to enjoy the rest of the evening, then we ultimately ended our rendezvous after polishing off our dishes. Indubitably, she and I had a splendid evening, but most of all, we enjoyed each other's company at our spot.

On other occasions, we accompanied each other to different locations, in both public settings, and at her place of residence. Aside from those outings, I can recall the two of us, her little one, and her niece at the Coastal Carolina Fair that comes to town each year in the fall. I can also recall her and her little one accompanying my nephew and I on a playdate at the movie theater.

From the time of her return, the friendship between us flourished like never before. As time progressed, the bond between us became tighter. All in all, things between us were clearly looking up, so much so, that we astoundingly maintained a connection this time around.

CHAPTER 13

At the beginning of spring 2008, a seed that God planted within me began to take root. The bud that began to develop through and out of me was my God-given purpose. And who would have known that I would be able to reverse the mistakes of my past, and draw men unto the God of the living by living on this purpose? Several years prior to taking on this amazing task, two young ladies who were longtime friends of the family told me on separate occasions that God had spared my life solely for this purpose, but I immediately rejected the calling and said, "Who? Do what? Oh no, dat ain't gonna happen." In response to my rejection, both ladies asked, "Why not you?" They said, "Think about your past experiences, and the adversities you are currently facing, then look at the issues in today's society. You are the perfect candidate, wouldn't you say?" Although I agreed to what both ladies said, I was still reluctant about the whole ordeal. Despite my reluctance, both ladies did not try to pressure me; however, their last words to me were, "You will be ready when the time comes, but until then, prepare yourself, because it's going to happen."

As time went on, however, the talk about my God-given purpose resurfaced in the spring of 2008, and hearing those words was like

Deja vu. Around this time, my loved ones and I had been living in the Rosemont community approximately three years. The person who brought up this conversation was the first caregiver I had with Nightingale's Nursing attendants. As I reflect on the past, I can remember that moment just like it was yesterday. It was in the early afternoon, as I recall, when the aid entered my room after prayer and said, "You do not know this, but I'm an evangelist." She said, "And I must be honest, I'm not doing all that I'm supposed to be doing, but God told me to tell you what he wants you to do, and he wants you to do it now."

Just as the aid was prophesying to me, my eyes immediately popped open, because I hadn't known she was an evangelist, but I must admit there was a tender expression on my face, because like Sunshine Anderson said, "I heard it all before." The aid thought I did not believe her, but I said, "It's not that I don't believe you, because I do. It's just that my reaction is more of, 'Here we go again.'" After all was said and done, the aid took the same approach as the other two young ladies, by not pressuring me, but she did advise that I pray about it.

Within an hour or two after that prophecy, I got an unexpected visit from my pastor, who visited with me for a while. During that visit with my pastor, he and I were having a casual conversation that led to a dialogue about his vision concerning the future of our church, and his agenda to help all members grow as a unit, as well as individually. Towards the end of our visit, my pastor revealed his purpose for popping up at my home unannounced. "God put me in his spirit to take on a specific task," he said. He told me that God had been speaking to him for some time prior to his visit, but due to his schedule, he kept putting it off. According to my pastor, God then spoke to him on another occasion concerning this task, but instead of putting it off again, he obeyed God's command.

As you can imagine, I was thrown for a loop the instant my pastor uttered the same exact words the aid had, because she and I'd just had that discussion prior to his arrival. It really blew my mind as I thought about the other half of that discussion between me and the aid. In the other half of that discussion, she and I were basically exchanging information with each other about who our presiding pastors were, the location of our churches, and the areas where our pastors were from. And in that discussion, she and I both quickly learned that neither one of us was familiar with either pastor, the location of either church, or the area where either pastor was from.

As I thought about that part of the discussion, I said to myself, "This has to be God." I mean, think about it, who else could it have been, considering that neither my pastor nor the aid knew a thing about each other? Before my pastor left, he, just like the others, did not try to pressure me, but he did advise that I pray about it, and said that he was most certain this was what God wanted me to do.

Later that night, I took that calling to God in prayer, and as I slept the night away, I saw myself in a dream doing thus saith the Lord. My purpose from God was to become a youth speaker, and although I was reluctant about taking on this significant task, I am honored that he chose a wretch like me. Never in a million years did I imagine ministering to the youth, but when God calls you to a service that is far beyond your imagination, you must answer. Needless to say, I contacted my pastor the next day to inform him that God had confirmed his calling for my life, and within that week, I had my first speaking engagement. It was at my church amongst the younger and older generations, that following Sunday.

Before I get into sharing my testimony, I generally take these steps: I greet the congregation/audience, be it a church congregation, group of students, etc.; render credit to God for all he has done, and who he is; acknowledge my loved ones and/or peers, if not both, for their support; reintroduce myself by stating my name, age, and the county where I'm from; then I explain to everyone that I'm going to share my testimony with them, my testimony about life before my injury, after my injury, and the incident that led to my injury in full detail.

The first time I spoke, however, I must say I was pretty darn nervous, to the point where I got teary-eyed. In fact, I asked the congregation to bear with me as I held back tears that were seconds away from trickling out of my tear ducts. As a result, I only took the first and last step out of those previous five steps I mentioned. Then I quickly proceeded with the assignment, and began.

"Coming up as a child, my siblings and I were brought up with both parents under the same roof. In our household, my parents always taught us right from wrong," I told the congregation. "They taught us to respect others, no matter who they are, because respect will take you places where money won't. My parents also taught us to stay in school, get an education, and make something out of ourselves. They instilled in us that we could be whatever we wanted to be, as long as we put God first, and worked towards our goals. As I think back, I can remember my ole lady driving me and my siblings to different communities of North Charleston and downtown Charleston, and showing us drug addicts, drug dealers, prostitutes, alcoholics, and the homeless, to let us know that that was how our lives could turn out if we didn't take heed to the wisdom and knowledge given to us.

"In addition to that, my ole lady also brought my siblings and I up in church, attending every service you could imagine. As time progressed, I began to go astray from those teachings by receiving in-school suspension, out-of-school suspension, detention, as well as expulsion. As I got older. I began to venture off into a much more destructive lifestyle, such as running the streets and dealing drugs, preferably crack cocaine. Instead of me lying in bed, preparing myself for school the following day, I was outside during the wee hours of the morning selling drugs, smoking marijuana, drinking alcoholic beverages, attending block parties and club events, and fornicating. While in the streets, I got myself arrested and locked up twice. I also got myself acquainted with a group of people whom I considered friends. Out of the group of people I chose to associate myself with, there is this one person in particular, who I later found out wasn't—and still isn't—a friend of mine. In fact, he is the person who has me in the predicament that I am in now, which I will explain."

After sharing my testimony with the congregation in its entirety, I then explained to everyone why I chose to share my testimony with them, then I immediately exited the church like a bat out of hell to exhale, as the congregation gave me a standing ovation.

I generally open the floor for those who may have any questions, but I didn't implement this specific step until several speaking engagements later, courtesy of a youth group and their advisors who attended charity Missionary Baptist Church. If I may, allow me to explain how this step came about.

It was at a local church event where I was scheduled to speak, and at the end of sharing my testimony, a group of inquisitive church members wanted to go in depth about what I'd said, so their youth advisor asked if it was okay to have a panel discussion, and I replied, "Yeah, I don't mind." As the congregation asked their questions, in that moment, I decided to incorporate that step into my sessions, because it not only allowed me to speak upon things that I may not mention, it also gives the audience a clear understanding of the message I'm trying to get across.

From that day forward, word about me speaking began to spread rapidly like wildfire; well, I'm over exaggerating, but it got around. And ever since then, I have received invites to attend local events as a guest speaker. In addition to attending local events, I wrote letters with my testimony to several loved ones and peers who were incarcerated at the time, in hopes they, too, would acknowledge God, reevaluate their way of living, and work towards change. All through the first half of 2008, I was faithfully living my God-given purpose, so much so, that I broadcast the good news any time the question, "What's new?" was asked.

Throughout that time, there were acquaintances and strangers who asked if I'd ever considered taking other avenues to tell my story. In fact, they all suggested that I take one avenue in particular, stating, "You have a very interesting story that the world would not only love to hear, but *needs* to hear, and I believe that it will inspire today's society, especially the youth." I told those individuals I had not considered other avenues beyond the speaking engagements, especially not the suggestion that everyone seemed to single out.

Years prior to encountering those individuals, a close relative of mine was the first to ask the question, but even then I gave it no thought, considering my lack of interest in what they were asking. Over the course of time, I continued to broadcast the good news to those whom I encountered along the way. The suggestion that I consider other avenues to tell my story became a frequent thing from those individuals. Surprisingly though, I took the idea into consideration, and in that process I said to myself, "Why not give it a whirl?

Why not take a stab at writing an autobiography of my life story?" The reason I'd been dead set against it was because I didn't like to bury myself in books, let alone do what everyone was suggesting, so in my mind, I knew it wasn't going to happen.

Upon proceeding with the assignment, I brought the idea to my ole lady for her consent, then I contacted my cousin to inform him that I'd decided to take his advice. As I broke the news to my cousin, he was as lost as the Israelites in the wilderness, because it had been years since he and I had had that discussion, but as I refreshed his memory, he got excited. He asked, "Why the sudden change?" I told him about the encounters I'd had with those acquaintances and strangers who'd suggested what he and I had discussed long before then. I told him about the discussion I'd had with myself, where I said, "For everyone I encountered to suggest that I take this avenue in particular, it has to be part of my God-given purpose, and rather than live the rest of my life saying to myself, "I wonder what if?" I'd give it a try.

Immediately after explaining to my cousin the reason for the sudden change, he offered his assistance to help with the writing process. Needless to say, I took him up on that offer, but it wasn't until the second half of 2008 that I began working on this project. In fact, it was in the fall, which is also when I purchased an HP desktop computer solely for the purpose of writing my autobiography. In the beginning stages of writing this book, it was a struggle, because I knew what I wanted to write about, but it was difficult finding ways to articulate it.

I asked my cousin repeatedly about the dilemma I was facing. "How do I go about writing the opening paragraph? What do I say?"

He simply said, "You could start with introducing yourself."

"Am I able to do that?" I asked him.

"Of course," he replied, "authors do it all the time." Then he said, "It's your book. You can write whatever you want."

I took my cousin's suggestion to introduce myself in the first chapter, then I proceeded to complete the sentences that went along with the introduction. After I completed the introduction in chapter one, I turned to my cousin a second time and asked, "How do I go about writing the opening paragraph in topic one? What do I say?"

"Think of what your topic is about—the incidents that occurred, be it good or bad—and that should give you a jump start with the opening paragraph of topic one," he responded.

Without question, I took my cousin's advice, however, I must admit, the topic lingered with me a while and I kept asking myself repeatedly, "What is the topic about?" That's when it hit me.

Shortly thereafter, my cousin advised that any time I write a book, I should take these steps: write out my life timeline; identify the main characters; pull out the best stories; write in my own voice; be revealing; and capture the spirit of the times.

I told my cousin, "I didn't have the patience to take step one." However, I did take the following five steps, as he coached me through the first three chapters. Three chapters in, I was beginning to get the hang of it, courtesy of my cousin, so instead of having him travel back and forth to my home to help me with the editing, I told him at our last visit, "I greatly appreciate the contributions that you made to this company, but unfortunately I have to lay you off. You are fired!"

In all seriousness, that is not how I broke the news to my cousin, I simply said, "Now that I got the hang of writing, I could ask my youngest sibling to do the editing instead of having you burn your gas and mileage." The instant I informed my cousin about my decision he expressed that it wasn't an issue for him to assist me with the editing. He also agreed that it wouldn't be a bad idea to have my youngest sibling assist me with the editing as well, considering how I stored days of material in my brain.

Due to my cousin's coaching, I was able to proceed with the writing process on my own, but I must admit, it wasn't such a bad idea to have my youngest sibling assist me with the editing, because the material was flowing out of me like streams of water. The decision to allow her to assist me worked out for us both, because I obtained what she so desired, and vice versa.

In the home where I began working on my project, there was an internet connection in both my youngest sibling's room, and mine. However, her desktop crashed and left her without access to social media. Considering that my desktop was still up and running, I was the only one with internet service. In order for my youngest sibling to access social media, she had to go through me. Because we needed each other, my youngest sibling and I negotiated a deal that benefited us both.

In this deal, it was agreed upon for her to use my desktop at any time without limitations, on one condition: She had to assist me with the editing of the project at any time. For example, if my youngest sibling was in another area of the house, and I needed her assistance with the editing, it was agreed upon that she would drop everything and assist me (depending on what she was doing). If my youngest sibling was already present in my room using the computer, and I needed assistance with editing, it would be the same scenario as in the first example.

As my youngest sibling used the computer, I would either be lying or sitting there putting together paragraphs of material for this project in my mind. Once I stored what I thought was enough material, I would then ask my youngest sibling to record the information on the computer for me. Without question, my youngest sibling hid the site she was occupying, pulled up the tab that I used, and recorded the material. Then she would resume with what she was doing. This system that she and I agreed to went on for months at a time, and needless to say, it worked out just fine.

With her assistance, I was able to navigate through the rivers of chapters four, five, and six like a white-water rafter. Navigating through certain parts of the rivers that followed—chapters seven, eight, and nine—was like maneuvering through class one rapids, but other sections in those chapters were more like class four rapids. The reason I chose to use white water rafting levels of difficulty as an illustration is simply because both levels, class one and four rapids, are symbolic to what I began to experience throughout those chapters I recorded, and more. In the process of writing this book, I was fortunate to encounter stretches of class one water, which created a pleasant break for writing between rapids, but on the other hand, I encountered turbulent waters—a.k.a. class four rapids—that required precise writing, which made things a tad bit difficult.

As I reflect on writing this book, I can recall myself completing chapters that contain paragraphs with common mistakes as far as spelling, punctuation, or grammar. Despite the mistakes made, I kept writing, because the material was flowing fluently. As the writing went on, however, I became exceedingly comfortable with the flow of it all, but much to my surprise, I encountered turbulent waters that disrupted my bed of roses. The instant I encountered the disruption, I was stumped, trying to figure out what happened, how it had happened, and what I could do to rectify the problem. In the puzzling moment, I sat there in a daze, asking myself repeatedly, "How do I rectify the problem?" And soon it hit me—I needed to carefully reread the written material from top to bottom, and visualize what I was reading.

Once I did that, I was able to get back in the flow of writing; granted, it wasn't the flow of a class one rapids, but it was a flow. Being that I encountered this issue in the beginning stages of writing this book, it should have been a no-brainer to take those steps listed, but considering all the confusion, it didn't dawn on me at that juncture to do so. Aside from that, encountering both levels of difficulty was a blessing; class one rapids allowed me to complete chapters without any disruptions, and class four rapids taught me to critique my writing skills.

As I set off to proceed traveling along this journey, I added another assignment to my agenda. Prior to following through with this additional assignment, I had to meet certain requirements, such as having to be seventeen years or older; acquire a transcript; and pay a registration fee of ninety-five dollars. In addition to those things, I had to take a placement test in different subjects to check my academic skill level so I would be placed with assignments that were at the right level.

Without question, I met the requirements, and in the following weeks, I was able to begin the first preparation class. The additional assignment added to my agenda was my decision to pursue a GED. If you can recall, I wrote about taking on an assignment quite similar to that in previous chapters, my goal to obtain my high school diploma, which I achieved. However, a conversation took place between myself and a permanent aid where I later found out the diploma was no longer valid . As soon as I learned that, I told the aid, "Hell no, that can't be. I spoke with a close relative of mine, who's employed with one of our top community colleges, to make sure it was valid."

In that conversation, I'd specifically asked the relative, "Do y'all college accept diplomas from this anonymous school?" The relative said, "I'm not sure, let me look into it, and I will get back with you." Later that week, it was confirmed that the college at which the relative was employed did accept diplomas from this anonymous school, considering the school was accredited.

The aid agreed they accepted the diplomas, but could not explain why they stopped so again, I contacted my close relative in search of answers. Due to a thorough investigation, the close relative said the community college where she was employed no longer accepted diplomas from the anonymous school, because they were not accredited. As I listened to the close relative of mine, I thought to myself, *What a bummer. Just put a dagger in my heart, why don't ya?*

Instantaneously, after such a let-down, I began searching for a GED program to enroll in, but unfortunately the programs I contacted did not accommodate spinal cord injury patients with my level of injury, so instead of attempting to contact another GED program, I decided to contact my anonymous lady friend; contacting those GED programs was getting a tad bit discouraging.

The instant I got in contact with her, I asked myself, "Why did you do that? Confiding in her is like shooting oneself in the foot," and I say this because her initial reaction was laughter the second I told her about my dilemma.

As she laughed, she said, "I thought the school you got your diploma from was accredited."

I replied, "I thought so, too, but according to the aid and close relative of mine, it's not."

As I confided in her, she then asked, "What are you going to do?"

And that's when I informed her about my efforts to find a GED program. She, with the assistance of her mother, then took the liberty to search for a program that accommodated spinal cord injury patients, and in no time, both ladies discovered a program. The program was at Dorchester County Adult Education in Summerville, South Carolina, located on 1325 Boone Hill Road.

The Summerville adult education program was a place where adults could go to achieve vocational skills, learn basic education, network with others within the community, and so much more. There are a variety of different types of learning centers for adults in Summerville, such as the adult learning center for low-income or unemployed adults, and the adult learning center for those looking to obtain a GED. Whatever the type of adult learning center, there are many benefits to lifelong learning. One of the major benefits is that it teaches adults marketable skills.

The adult learning center is extremely important for those who may lack a high school diploma and are attempting to obtain a general equivalency diploma. The test to obtain a GED is one that could be challenging for many people, but this diploma is required for almost every profession in the country today. Fortunately, the adult learning center is geared toward this type of instruction, and can make a huge difference in the life of someone seeking their GED.

During the first preparation class I focused on areas of different subjects that show my weakness. In fact, I was more focused than ever; I wasn't letting anything or anyone deter me from completing this course. In the course of time, however, I was able to improve my academic skill level by committing my time to the assignments that I was placed with in class or at home. After spending weeks on improving in the areas where I was weak academically, I was presented with the opportunity to advance into the second preparation class, but in order to do so, I had to take the GED assessment to determine strengths and weaknesses. I took the practice test, and with my test scores, the test administrator said I was able to advance into the second preparation class; in fact, the test administrator said if it had been the actual GED test, I would have passed with flying colors.

I gave this second preparation class my all, because receiving my GED was a goal I'd wanted to achieve not just for myself, but for those who were near and dear to my heart. While things were looking up in terms of my academics, I unexpectedly took sick and my health began to decline significantly. In the process of taking sick, I did not notice my illness until I developed uncommon symptoms, like fevers with temperatures of 100.4 degrees or higher, chills, malaise, dizziness, a cough, and breathlessness. The instant I noticed these symptoms, I ignored all signs, thinking it would run its course, rather than check myself into the ER. Because I was stubborn, my health proceeded to decline, and I unexpectedly developed a symptom that I did not anticipate.

I developed mankind worst enemy, diarrhea. On the evening I developed this symptom, it was between travel from school to home, but no one was aware of it until my ole lady was about to transfer me out of the van. The reason no one, including me, was aware of my accident was because my body did not react in the way it normally did when I had a bowel movement, nor did my stool have an odor. As soon as my ole lady became aware of the accident, she laid me back in the passenger seat for a split second, got a sheet from out the house to put under me, then carefully transferred me out the van into the house.

I stubbornly continued to ignore all signs, but my decisions to ignore them was short-lived later that night, thanks to my stepfather. Later that night, during the wee hours of the morning, around two or three o'clock, I suffered from a low-grade temp, hot and cold body temperatures, and shortness of breath, some of the symptoms I suffered from long before I developed diarrhea. I unfortunately had to wake up my ole lady and repeatedly ask her to fix me cups of ice water, given my low-grade temp; pull the covers on or off, with my changes in body temperature; and bend my legs (hip flexion), with my shortness of breath.

While this was happening, my stepfather silently observed, and eventually he told my ole lady, "Enough is enough. We taking Mann to the hospital."

On the way to the hospital I wanted to strangle the living daylights out of my stepfather, because he got me up during the wee hours of the morning to transport me to a place that I was trying to avoid going to. As soon as I arrived at the ER, I was immediately checked in and escorted to the back. Immediately, a phlebotomist came in to insert a winged infusion set, also known as a "butterfly" or "scalp vein" set, a device specialized for collecting blood samples, intravenous drugs or fluids, or saline fluids. Once she'd inserted the IV tube, the nurse collected blood cultures, then began IV rehydration treatment. I waited, then the nurse came back with the lab test results. Unfortunately, I had to be admitted to the hospital due to a serious MRSA infection that was in my bloodstream. Methicillin resistant staphylococcus aureus (MRSA) is a bacterium that causes infections in different parts of the body. It's tougher to treat than most strains of staphylococcus aureus—or staph—because it's resistance to some commonly used antibiotics.

The moment I learned about MRSA, I no longer wanted to strangle my stepfather. I thanked him for his decision to transport me to the ER, because had I waited any longer, the infection could have became life- threatening, said the medical staff. During my stay at the hospital the medical staff began treating me with antibiotics in hopes of curing the infection. They also proceeded with the

IV rehydration treatment so I would stay hydrated, considering that I still had diarrhea. The fact the diarrhea still persisted days later, drew concerns, because I thought it would have gradually cleared up, considering I was being treated for the infection, but the medical staff said to not be alarmed; it was just my body fighting off the infection. After speaking with the medical staff I was at ease. They reassured me that there was nothing to worry about.

Soon after the previous conversation, I was discharged from the hospital because the medical staff said the infection had cleared up enough for me to be released. In addition to that, the medical staff faxed an authorized order to the pharmacy to continue the antibiotics I was being treated with. I was discharged from the hospital after my health had gotten back to normal; however, the diarrhea symptoms I suffered from were still a factor. It seemed uncommon for the diarrhea to persist longer than I expected. I notified my primary care doctor, and as a result, I was readmitted to the hospital a time or two.

The medical staff wholeheartedly focused on finding the cause of the issue. In their efforts, the medical staff asked me for some information: How long had I had diarrhea since my discharge date? Did the diarrhea come and go, or was it continuous? Did certain foods or situations seem to make the diarrhea worse, or better? I told them that I had no symptoms; the diarrhea never stopped, but there was nothing that made the diarrhea worse or better.

The medical staff continued the antibiotic treatment, considering that I had not quite finished the authorized prescription that I was sent home with, and they also began IV rehydration treatment because of the fluids lost from diarrhea. Throughout their search, their chances of finding the cause of the issue were getting slim, so they decided to change the liquid feeding formula for my feeding tube to see if it had an effect. We learned that it was not the daily liquid feeding formula, so as a last resort, the medical staff decided to discontinue the meds they were treating me with—and voila! There you have it. It was the antibiotics all along.

The instant the medical staff found out what caused the diarrhea, they didn't just discontinued the antibiotics that I was treated with, they discontinued it indefinitely, and I no longer had to endure that whole ordeal—what a relief.

As far as the schooling was concerned, I was unable to attend my GED program due to my health complications. I notified the school a few times and informed them of my health issues in hopes of not being withdrawn from the program; however, the whole ordeal took a toll on me over time to the point where I lost interest in school, and I unfortunately blew my chances of becoming an Summerville adult education/GED grad. Around the time my interest dissipated, I decided to return to therapy, but rather than attending outpatient therapy at the Medical University of South Carolina, I chose to do home health therapy with Pharmaceutical Healthcare.

During the first session, the therapist asked what were my goals in terms of therapy.

I told the therapist I wasn't expecting anything miraculous. I said, "My goal is to maintain the strength and mobility that I currently have, and to prevent my muscles from contracting. But if I regain more strength and mobility in my upper extremity, that's cool. If I don't, that's cool as well." She stated those were reasonable goals that could be achieved. Then she began examining the strength and mobility in my upper extremity by performing range of motion. Subsequently, we were able to design a plan of care that included long- and short-term functional goals, that consisted of neck exercises, shoulder exercises, arm exercises using resistance exercise bands, and leg exercises.

After designing the plan of care, the therapist said, "Now that we have developed a list of exercises that can help you achieve your long and short-term goals, these are the exercises that we will use during our next visit. In fact, you don't have to wait until our next visit," said the therapist. "You can have your nurse assist you with these exercises until I return, considering she's here from eight to four."

Shortly thereafter, the therapist and I agreed she would schedule me for at least two to three sessions a week, then she left because our session had exceeded its time.

She and I diligently worked on that list of exercises developed with the usage of a resistance exercise band. In addition to those, I agreed to go outdoors with the therapist and drive my power chair around the empty lot across the street from my home as a part of therapy. (That workout wasn't implemented until weeks later.) Two weeks in, however, the therapists decided to discharge me, stating that my prognosis was what it was, and there wasn't much she could do in terms of my mobility.

She also said the exercises she and I worked on were exercises I could do on my own, and with the assistance of the aid, I pretty much had no need for her. Then she went on to say, "I know you are a man of faith, and in no way am I trying to discourage you, but I'm limited with what I could do." In light of what the therapist said, I became a tad bit discouraged, but I understood where she was coming from, so I expressed my gratitude for her assistance, then she and I parted ways.

As time progressed, a new year arrived, but I'm sad to say it wasn't happy due to the death of a fallen soldier. In January 2010, I received an incoming call about the death of this gentleman. The caller stated that the gentleman had been fatally shot and killed. As the caller broke the news, it was hard to believe, considering that I had just spoken to the gentleman prior to his death. Later in the day, I received another incoming call from a different person, who made the same statement as the first caller. That time around, I was convinced.

Hours later, I got in contact with the gentlemen's brother, and I learned how the incident had occurred. According to his brother, the gentleman received an incoming call to come outside on the evening of the incident in question. Straightaway, he went outside to meet the caller, and as soon as he did, shots were fired. As the gentleman's brother filled me in, all I could think about was the conversations the gentleman and I had, which consisted of him getting himself together for the better, and him working towards pursuing his music career as a rapper and singer.

The more I reflected on those conversations, I recalled the gentleman telling me about an opportunity he had in Florida to pursue his music career; he also told me about when he presented his opportunity to his parole or probation officer, hoping that he or she would grant him permission to leave the state of South Carolina, and due to legal stipulations, his PO denied his request. Truth be told, if the gentleman's PO had granted him permission to leave the state to pursue his music career, I truly believe he would still be among us today, alive and well.

On Tuesday, however, January 19, 2010, the relatives of my partner Patrick Darnell Young, a.k.a. Lil P, Da Ghetto Priest, had a home going service for him at St James AME Church off of Highway 17 North in McClellanville, South Carolina, where he was fatally shot and killed. Unfortunately, though, Patrick, at the tender age of twenty-five, left behind his loving parents, grandparents, siblings, and daughter. He also left behind a host of nieces, nephews, other relatives, and friends who loved him dearly.

Soon after my partner was laid to rest, I found myself preparing for a ceremony that wasn't death related, a wedding ceremony that my ole lady (the bride-to-be) was having. Back on January 8, 2009, said my ole lady, she'd encountered my stepfather (the groom-to-be) at a local juke joint called Six Mile Tavern located in the town of Mount Pleasant, South Carolina, off of Rifle Range Road. On the evening of that encounter, she said that the legendary Six Mile Tavern was having a mother-daughter event that my eldest sibling had invited her to. Initially, my ole lady wasn't interested in attending the event, but after a pep talk with me and my eldest sibling, she decided to go.

My ole lady got herself squared away, then immediately she and my eldest sibling left for the event. Shortly after reaching their destination, they exited their vehicle, linked up with a couple of female acquaintances, then entered the tavern. As the evening went on, said my eldest sibling, the ladies were enjoying themselves, so much so that she and my ole lady got up and danced with each other.

Following that dance, a gentleman (my stepfather) approached my eldest sibling and politely asked if he could have a few moments of my ole lady's time. In response, my eldest sibling said sure, then gave both my ole lady and the gentleman their privacy. According to my ole lady, she and the gentleman were cordially conversing with one another, until they were disrupted by my eldest sibling who pulled my ole lady aside for a brief pep talk, because she noticed the glazed look that masked her face.

Subsequently, that pep talk with my eldest sibling must have worked, because my ole lady went back to speak with the gentleman, showing interest the second time around. Before long, my ole lady reunited with my eldest sibling and their female acquaintances the moment she and the gentleman ended their conversation. Shortly thereafter, the owner of the legendary Six Mile Tavern began to wrap things up and shut the tavern down for the night.

As they exited the Tavern and walked to the car, my ole lady said, an unmarked car pulled up in front of her. When the driver pulled up, she sarcastically said, "Damn, dat's a nice ride. I wonder who driving dat?" The driver rolled down their window, and much to my ole lady's surprise, it was the same gentleman she'd chatted with in the tavern, and asked if she needed a ride. In response, my ole lady told the gentleman, "No thank you, I have my own transportation," as she proceeded to be sarcastic. Then the two ultimately exchanged numbers and parted ways.

Later on, during the wee hours of the morning, the gentleman contacted my ole lady. According to her, they sat on the phone conversing till dawn. From that day forward, they stayed in contact, and the two quickly developed an inseparable bond through phone conversation, visitations, and outings. In fact, within a matter of four months, the gentleman decided to take their relationship to the next level, and he appeared at her workplace on May 13, 2009, to pop the big question.

Upon my stepfather's arrival, he contacted my ole lady to inform her that he was on the way with a surprise for her. He said he would call back the instant he arrived so she could come outside. Just as my stepfather said, he arrived and contacted her so she could come outside. Instantaneously, my ole lady came downstairs prancing, along with a coworker, as my stepfather patiently waited in the back by the red awning. My ole lady come outside to the red awning, and my stepfather presented her with an engagement ring, and he proposed.

My ole lady ran around the area once, then went to accept the proposal and place the engagement ring on her finger.

She then went back upstairs to the unit where she worked and shared the glad tidings with her coworkers, who were just as excited as she was. My ole lady was overwhelmed with joy, and proceeded to share the news with loved ones and peers from that day forward. As time progressed, those same people they shared the glad tidings with began to chatter about the two.

Because they'd gotten engaged and married in a short period of time, people couldn't understand for the life of them how that was possible, saying the two must have known and had dealings with each other prior to the passing of my stepfather's deceased wife. This same group of people also speculated about the groom-to-be employment status, stating that he was no longer employed with the company he claimed to be employed by, nor did he possess the assets he claimed to possess.

The last of the chatter centered around a domestic dispute between the bride and groom—*that didn't occur*—and the gradual changes the bride was making. Certain loved ones of hers talked about how she no longer came around and visited like she used to. They also felt she was moving too fast, considering that she and the groom had just met. According to the bride-to-be—my ole lady—those people who felt she was moving too fast were jealous because the Lord had blessed her with a husband, and she was no longer enduring the hell they were within their relationship. She also said they were simply upset because she was no longer lending the helping hand she'd previously extended.

Certain people contacted me, or pulled me aside in passing, to inquire about the chatter, and I told them to disregard it. "Homie good people," I said, about the groom. "Dey just mad cause dey miserable, and dem boy happy [the bride and groom]." Once I reassured them he was a stand-up guy, they were all relieved, and said something told them to "Go holler at Lo Mann. 'Cause if anybody know the truth, it's him."

I can also recall my ole lady querying about the matter as well. I can see her turning down the radio as she and I sat at the traffic light on the top of Stall Road. She brought up the issue about the chatter, and the loved ones and peers who were circulating it.

Moments later, she asked me, "How do you feel about our decision to get married?"

Being that the groom had never displayed any signs of negative behavior, I told her, "He's cool." I said, "As long as he do right by you, and don't cheat or verbally and/or physically abuse you, y'all got my support."

She ended our conversation with these words: "After all that I've been through in my first marriage, God blessed me with a good man, and I'm happy so whoever don't like it, da hell wit 'em."

Despite the chatter, they proceeded to follow through with the planning of their wedding event. And by the grace of God, the two officially became husband and wife on Saturday, June 5, 2010.

The next month, I got the most exciting news that I'd ever gotten. I was lying in bed working on the rough draft of what you are currently reading, when an incoming call came to my phone. Much to my surprise, it was my eldest sibling.

The instant I answered the call, my eldest sibling and I greeted each other, then she proceeded to ask, "Have you heard the exciting news?"

In response, I said, "Nah. What news?"

"Have you received any calls?" she asked.

"Nah."

"So ain't nobody call you?"

"Nah."

"How about text?" she asked. "Did anybody text you?"

"Nah,"I replied.

My eldest sibling then asked, "Did you hear anything on the radio this morning?"

"Nah, I'm generally snoozing in the morning, especially at the time you mentioned."

"Oh yeah, you got a point," she said, then laughed.

Becoming impatient, I said to her, "Hey, quit beating round the bush and say what you gotta say."

"So you sure you ain't hear nothing?"

"Hey,"I said in a deep, demanding voice.

"All right, all right, I quit. Well, if you insist," she said. "The good news I called to tell you is, your wife is coming to town."

"Hey, quit bullshittin'!"

"I'm not playing," she said. "I'm for real."

Where you get your info?"

I know you're thinking that I got married, but I didn't. In fact, I'll explain further into the story. According to my eldest sibling, she'd heard the announcement early that morning over the radio, either prior to, while, or after transporting a client. In fact, before she contacted me later that morning, she said the instant she heard the announcement, she thought, *I wonder if my brother knows his wife is coming to town.* Truth be told, I was a tad bit skeptical about the exciting news she'd delivered, but considering she had nothing to gain by delivering false information, I gave her the benefit of the doubt in hopes that the truth would be revealed.

Within that same hour, I got another incoming call, but this time it was Mama G, my partner's mother). The instant I answered, Mama G and I greeted each other.

Mama G asked, "Son, you sitting up in ya chair?"

"No, ma'am, I'm lying down."

"What happened? Your nurse didn't come today?"

"Oh no, she here. I'm just giving my body a break," I replied.

"Is it painful to sit up?"

"I wouldn't say that, but in terms of comfort, there is a difference between sitting up in the chair and lying down in bed."

Further into our conversation, we both asked about each other's loved ones, then she asked when the last time was that I'd spoken to my brother (referring to her son).

As the conversation seemed like it was coming to an end, Mama G said, "Son, I know you thought Mama just called to check on you, huh?"

"Yes, ma'am."

"I know." She laughed. "I did call to check on you, but I also called to tell you the good news."

"Good news, huh? I wonder if this is the same news I heard not too long ago."

"What you hear, son?"

"I tell you what," I said, "how about you tell me what you heard, then I'll let you know if it's the same thing I heard."

Mama G was eager to know the good news and she insist I tell her what I'd heard. I was very adamant about not telling her until she broke the news first; I wanted to know if my eldest sibling was telling the truth.

Ultimately, Mama G and I came to common ground, and she broke the news first, uttering the same exact words as my eldest sibling. "Your wife is coming to town," she said. I laughed, then I told her what I heard prior to her contacting me.

"What I want to know," she asked, "is who beat me to the punch?"

"Kesia."

In response, Mama G confirmed for the second time that my eldest sibling was being truthful, stating that she'd heard the announcement over the radio as well. Both Mama G and my eldest sibling offered to purchase me a ticket to attend the event before each phone call was over. Both ladies said to give them time to check ticket prices and the date, time, and location of the event, and they would get back with me. I thanked both ladies, and gladly accepted their offer, then said I'd inform them about who purchased the ticket first so money wouldn't be wasted on an extra ticket. Within a week's time, my eldest sibling once again beat Mama G to the punch by being the first to purchase the ticket on her lunch break, on July 1, 2010, approximately three months before the event.

On Saturday, October 2, 2010, the moment that I had been waiting for arrived, so I put on my Sunday best, then commuted to Daniel Island to the Family Circle Stadium, where two-time Grammy-Award-winning R&B Superstar Patti LaBelle, and the most commercially successful R&B male group of all time, Boyz II Men, headlined the MOJA Arts Festival finale concert.

As I arrived at the stadium, my ole lady found a nearby parking space where she was able to transfer me into my power chair and get me squared away. Shortly thereafter, she and my stepfather escorted me to the entrance gate, where all tickets had to be scanned prior to entering. From there, they escorted me to the section where I was to be seated. Once I was seated, my ole lady and stepfather sat around for several moments to make sure I was okay, considering I was by my lonesome, then they finally left.

When the headliners graced the stage, fans wasted no time packing into the venue. By the time the fans had filled the majority of the venue, the lights were completely shut off, and out came the first headliner, Boyz II Men. At the start of the group's performance, they opened up with a number countdown, then they had the spotlight shine upon them as they performed one of their hit singles. Following their opening performance, they performed other hit songs that earned them four Grammy's, nine American Music Awards, seven Soul Train Awards, and two World Music Awards.

What intrigued me most was their performance as a whole. What was so fascinating was their ability to keep up with the choreography and lyrics as they performed a list of their selections. For example, as soon as those gentlemen graced the stage, their energy levels were through the roof, and not once had I seen the group take a break between ballads, considering their ages. In fact, at the end of one ballad, the group jumped straight into the next ballad with the participation of the fans. All in all, Boyz II Men gave the fans their money's worth by opening and closing with a bang, and if I had to give a one-word description of the group's performance, I would say it was *epic*.

At the end of the show, Boyz II Men showed their gratitude to the fans by thanking them for their many years of support, then they exited the stage with style and grace. Next to the stage to make her debut, came Patti LaBelle, a veteran vocalist who'd belted out classic rhythm and blues renditions, pop standards, and spiritual sonnets for decades. Upon gracing the stage, the lights were shut off, then moments later the sound of her explosive, powerful, and incredibly emotive voice pierced throughout the stadium as she made her grand entrance under the spotlight.

The moment fans heard that notable and distinctive voice, Miss LaBelle got a standing ovation as we all braced ourselves for a stellar performance. About midway into her performance, Miss LaBelle paused a few times as her band and background vocalist kept performing. Shortly thereafter, Miss LaBelle could no longer hold her peace, so she copped a squat on stage near the band and background vocalist as she informed the fans about what was occurring. According to Miss LaBelle, she was beginning to have a diabetic moment, and as a result, the symptoms that she was experiencing ultimately began to affect her performance. An order of chicken from a nearby chicken joint was placed and delivered at Miss LaBelle's request.

The delivery arrived, and Miss LaBelle, in her intense hunger and fatigued state, began to chow down on stage immediately. Fans were disappointed in Miss LaBelle because of her lack of ability to perform. In fact, they were beyond disappointed; they were livid with the singer for eating on stage during her performance. Truth be told, I understand the fans' frustration in terms of paying for a show that they didn't get to see; I also sympathize with Miss LaBelle.

Despite her inability to perform, she allowed the band and her background vocalist to proceed with the show as she introduced them all. In fact, Miss LaBelle unexpectedly stepped away from the spotlight and allowed one of her background vocalist, a Hurricane Katrina survivor, take center stage. The instant the Hurricane Katrina survivor took center stage, she took the audience by storm as her sonorous voice pierced through our souls, demanding our attention. During that performance, the young lady kept the fans on their toes as Miss LaBelle recovered, and it blew me away to witness someone who was no bigger than Tinkerbell produce a strong, deep sound in a pleasant way.

Ultimately, Miss LaBelle recovered and took center stage with the Hurricane Katrina survivor. As the show went on, I can recall Miss LaBelle performing one of her most popular hits, "Lady Marmalade." In the course of that performance, Miss LaBelle invited several fans on stage to perform that hit single along with her. Miss LaBelle also had those fans harmonize to the words as the band and background vocalist backed them up. As those fans singing along with Miss LaBelle had the time of their lives, so was I, because their performances were quite amusing.

All in all, I sincerely enjoyed Miss LaBelle's performance, and if I had another opportunity to see her live in concert, I would be one of the first fans gunning to the box office to purchase me a ticket.

Weeks after attending the concert of a lifetime, I again had to prepare myself for another upcoming event, but this time around it was my twenty-fifth birthday bash. Upon planning that event, me and an aunt of mine were conversing on the phone.

During our conversation, my aunt calmly said, "Someone has a birthday coming soon!" My aunt asked if I had any plans.

I said, "Nah, you know I don't celebrate my birthday."

"I know," said my aunt in a soft voice, "but it's your twenty-fifth birthday. You lived to see a quarter of a century. You have to do something, even if it's a small gathering."

With all things considered, I understood her point of view, and took what she said into consideration. After giving it some thought, I decided to celebrate my twenty-fifth birthday. In the process of planning that event, me and the event planners (my ole lady and aunt) were in contact with one another about the details. We discussed the date, time, location, the menu, and who the guests would be. Several calls later, we ultimately worked out the details weeks prior to the actual event.

On November 13, 2010, I had a birthday bash thrown by my ole lady, stepfather, and aunt a couple days before my actual birthdate. Upon my arrival, there were chafing dishes set up to keep the food warm; the grill was being prepped, and the DJ booth was being assembled. In addition, tables and fire barrels were being set up throughout the yard, considering it was an outdoor event. Shortly after my arrival, the guests gradually began to arrive, and before I knew it, we had a crowd.

My loved ones, childhood peers, friends of the family, and strangers all attended my twenty-fifth birthday bash. Once the majority of them had arrived, my aunt (event planner number two) politely asked everyone for their attention. After she had their attention, she thanked them all for coming out and celebrating my birthday along with me. Immediately after, my aunt was signaled to bless the food because it was ready to be served. While everyone was feasting, my ole lady and aunt supervised the event, making sure we were all satisfied.

As the event went on, my ole lady took a moment to say a few remarks about me and wish me a happy birthday. When she was finished, the other guests gave their remarks and birthday wishes as well, then immediately after, everyone gathered around me to sing "Happy Birthday," the song written, produced, and performed by Stevie Wonder. After that serenade, and the cutting of the cake, the guests went back to their seats, but not for long, courtesy of my ole lady and her song request the DJ played.

My ole lady said, "Look at 'em, dey done eat so much til dey can't move. I got sum' fa dat. Watch dis!"

As suspected, my ole lady escorted several guests from the comfort of their seats to the center of the yard, and began rump shaking. The instant she started rump shaking like Wreckx-n-Effect, the guests who had never seen her behave in that manner were astounded, so much so they immediately stood up and came closer to the center of the yard because they couldn't believe their eyes. The guests who were aware of my ole lady's behavior in the past were laughing their butts off, because they knew it was Paulette. Before you knew it, all the guests ultimately let their hair down and joined her, as she and the DJ proceeded to set it off like Strafe, the American electro and old school hip hop group. Several tracks later, the elder generation retired for the night, but the younger generation kept on grooving until the DJ played the last call.

During the event, we had the time of our lives. The spread was fulfilling, the drinks were thirst-quenching, and the DJ was lit. Aside from that, my ole lady and aunt (the event planners) were very courteous to the guests, and the guests were courteous to everyone in general. Despite the fact that I didn't generally celebrate my birthday, that fun-filled event left me open minded about other birthdays of mine to come.

CHAPTER 14

As I embarked on a journey eleven years ago (2002) to climb this mountain step by step, there were many turns of events I encountered along the way. Throughout the years of my physical disability I have struggled with health issues concerning nausea, loss of appetite, and weight. Around the time I was pursuing my GED at Summerville Adult Ed, I made an important decision to have myself admitted at Roper St. Francis Hospital, located in downtown Charleston.

On the day of admission, I informed all physicians about my difficulties with tolerating the tube feeds, eating solid food by mouth, and losing a huge amount of weight as the end result. The physicians' plans were to schedule X-ray exams and barium swallow during my stay at the hospital, as well as run the tube feeds overnight in hopes of finding the cause to the health issues.

Within my two-week stay at Roper St. Francis, all physicians, including the caretakers, followed through with their plans to find the cause of these health issues I was currently struggling with. According to the doctor's report concerning the X-ray exams and barium swallow, there were no signs that pointed towards the cause;

however the tube feeds that I was given left me nauseated, and I ended up vomiting the morning prior to my original discharge date.

Due to this incident, they held me as an inpatient a week longer than we'd all intended. In the extended week of my stay at Roper St. Francis, the physicians took additional X-ray exams. After witnessing what I'd been telling them all along, they also ordered that I take medication, such as promethazine, to help with nausea. As suspected, the additional X-ray exams continued to show no signs as to the cause of my health issues, and the medication had no effect on the nausea. In fact, it only made me drowsy. With this being an ongoing issue, words cannot express how frustrating it was for me to deal with on a day-to-day basis; however, I dealt with it because I knew this was life as a spinal cord injured patient.

Throughout my two weeks stay at Roper St. Francis, I ate small portions of solid food by mouth, as ordered, to help prevent my swallow glands from resisting food intake; increase my appetite; and expand my stomach so it could contain larger quantities of food. I also partook in Roper St. Francis's physical and occupational therapy activities, as I was on the eighth floor, which is their rehab unit.

In the course of time, once discharged from Roper St. Francis, I attended the grand opening of the center for spinal cord injury patients. This clinic that was developed by Roper, MUSC health, Carolinas Rehabilitation, and the Spinal Cord Injury Research Fund was a new collaborative program that would improve patient care for hundreds of people in our area living with spinal cord injuries. The Center for Spinal Cord Injury (CSCI) opened July 15, 2011, with a special ceremony on the sixth-floor rehabilitation gym at Roper Hospital.

During the ceremony, there were reporters who interviewed me, and leaders of the Center for Spinal Cord Injury patients, such as Dr.

Nancy Tsai, a board-certified physiatrist and the medical director for CSCI, and Charles T. Cole, a retired bank executive and active member of the Charleston community.

"The new center is a blessing," I said in my interview. "It's a wonderful thing. It's going to be so much easier for me to make one appointment, and know that I will be able to receive all of the medical attention I need."

While at the Center for Spinal Cord Injury, a team of medical specialists from Roper Rehab and MUSC Health escorted me to a cubicle in the clinic, where they later transfer me to a bed and began the assessments.

As I continued to climb this mountain higher and higher, there was a sudden change in climate that I never saw coming: the departure of my relationship with my anonymous lady friend. Between the years of 2007 and 2011, she and I had knit a bond I thought to be inseparable. Within that timeframe, there were issues in her personal life that I didn't approve of, and refused to accept. Due to these issues, I felt it was in our best interests to part ways, so I initiated the departure.

Around the time I decided to part ways with her, she and I were on the phone, and I distinctly remember sitting there in silence, pondering how to bring it up. Once I collected my thoughts, I took a deep breath, and calmly said, "Hey, I think it's best that we part ways." The initial reaction I got from initiating the departure was, *click*, when she hung up. In my mind, I said to myself, *Damn, it was that easy.* But lo and behold, I received an incoming call moments later from her, and she asked me to repeat what I'd said. As I went back and forth with her, she then asked for an explanation. Truth be told, an explanation was something I did not want to give her; in fact,

I was hoping she would accept what I said and leave it at that, but she insisted that I explain why.

"It's just not working out," I said.

She replied, "You are still not telling me anything, but whatever," then hung up once again after she uttered in fierce anger, "I ain't got time for this shit!"

Within that same week, I received several incoming calls from her that I ignored; she also came to my home several times unannounced, demanding an explanation. Considering the explanation she was entitled to, it was only fair that I gave her what she deserved. There were several reasons I decided to part ways with her: a lack of honesty; lack of support; lack of affection; and infidelity.

Early on at the beginning, when we'd first reunited, she and I had an open relationship, but as time progressed, things begin to change. Before that, we confided in each other about our pastimes, personal issues, and long-term goals. As we took the time to get to know each other on a personal level, she and I grew closer like never before. In the process, she became comfortable enough to confide in me about the rocky relationship between her and her male acquaintance she was dating at the time.

Over the course of time, however, she had reached a breaking point, and decided to end their relationship and focus on co-parenting. As their connection grew further apart, the relationship between me and her plunged deeper, to the point where she and I developed a strong affection towards one another. The closer I got to my anonymous lady friend the more she made see; by giving me all she had, her love captured me.

By that time, I was caught up in the rapture of love! I was fully convinced that the relationship between her and her male acquaintance was past tense, but little did I know, it was still present. Prior to discovering this disappointing information, I took those confidential conversations between us at face value; I was also sold on the dreams of her openly saying how she would no longer make things convenient for her male acquaintance, or allow him to do this or that. As time went on, however, the things she once enforced changed to "Okay, I'll give you another chance"—after chance, after chance. If things do not go her way, or her male acquaintance did not follow through with his end of the bargain, all hell would break loose.

On any given day I would receive incoming calls from her enraged about what her male acquaintances had or had not done, saying, "This is why I no longer allow this or that." At times she called my cellular device and tagged my line onto their conversation, as they were in the heat of an argument. As I sat on the line, tuning into the argument, I said to myself, "This is news to me, because I thought you no longer allowed these privileges."

Observing her back pedal and react to things she no longer reacted to led me to believe that she was still emotionally attached to her male acquaintance; it also created a lack of honesty issue, which stemmed from that problem, because she went from being open about their relationship to withholding specific details, and had her male acquaintance not ticked her off, I would not have known. When she expressed how she truly felt about her male acquaintances without saying I did not question her, but I kept my mouth closed from that day forward.

As I silently proceeded to observe her, there were no changes; in fact, it seem as though the issues between her and her male acquaintance had gotten worse. It became so obvious, because she could no longer hold her peace, and to make matters worse, she at times took her anger out on me, instead of applying for a gym membership at Planet Fitness. The issues between them led to her metamorphosis;

it literally transformed her into a woman scorned, who at times uttered the words, "Why is it so hard for men to do right?"; "Fuck all men"; and, "It's about me and my child."

It also led her to disappear days at a time, without anyone knowing her whereabouts. At times, she gave me the silent treatment while on the phone. Eventually, her frustration created the lack of support and affection issues I had with her; it also led me to deeply consider parting ways with her due to the nature of her irrational acts. Prior to their issues getting worse, I started doing speaking engagements a year after reuniting with her, and a couple of years later is when I enrolled myself into the Summerville Adult Ed program to pursue my GED.

In the beginning stages, my anonymous lady friend was a shoulder to lean on; she leant a helping hand if ever I needed or wanted anything. She would spend quality time with me at my home, or on outings. After her metamorphosis, our relationship went south, and in the course of our down spiral relationship she cut back on our visits, as well as brought the support and affection she showed me to a screeching halt.

If I may, allow me to elaborate on the reason that prohibited her from supporting my speaking engagements. At the time I started speaking, I hid that important information from her because I was nervous to speak in front of her, and I didn't know how she would accept it; however, once she found out about it through a twenty-third "betrayal" party my loved ones surprised me with, I informed her about an upcoming engagement, as she'd requested. To my surprise, she did not attend the engagement due to a lame excuse she gave me. The moment she told me why she wasn't going to attend, I made it my business to no longer inform her about upcoming events.

Around the time these issues between us occurred, I had not reached my wits end, because I sympathized with her as a human being and a friend, but I will say this, I wasn't far from it. The deal-breaker that led to the end was the infidelity issue.

One evening while on the phone with her, I asked a question in search of an honest answer: "Are you having sexual intercourse with anyone? And if so, or not, when was the last time you had sexual intercourse with someone?"

She answered no, then stated, the last time she had sexual intercourse with someone had been a month or two prior to me asking that question. At that moment I knew our relationship had reached its time limit, because she once again backpedaled on a previous conversation we'd had, where she openly stated her take on the issues, but unlike others I did not part ways with her right away because of my emotional attachment towards her.

Apart from these issues, there was a strong magnetic force that kept pulling me to part ways from her. I don't know why, but I knew I had to let go. Once I broke it off with her, she and I sadly went our separate ways. The changes she made left me distraught and embarrassing as it is to say, there were times when I could not eat or sleep, but through the grace of God, I took Mariah Carey's advice, and shook it off. Despite the issues, my anonymous lady friend irrational behavior towards me does not define who she is, because deep down inside, she is a wonderful person who allowed the issues between her and her male acquaintance get the best of her.

As I weathered the storm, a discussion between my ole lady and stepfather sprung forth once again. This discussion between them had taken place prior to their marriage, and they'd talked about relocating. As my ole lady and stepfather debated their plans to relocate, they collectively decided to give my eldest sibling the home we were in, and relocate.

On the first week of November 2011, my family and I moved into my stepfather's three-bedroom, two-bathroom mobile home located in Mount Pleasant, South Carolina. In that community, we were surrounded by my stepfather's loved ones and peers, who each sat on at least an acre or two of land, if not more. Upon moving into my stepfather's home, he informed us of how safe and peaceful his community was; he said the wild and crazy things that took place in the City of North Charleston did not happen in the town of Mount Pleasant. Then he went on to share stories about him sitting in his yard by his lonesome, listening to the radio, saying, how my family and I would enjoy the comfort of sitting outdoors through all seasons.

In the beginning stages of adjusting to my stepfather's home, I immediately noticed within the first three months, there wasn't much of a difference between the City of North Charleston and the town of Mount Pleasant, as I sat outdoors and watch the local news. The only things that separated the two were their names and locations, the crime rate, and the public schooling grade ratio. Other than that, I believe that it's safe to say that both areas are one and the same.

Once I'd adjusted to my stepfather home, I pretty much picked up where I left off. I proceeded with my activities of daily living as scheduled, and within the time span of those first three months, I continued writing this book. Before I resumed the writing process, I decided to put together an execution plan of how I was going to complete this book. I put together a list of topics I needed to write about in the final three chapters, and the plan would also help keep track of what I'd already written as well as what I have left to write.

The initial step, however, was prayer. Completing this first step was a vital step that I have always taken from the beginning, because it opens a channel between myself and God, implying that I desperately need and desire his help. After prayer, I started with a new strategy, which I call outdoor meditation. Outdoor meditation is very essential to the writing process, simply because it helps me articulate my story in a way where you will be able to better understand. Once activating this new strategy, putting it in motion, I then jot down all that I have stored in my noggin with the assistance of a willing writer, be it my ole lady, caretaker, etc.

Every morning before starting my day, I turn my television on to the Word network at nine thirty to watch Bishop TD Jakes' televised sermon. One morning, I tuned in to his sermon from his four-part series titled "Live on Purpose." In that sermon, all I can remember him saying is "Your purpose is tied to your passion." He said, "Whatever you have a passion for is more than likely your purpose." In that moment, hearing such profound words, I immediately began to reevaluate what my passion was, and in the process, I quickly discovered my passion.

Prior to this discovery, I did a rundown of my list of things I was passionate about, and in that assessment I had to eliminate truck driving, which was my first true love, because I knew it wasn't an option, considering my physical disability. As I further examined my list, it was a no-brainer to acknowledge that my passion as a youth speaker was my purpose, because it was the only other thing that I'm passionate about. After this discovery, I confidently proceeded to live on purpose as a dedicated youth speaker.

Once again, however, I began to question God about my purpose, asking, "Is this really what you want me to do? Because I have made efforts to humbly serve you, but I haven't seen any changes or progression in certain areas of my life."

Thinking back on this day in particular, I can remember questioning God as I completed my activities of daily living; I can also remember questioning God as I tuned into one of Bishop TD Jakes' televised sermon; but more than anything, I can remember feeling like something was about to happen. Around noon that very same day, Tel-A-Ride picked me up from home as schedule to attend an appointment for wheelchair evaluation with Jill Mongers on the third floor at the Medical University of South Carolina.

As the driver arrived at our destination and unloaded me off the bus, I was trying to decide whether or not I wanted to enter the building or linger outdoors, considering I was ninety minutes ahead of schedule. Needless to say, I was still undecided about what I wanted to do once I'd gotten off the bus, so instead of entering right away, I drove my power chair towards the facility at least fifteen steps from the hospital entrance, where I made a sudden stop to check my voice-mail. In the process of checking my voicemail, this strange woman I'd never met before mysteriously appeared out of nowhere, like a ghost in a horror film.

As she stood there looking hesitant but anxious to speak, she eventually spoke. "I just want to tell you how much you encourage me. I saw you getting off the bus, and I just had to say something."

In that moment I couldn't tell you who left a voice message, or the time they left it, because she had my undivided attention as she spoke. Within seconds, it all began to make sense as to why she approached me. I quickly learned about her youngest son, who had just gotten into a tragic motorcycle accident that left him in the same condition as me, on June 2, 2012, which was two months prior to our encounter. Without question, I asked the woman, who later introduced herself as Amy, if her son was still in the hospital, and she said yes, so I kindly asked her to escort me to his room, where he and I met shortly after.

The moment I entered her son's room, it felt like Deja vu all over again, because in this gentleman, I saw a reflection of myself; in his mother, I saw a reflection of my ole lady; and in his sister, who sat along his bedside, I saw a reflection of my youngest sibling. Truth be told, I couldn't help but reflect on the olden days of being a newly spinal cord injury patient. As I was caught in trance by this encounter, Miss Amy introduced me to her son, whose name was Javontae. I learned that Javontae had just turned eighteen on July 14, 2012, which was a month before his injury. I also learned that he and his family hailed from Beaufort, South Carolina.

Considering the time I had left, I asked Javontae and his ole lady to brief me on how he got injured, then I immediately began sharing my testimony with them in hopes of having a positive impact on their lives. At the end of our visit, his mother expressed how she wished his father had been there to meet me. I told her that I had plans to come back over the weekend to visit with them, so if he could come then, that would be great. Just as my caretaker and I exited Javontae's room, his father came, so his mother introduced us to each other, then asked that he escort us to the elevator.

During our brief visit, I shared my story with Javontae's father of how I got injured, and in doing so learned that the day his father and I met was the first time his father came to visit his son. He said, in addition to having transportation issues, he did not want to see his son in that predicament; he also expressed how he blamed himself daily on his son's accident, because he was the one who introduced him to off-road bikes and motorcycles as an adolescent.

I told him that I understood, because my eldest sibling still struggles with seeing me in this predicament to this day, considering that it was just me and her prior to our younger siblings' conception and birth. However, the only way he would be able to adapt to this new adjustment was by coming around, or else he would always struggle with it. I also told him not to blame himself for his son's accident, because it wasn't his fault. I said, "Freak accidents happen, and unfortunately it's one of those things that we as human beings don't have any control over."

For the remainder of that day I could not help but think about that encounter with Javontae and his family; I could not help but think about when I'd questioned God about my purpose earlier that morning. In fact, I could not help but imagine God saying to me, "Any more questions?" If I was uncertain about my purpose in life before that encounter, I knew then in that moment, without a shadow of doubt, what God had chosen me to do. And from that day forward I have yet to question God about what he has strategically confirmed through this family.

That coming Saturday, I visited Javontae and his family as promised. However, I didn't go alone, I brought my ole lady along so she could share her testimony with them, and give his mother insight on how to deal with a new spinal cord injury patient. Twenty-two months later, I had the pleasure of meeting with Javontae again when he was admitted to Roper St. Francis Hospital. When I was told about him being in town under those circumstances, I took advantage of the opportunity to see him, since he lived in Beaufort. The first day I visited Javontae, his face lit up as he yelled out, "Wendell!" with such excitement. I did the same in return to he, and to the staff members of Roper Rehab unit who was present at the time.

After greeting everyone, I trailed behind Javontae and the physical therapist, who was working with him at the gym on the third floor, where he finished his therapy session. Shortly after, he and I went to sit outside and updated each other on our lives, but unfortunately our visit was cut short when Tel-A-Ride arrived with my return pick-up as scheduled. Due to Tel-A-Ride arriving on time, I once again made a reservation to visit Javontae the following week, with a later return time.

The second time I visited him, he and I sat outside as usual, checking out the view. And when I say the "view," I'm not talking about the daytime Emmy award-winning talk show. In addition, he openly shared with me how he'd gotten injured in full detail. One evening while out on the town, Javontae heard the sound of a biker's engine, and shortly after, that same biker pulled up, then backed up alongside Javontae as he revved up his engine. Being the outspoken person Javontae was, he told the biker, "You ain't trying to do nuttin," and in response, the biker asked Javontae, "What you wanna do?" With Javontae having a competitive, need-for-speed spirit, he boldly told the biker to line up.

As Javontae lined up his Suzuki 1500 alongside his opponent, both bikers took off full speed ahead within seconds. According to the information Javontae gave me, he and his opponent had quickly reached a certain distance as both bikers dragged off alongside each other. As they both speedily excelled along the strip, his foot pedal broke, which then caused his foot to drag and entangle with his opponent's foot. Both bikers became untangled, however, Javontae began trailing behind his opponent due to the mishap. As Javontae rode a distance behind his opponent, he noticed the biker's bike fishtailing as if he was trying to slow down, but unfortunately for Javontae, he blacked out, wobbling at 120 miles per hour.

The eyewitness who was present on the scene said Javontae ran into a drain pipe and the impact of that collision threw him at least ten feet or more from the bike, but here is the ironic part, Javontae was just miles away from a loved one's home. Despite his injury, he was in good spirits; in fact, it seemed as though he was doing better now than he was when he and I had first met. Believe it or not, I was encouraged by his joyful and outgoing spirit to proceed through all adversities in good spirits continually, because truth be told, life must go on.

What a journey this had been; the pain I inflicted upon others, the losses that I took, and the anger of God that I kindled. If you were to ask me, what would I take from this journey, my response would be "Nothing." If you were to ask me what I've learned from this journey, my response would be "To keep and fulfill God's statutes and Commandments." And if you were to ask me what I'm going to do with my life from this day forward, my response would be "Stay in God's will." Although this course I'm currently on may be in the latter stages of all I've endured, I truly believe it is also the new beginning of a new journey with God.

MESSAGE 1

To the youth:

If you read my book carefully, you will notice I had the same opportunities that you have. For example, I had the privilege of having both parents present in my life, as well as family members, friends, etc., who tried their best to lead me and my siblings in the right direction. I had the opportunity to complete a twelve-year education through public schooling, free of charge, with the possibility of a full scholarship to any college of my choice. I had the opportunity to make an honest living on several paid jobs that hired teens. I also had the opportunity to not grow up fast, but to stay a child, as I should have done.

However, I disregarded the knowledge that I was taught by both parents, family, and friends. I disregarded the rules and regulations of the school houses by disrupting their classes. I disregarded the law by distributing narcotics. I also chose to grow up before my time, and not stay a child, as I should have done. As a result of the poor decisions I made, I got my behind cut, and was grounded frequently. I flunked twice, and I received in-school suspension, out-of-school suspension, detention, and expulsions. I got arrested and locked up twice, which led to probation, house arrest, drug court, and drug class. I also had to suffer the consequences of my actions as an adult would.

As a young man, being equal to all mankind, I can relate to being inquisitive. For example, I can relate to being curious about what it is like to use controlled substances, get high, drink alcoholic beverages, or have sex. I can relate to being curious about what it is like to distribute drugs, and attend block parties or club events. I also can relate to being curious about what it is like to do what you want to do, when you want to do it, and how you want to do it, because I, too, was there. I, too, was inquisitive about the examples I just gave. In fact, there are certain things in life that I am still curious about, but coming from a person with years of experience, it is in your best interest to be mindful about the decisions you make. With all things considered, I am not saying don't have fun, I am simply saying be conscious of how you go about having fun, because if not, it could lead to fatal consequences, such as a lifetime addiction, a sexually transmitted disease you may or may not be able to get rid of, prison time, or even death.

If you can recall, I also wrote about betrayal, as well as withdrawal in later chapters, for example. I was betrayed. I wrote about the betrayer, as well as the relationship we had. I wrote about associating myself with people I considered to be friends. I also wrote about family and friends who withdrew themselves from me. Throughout my childhood upbringing, both parents of mine, along with family and friends, warned me about incidents such as these, and told me, "Choose your friends wisely"; "Beware of the crowd you keep"; and "You will find out who your real friends are when you are down and out."

However, I once again, like an idiot, chose to disregard their knowledge about life, and as a result, I got lynched by a group of guys, one of whom was a friend. I got shot by a person I consider a friend. I also had family and friends I considered genuine, turn their backs on me once I got injured, or shortly after.

Everything that I have just written could have been avoided if I had taken heed to the knowledge that was given. Everything that I have just written could have been avoided if I had taken heed to the warnings God gave me before the destruction. It also could have been avoided if I had not taken for granted the opportunities that God gave me to get myself together.

MESSAGE 2

To parents or guardians:

Although I am in my late twenties, I still consider myself to be a descendant of the youth, and as a spokesman for the younger generation, I speak on their behalf, by saying instead of constantly fussing at your children, going off the deep end about every little thing, calmly talk to them as the civilized adult you claim to be.

Take time out with your children. Find out what is on their minds. Find out what is going on in their lives outside of your household. Gain their trust, that way they will feel comfortable talking to you about their issues.

If you fail to do as instructed, you will push your children away, and as a result, they will seek comfort from someone else to confide in, and that person who they seek may entice them to do the things you and I are trying to prevent, like abusing controlled substances or alcohol, getting involved in gang activities or prostitution, or commit suicide.

There is an important lesson that you must learn—in fact, it is mandatory that you learn this, because it could either be detrimental or beneficial to the relationship with your children. The important lesson is simply this: *Listen*. Sit back, take a chill pill, and listen to your children. As children, we know, understand, and respect your position as our parent/guardian, and in all honesty, we are not asking that you take off your parenting attire, or become our friend. However, we are asking that you listen.

Listening to your children, will help you better understand who they are, what is on their minds, and why they do the things they do; it may also knit an inseparable bond between you, so rather than flying off the handle, pause for a moment, and quietly listen to your children as you find out what the issue is by allowing them to speak. Capiche? If I know any better, you're probably saying that the insight I've given you concerning the youth will not prevent all problems. In all honesty, you are right, it won't prevent all problems, but keep in mind, it is a start towards change. Trust me, I know.

I want to leave you with this: If you are training your children in the way they should go, and they are not taking heed to your knowledge about life, do not blame or stress yourself about it, because it is not your fault. In fact, allow me to commend you on incorporating structure and discipline into your children's lives, because these days, it is not often that you witness parents instilling values in their children.

I do advise you to continue showing your children "tough love," as Judge Greg Mathis would say, then pray for them, and leave them in the hands of God. Truth be told, with things changing so rapidly in the world, it seems like the "real" parents and grandparents, ones who don't play any games with their children or grandchildren, are nearly extinct, and as a result, the youth today have no manners, no respect, and no home training.

Parents or guardians whose children are taking heed to your knowledge about life—I also commend you, as well as your children, and I pray that you all proceed with doing what you are doing, because it will pay off in the long run.

MESSAGE 3

To the young women and men:

If you are interested in the concept of dating, listen up, and listen closely. Stay away from individuals who are only interested in withdrawing something from you, rather than placing a deposit within you.

Stay away from selfish people who are only interested in what you have to offer them sexually, financially, or emotionally. You should also stay away from selfish individuals who are only seeking shelter, because people like that clearly mean you no good, and they will leave you broken and lonely as the end result. I highly recommend you to associate with people who have your best interest at heart.

Associate yourself with considerate people, who love the seed of you, rather than just the fruit of you. In other words, associate yourselves with considerate people who love you for who you are as a person, intellectually, as well as spiritually. People like that are known to make great friends, or loyal significant others, who won't leave you broken and lonely, if it is in God's will. No matter what the outcome may be with your personal relationships and friendships, keep in mind that God strategically placed certain people in our lives for a purpose, so do not be afraid or dismayed, because who God intends to stay in our lives will do exactly that.

TO CONCLUDE

THESE THREE MESSAGES:

Youth, I know that you are tired of your parents/guardian jumping down your throat, constantly fussing at you. I know this because throughout my years on Earth with my ole lady, who is the queen of fussing, I, too, dealt with the same nerve-wracking issue that left me tired. However, you must understand this: Your parent/guardian is not taking disciplinary action just for their health; they are simply trying to prevent you from traveling down an avenue a self-destruction, one which they themselves may have embarked on, so instead of talking back to them, or saying to yourself, "Oh boy, you get on my nerves"; "I wish you would shut up"; or—here is an old one—"I wish you were dead," keep your mouth closed, carefully listen to them, and take heed to their knowledge about life, because they are not telling you something that will hurt you, they are telling you something for your own good.

If you don't remember anything else I've written, remember these words: Any time your parent/guardian takes disciplinary action, do not view it as if they are being mean. You should embrace it, because them being hard on you is always out of love.

EXPOSURE
TO GUN VIOLENCE

In today's society, gun violence has become an epidemic across the world, and as a result, casualties are left wounded or dead. As a victim of gun violence, I boldly ask that we, the citizens of the world [law enforcement included], refrain from gun violence, because it is a senseless act that has a domino effect on the lives of many. It affects not only the victim, but their loved ones and friends as well; the suspect as well, along with their loved ones and friends. It also affects communities, and the world as a whole.

If, however, we take heed and refrain from gun violence, and unite as one, then we will be able to reduce murder rates, create a safe environment for all citizens in the world, and bring together social groups and the government to engage in compassionate action, and stand together as a collective force.

KEYS TO SUCCESS

- Belief/faith in God

- Prayer

- Read the Bible

- Attend church

- Avoid temptation/sin

- Find your purpose/live on purpose

- Walk upright, and be in right standing with God

- Stay humble, and keep God first

- Mental and spiritual strength

- Have the ability to endure hardships and long-suffering

- Be a willing spirit to listen, learn, and take valuable advice

- Have the ability to deal with criticism

- Courage

- Passion

- Ambition

- Tunnel vision

- Consistency

- Instinct

- Education

These keys to success are a list of examples that I, myself, did not utilize throughout my upbringing, but once I became older, wiser, and more experienced, I incorporated them into my activities of daily living. I wrote this list in hopes that you'll take my advice and apply these keys to your life so you may obtain success.

THE AUTHOR'S SCRAPBOOK

IMAGES THAT SHOW THE AUTHENTICITY
OF WHAT YOU'VE JUST READ.

My Great Grandparents Home

My great grandparents' home were the history of me, my eldest sibling,
our ole lady and her sibling's lives began

My great grandfather Rev. Tindal whom my ole lady cared for
along with other relatives

Me, my eldest sibling our parents and Uncle Bernard standing outside
of our great grandparents' home

Me and my eldest sibling playing in the playroom that our great grandfather built for us

MY OLE LADY'S PUBLIC HOUSING APARTMENT IN THE THREE OAKS COMMUNITY

Me, my eldest sibling and our ole lady standing outside the door
of our public housing apartment

Me and my ole lady standing in the driveway at
Three Oaks Apartments on Easter 1990.

Me and my eldest sibling Easter egg hunting in the backyard
of our apartment complex

Me sitting on my bike in the kitchen of our apartment

My eldest sibling and our Uncle Robert sitting in the
living room of our apartment

Me, my great grandfather and eldest sibling sitting in the
living room of our apartment

Me, my eldest sibling our ole lady and Uncle Ronald
looking at the snow back in 1989

Me, my eldest sibling and our Uncle Ronald playing in the snow

Me and my eldest sibling class photos at Pepperhll Elementary

My second grade class portrait at Pepperhill Elementary

My eldest sibling fifth grade portrait at Pepperhill Elementary

MY BIOLOGICAL PARENTS' WEDDING

My parents and Uncle Bishop Sharper the wedding officiator

My parents and the wedding party their friends
James Morton and Leatrice Hardee

My parents and grandparents Robert and Elizabeth Manigault
and Robert Tindal

Me, my sisters our parents and cousin Star

My Biological Parents' home in Trailwood Trailer Park

My Granny Liz standing on the deck of my parent's mobile home in Trailwood trailer park

My parents playing foosball in the living room of our mobile home

Me and my sisters sitting in the living room of our mobile home

My Aunt Gloria and her offspring's Jimmy, Big A, and Deidra sitting in the living room of our mobile home

REPORT CARD

Ronald E McNair Elementary

CHARLESTON COUNTY SCHOOL DISTRICT
TUITION SUMMER SCHOOL

ELEMENTARY SCHOOLS
STUDENT'S REPORT

Summer 19 _97_

STUDENT'S NAME _Wendell Manigault_

GRADE _5_

HOME SCHOOL _Goodwin Elem._

SUMMER SCHOOL _McNair Elem._

SUMMER SCHOOL TEACHER _J. Neider__

SUMMER SCHOOL PRINCIPAL _M. Hedge_

Proof of attendance

NAME _Wendell Manigault_ GRADE _5_

METHOD OF GRADING 1-3:
+ = 90-100
80-89
- = 75-79
! = 70-74
! = 0-69

METHOD OF GRADING 4 AND UP:
A = 90-100
B = 80-89
C = 70-79
F = 0-69

Passing = 70 & above)

ATTENDANCE	PERIOD 1	PERIOD 2	TOTAL
DAYS PRESENT	11	23	24
DAYS ABSENT	0	1	1
TIMES TARDY	2	1	3

SUBJECTS			AVERAGE
LANGUAGE ARTS			
MATHEMATICS	83/B	85/B	83/B
SOCIAL STUDIES			
READING	84/B	85/B	85/B
SCIENCE			

NOTES TO PARENTS
The spaces below will be used by the teacher when she feels
the need for explanatory comments or suggestions.

1st Period
Wendell is a good student and a joy to have in my class.

2nd Period
Wendell is a very bright student and I wish him all the best! Good Luck in 6th grade.

J. Neider

Proof of attendance

275

Brentwood Middle School

```
                    BRENTWOOD MIDDLE SCHOOL
                 Report Card Fourth Quarter 1997-98

Manigault, Wendell Maurice
248635092
Grade  6
Homeroom Teacher: D Bishop

                        1st 2nd 1st 3rd 4th 2nd  Ex  Yr      8/25/97 -  6/ 5/98
  Course/Teacher        Qtr Qtr Sem Qtr Qtr Sem             Absent  Tardy

Advisory / Hr                                                  24      2
  Per 1  D Bishop
              CONDUCT
-------------------------------------------------------------------------------
Science 6               87  83  85  71  76  73      79        10      0
  Per 2  L French
              CONDUCT S
              A PLEASURE TO TEACH AND KNOW.
-------------------------------------------------------------------------------
Social Studies-6        73  71  72  76  76  76      74        10      0
  Per 2  D Bishop
              CONDUCT NI
              A PLEASURE TO TEACH AND KNOW.
-------------------------------------------------------------------------------
Literacy                95  96  96  87 100  94      95        24      0
  Per 3  A Montgomery
              CONDUCT S
              A PLEASURE TO TEACH AND KNOW.
              PLEASE ENCOURAGE STUDENT TO READ FOR PLEASURE AT HOME.
-------------------------------------------------------------------------------
Math-6                  64  66  65  73  84  79      72        24      0
  Per 4  E Bernados
              CONDUCT S
              HAS IMPROVED STEADILY.
              KEEP UP THE GOOD WORK !
-------------------------------------------------------------------------------
Drama-6                                                        6      0
  Per 5  H Banias
              CONDUCT
-------------------------------------------------------------------------------
Art-6                               95  95                     1      0
  Per 5  T Hicks
              CONDUCT S
-------------------------------------------------------------------------------
P.e.-6                              89  89                     2      0
  Per 5  D Horne
              CONDUCT I
              STUDENT IS COOPERATIVE AND PLEASANT.
              A PLEASURE TO TEACH AND KNOW.
-------------------------------------------------------------------------------
Read/language Arts 6    84  68  76  60  88  74      75        24      0
  Per 7  C Bligen
              CONDUCT S
              PLEASE ENCOURAGE STUDENT TO READ FOR PLEASURE AT HOME.
-------------------------------------------------------------------------------
  O+   NOT PASSING          F   FAILING           I   INCOMPLETE
  W    WITHDRAWN            TR  TRANSFER IN        P   PASSING
  S    SATISFACTORY         I   IMPROVING          U   UNSATISFACTOR
  NI   NEEDS IMPROVE


Student is  √  Promoted _____ Retained _____ Placed
Set your goals for the 1998 - 1999 school year now! Have a safe summer!
```

Proof of attendance

276

RESIDING AT MY GRANDPARENTS'

Me and my Lil Sis at our grandparents (fathers parents) home
where I was residing at the time

Me at my grandparents' home

Me and my Partner whom I made the wager with

FAMILY PHOTOS

My ole lady, my sisters, lil' brother, and me

My ole man, lil brother and my nephew

My Lil Brother and Sister

Christmas Holidays

Me and my two sisters on Christmas morning back in the mid nineties

Me, my sisters and cousin — Deshawn on Christmas, early 2000

CHARLESTON COUNTY DISCIPLINE SCHOOL BOOT CAMP

Graduation

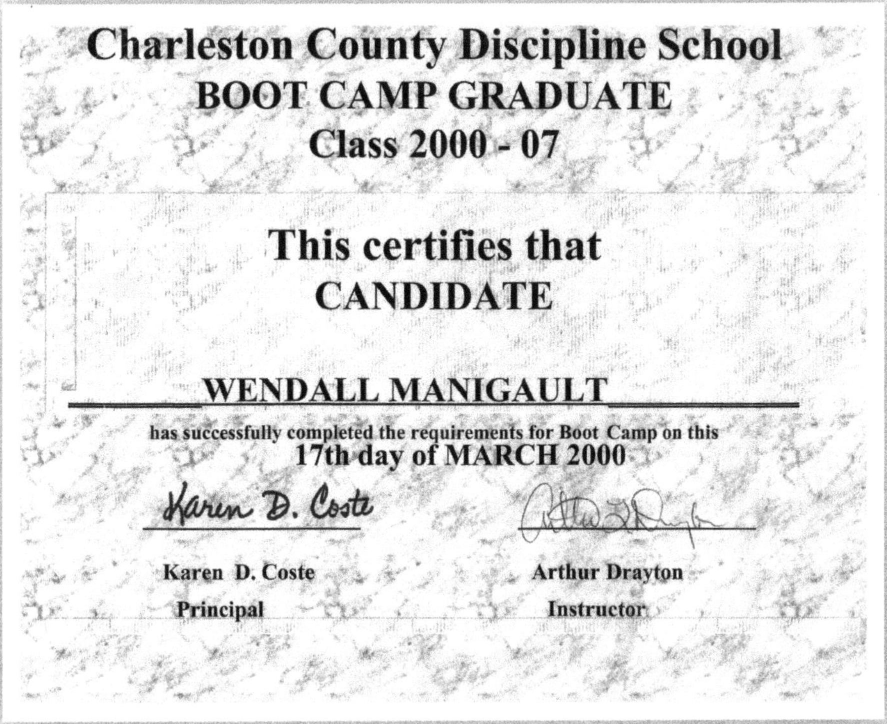

Charleston County Discipline School
BOOT CAMP GRADUATE
Class 2000 - 07

This certifies that
CANDIDATE

WENDALL MANIGAULT

has successfully completed the requirements for Boot Camp on this
17th day of MARCH 2000

Karen D. Coste

Karen D. Coste

Principal

Arthur Drayton

Instructor

Charleston County Discipline School Graduation Ceremony

Me after Graduation Ceremony at Charleston County Discipline School

BACK TO OUR GREAT-GRANDPARENTS' HOME

Me and my two sisters

My two sisters and our parents

My Lil Sister and Brother playing in the room I got injured (shot) in

HIGH SCHOOL MEMORIES

Me and my cousin Blinka outside of R.B. Stall High School

Me and my eldest sibling high school photo taken at R.B. Stall High School

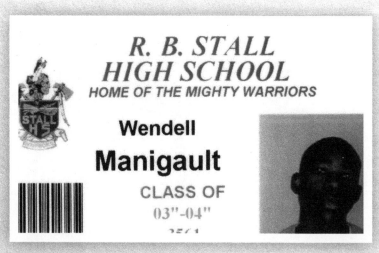

My student I.D.

The Post and Courier

LOCAL REPORT

Teen-ager hospitalized after being shot in neck

A 16-year-old boy was shot in the neck with a handgun Monday night in a residence off Ward Avenue, according to the Charleston County Sheriff's Office.

Medics transported the teen-ager, who was in serious condition, to the Medical University Hospital, the sheriff's office said. His condition late Monday night was not immediately available.

Deputies were called to the residence in the 6800 block near the Charleston Air Force Base around 7 p.m.

The teen-ager, whose name was not released, lives at the residence.

Investigators are questioning an 18-year-old man in connection with the shooting, said Lt. Don Martin.

Deputies are trying to determine the cause of the shooting, including the possibility it was accidental.

The news article that was typed and printed about the night of my injury

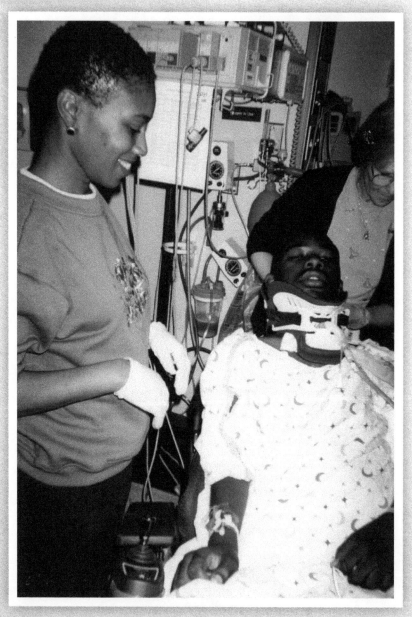

Me, my ole lady and nurse

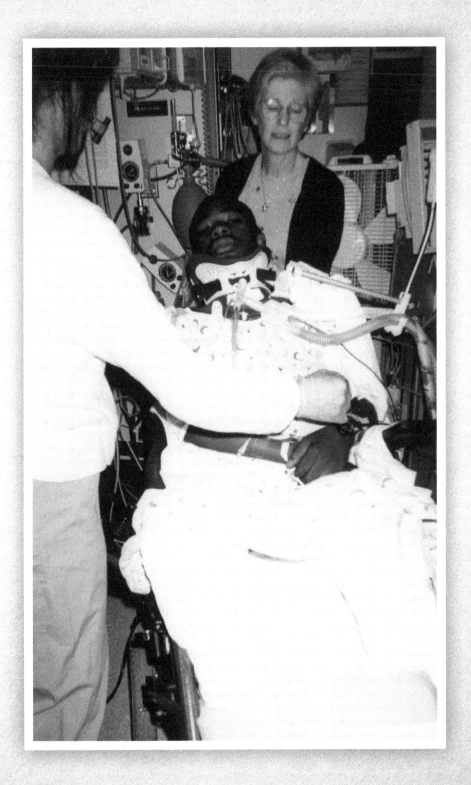

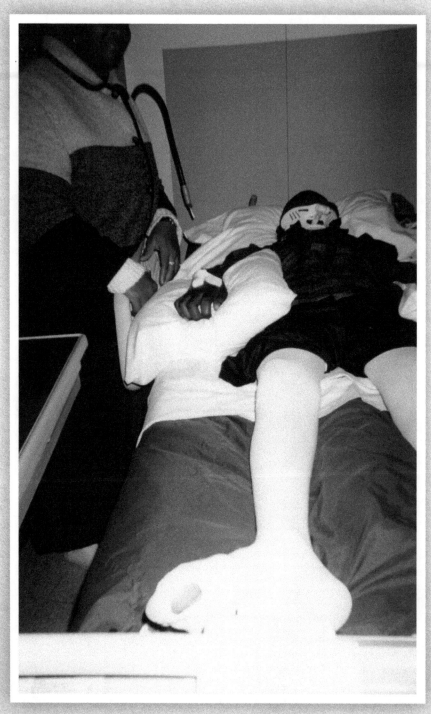

Me and my Aunt Wanda Reese

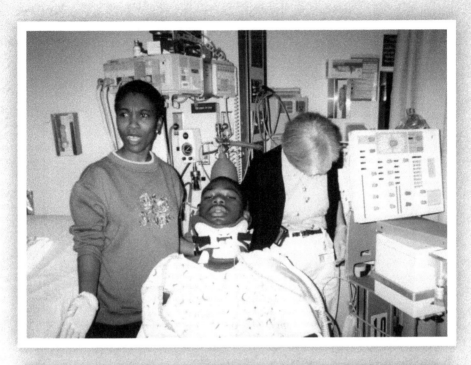

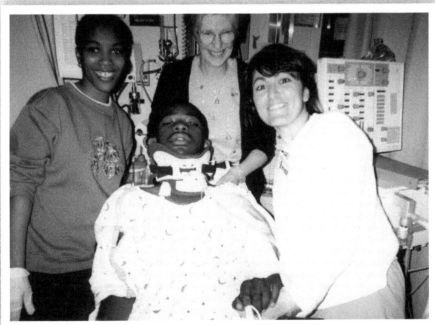

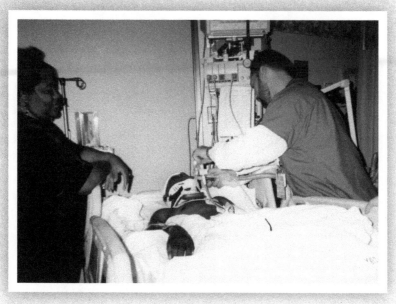

Me, my aunt Denise Robinson and the nurse who was suctioning the secretion out my tracheostomy

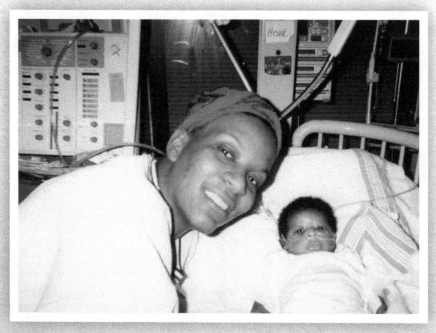

Tina Mack a young lady whom my ole lady linked up with during me and her baby's admission at the Medical University of South Carolina

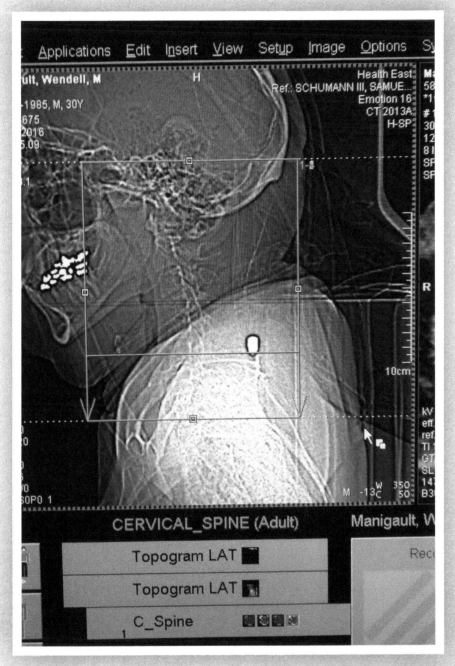

X-Ray image of bullet lodged in my neck

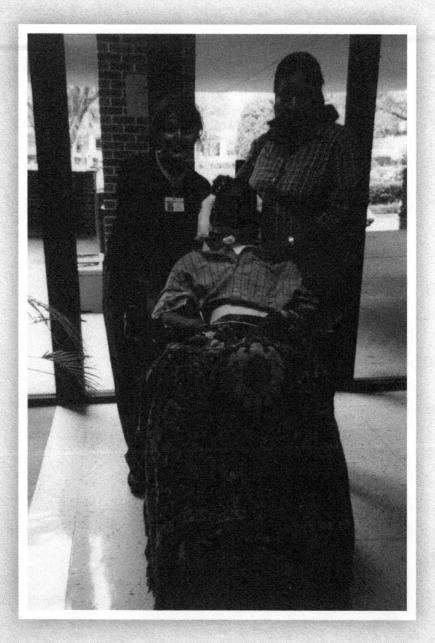

Me, the nurse and my Aunt Sharon Manigault who broke the news about my deceased grandfather in front of the children's hospital

LONG LIVE
ROBERT "BOY" MANIGUALT JR.

My deceased grandfather that passed 5 days after I got shot.

THE HEARTFELT BANNER FROM

MY TEACHERS AND SCHOOLMATES

Roper St Francis Rehab

Schoolmates/eldest sibling visiting me at
Roper St. Francis Rehab Unit "The Usual Suspects"

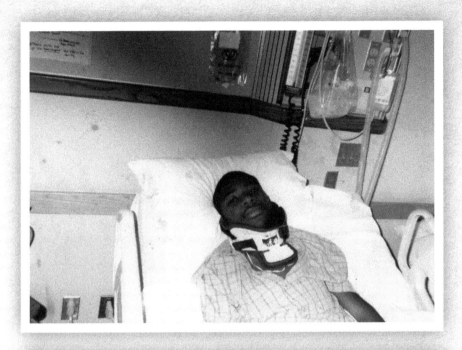

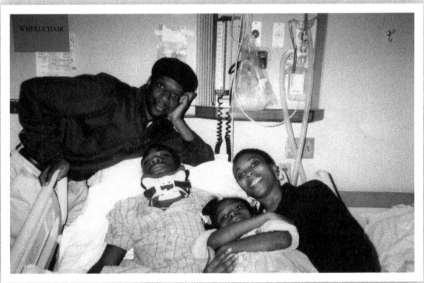

Me, my Lil Sister and our parents

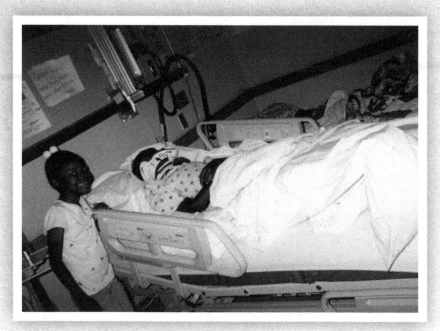

Me and my Lil Sister

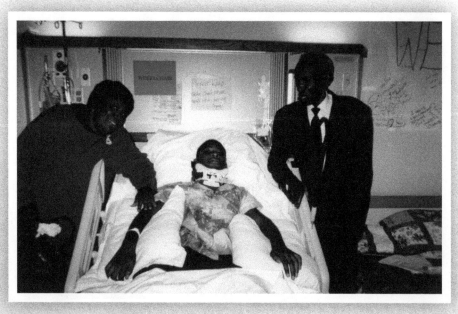

Me, my Aunt Willamena and my Grandfather Robert Tindal
(ole ladys father)

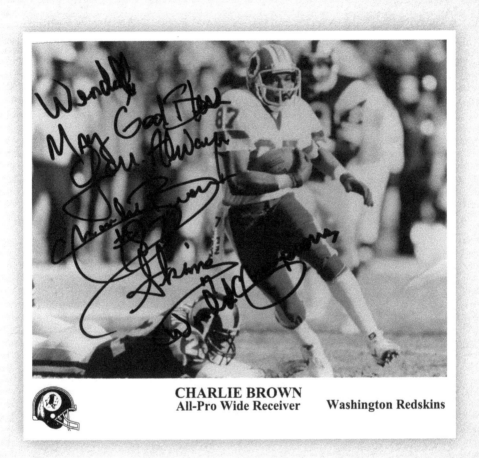

CHARLIE BROWN
All-Pro Wide Receiver   **Washington Redskins**

Signed autograph photos that was given to me personally by
All-Pro Charlie Brown (Image one)

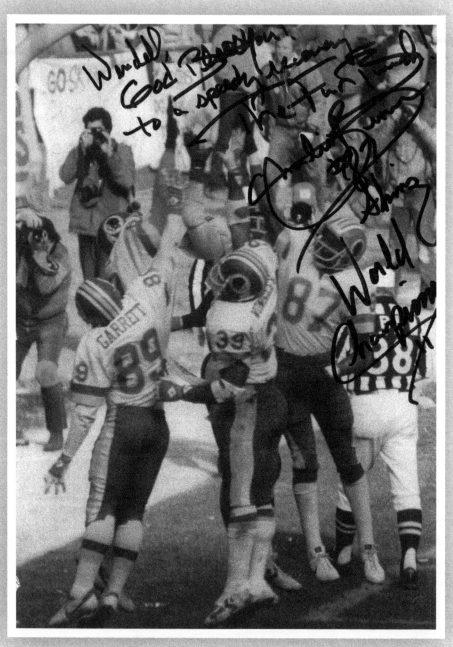

Autograph (image two)

LONG LIVE
CEE

JONES, Ricardo
The relatives and friends of Mr. Ricardo Terrell Jones, those of his parents, Ms. Lucille Jones and Mr. Samuel B. Crummey, III, those of his step-father, Stacy Salters, step-mother Janice Mayo, his sister and brothers, Shannon Denise Jones, Oatis Jones and Christopher Whaley, and all other relatives and friends are invited to attend his funeral services, Thursday afternoon, April 18, 2002, 2 p.m., at Victory Baptist Church, Remount Road, North Charleston, S.C. Reverend Clary Samuels, Pastor. Interment, Sunset Memorial Gardens. Mr. Ricardo Terry Jones will lie in state this evening at the North Area Funeral Home from 6 p.m. until 8 p.m. where the family will receive friends from 7 to 8 p.m. Services entrusted to NORTH AREA FUNERAL HOME (843)

My brother from another mother whom I made an instant connection with in times past

PROM NIGHT

Me and my prom date who escorted me to her senior prom

My eldest sibling and her prom date attending the same prom

17TH BIRTHDAY

My seventeenth birthday party that I almost didn't live to see
due to my injury

The young lady Shante who's attending the party is the nurse that was
assigned to my case at the time

MY BAPTISM

Certificate
of
Baptism

This certifies that _Wendell Manigault, Jr._

was baptized in the name of the Father and of the Son and of the Holy Spirit on

the _27_ day of _April_ , _2003_

at _Lovely Mountain Baptist Church_

of _6798 Ward Avenue_ , _Charleston, South Carolina_

THE MEANING OF BAPTISM

"Repent," Peter said to them, "and be baptized, each of you, in the name of Jesus the Messiah for the forgiveness of your sins, and you will receive the gift of the Holy Spirit." Acts 2:38 (HCSB)

MY CALIFORNIA FAMILY

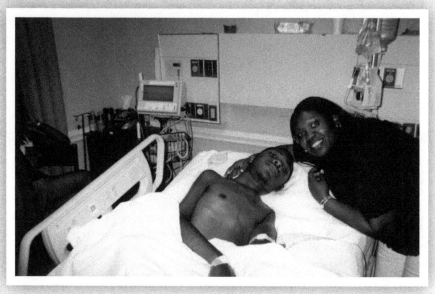

Me and my aunt Sharon during my short stay at Roper Rehab due to my urinary tract infection.

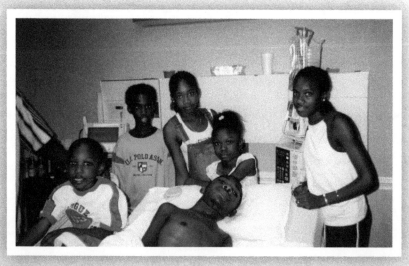

Me my cousins DeShawn, Bryan, Nebresha, Brittany, and my lil sister during my short stay at Roper Rehab

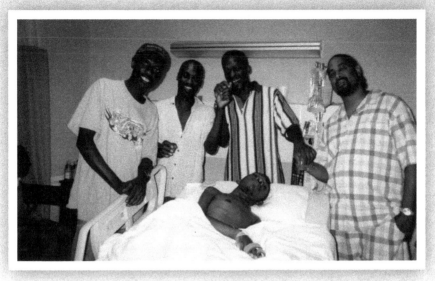

Me, my uncles Robert, Bernard, Bryan Sr. aka Big Red, and my father during my short stay at Roper Rehab

Noonie, my aunt and uncle from California baby boy who couldn't live without his pacifier

LONG LIVE
ROBERT MARION TINDAL SR.

My grandfather whom I love and miss dearly.

VOC REHAB GOING AWAY PARTY

Me and my partners David Graham, and KG enjoying the festivities of my going away party

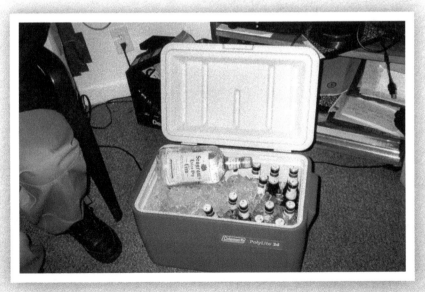

Me, my relatives and partners with a cooler full of booze

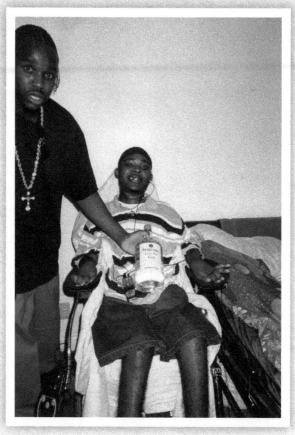

Me and my partner KG with a bottle of Bumpy. Sociably enjoying the festivities at my party.

Me and my cousins, Bubba and Cleo politicking

VOCATIONAL REHABILITATION CENTER

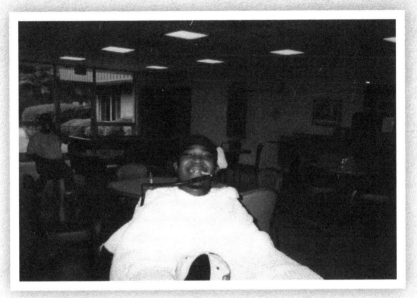

Me sitting in the dining hall at Voc Rehab

Me sitting in the Voc Rehab dining hall with one of the staff members

Me standing outside Voc Rehab Facility along with another staff member

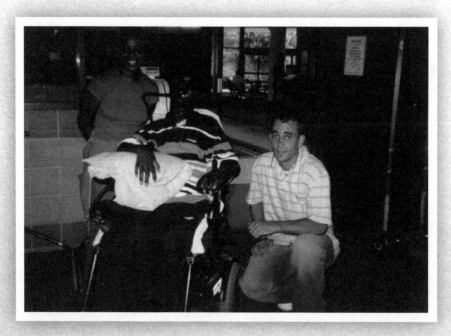

Me sitting inside Voc Rehabs muscular development center
along with two of their therapists

CHARLESTON HABITAT FOR HUMANITY

One news article about the history of the Rosemont Community
being built on backs of slaves

The beginning of construction in the Rosemont Community

Habitat for Humanities selected partner families and volunteer helpers on one of their construction sites

My ole lady, cousins and co-workers who supported her throughout the whole process

Another one of Habitats construction sites

The progress that Habitat staff, Selected Partner Families and Volunteer Helpers has made on our homes in the Rosemont Community

Mr. Joe Reed home dedication ceremony

Ms. Idell Sass home dedication ceremony

My ole lady's home dedication ceremony

My ole lady, Pastor Dayson and Rev. Bratton testing out my lift
during the dedication ceremony

Rev. Bratton, Pastor Dayson, Minister and Sister Ancrum
attending the ceremony in our new home

My Granny Liz, Mary Lee, Sister Dayson our First Lady, and Ms. Maggie
a longtime friend of the family attending the ceremony

SPEAKING ENGAGEMENT

My very first speaking engagement that God who has chosen me to speak orchestrated along with my presiding Pastor Curtis J. Dayson at our church

My speaking engagement at Wannamaker Park that was hosted by the youth advisors at Charity Missionary Baptist Church

My speaking engagement that was hosted by the youth advisors at
Community Baptist Church in the Rosemont Community

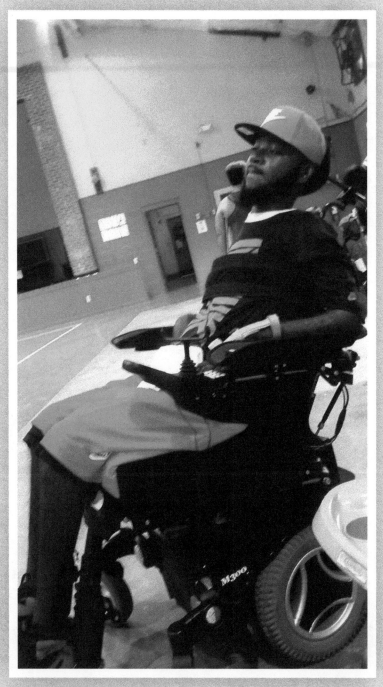

My speaking engagement that was hosted by Larry aka La La
inside the gym of Clark Academy that's located in James Island

LONG LIVE
LIL' P

My Partner who kept in contact and visited me throughout the years of my injury. In fact, he visited me at least three to five times out of the week when he wasn't incarcerated.

MR. AND MRS....

My ole lady and stepfather standing together in holy matrimony.

Moja Festival finale headliners Patti Labelle and Boyz II Men

Boyz II Men on stage giving their fans an epic performance

Here go Patti LaBelle demanding her fans attention as she make her grand entrance to the stage belting out one of her hits under the spotlight

Patti LaBelle background vocalist/ Hurricane Katrina survivor giving the
fans the performance of a lifetime

Patti LaBelle performing Lady Marmalade while interacting
on stage with fans

My 25th Birthday Bash

My scrumptious birthday cake

My aunt and ole lady presenting me with my scrumptious birthday cake

The DJ's, my ole lady and relatives singing happy birthday

Everyone is still singing happy birthday. However, this time around they're putting money in the hat that's placed on my lap.

Everyone is beginning to bring that sweet serenade to halt.

Two of Midland Parks finest DJ's on the ones and two's

Ernest Warring a longtime friend of the family getting the party started

Ernest Warring cutting a rug

My stepfather and granny having the time of their lives grooving

Relatives dancing to a popular line dance

Relatives dancing to another popular line dance

VITAL SIGNS

COVER STORY

Leaders of the new Center for Spinal Cord Injury at the facility's opening on July 15. The center is joint effort of F Rehabilitation Hospital, MUSC Health, Carolinas Rehabilitation and the Spinal Cord Injury Research Fund.

Spinal injury clinic team partners and treatment:

Wendell Manigault was 15 years old in the winter of 2002, a self-described people person with an eye on the future.

The normal life Manigault lived – school, friends, girls – ended on Feb. 11 that year, shattered by a fateful discovery and a bullet that should have never been fired.

FOUND AND LOST

Manigault and a friend found three handguns in a patch of North Charleston woods near Manigault's home two weeks before the accident that irrevocably altered his life. For whatever reason – novelty, bravado, boredom – the boys held onto the guns, which were loaded.

In the following days, the firearms provided sport for the duo, with the pair taking aim at each other while depicting would-be scenarios. "This is what I would do if somebody runs up on me," Manigault's friend said the night of the accident, according to police reports.

The boys were alone, with the guns, in Manigault's room that murky Monday evening. Manigault, according to autho dropped a 9 mm pistol and bent down to it up. His friend was aiming another gun, caliber pistol, at Manigault when he no that it was cocked. When the friend atter to pull the hammer back, the gun fired.

Manigault was shot in the neck remained conscious. His friend ran fro room shouting, "Call the police, cal police." Manigault, meanwhile, lay o bedroom floor, terrified as blood p around him and the feeling in his evaporated.

"The bullet entered my neck in such that it fractured my spine," Manigault 25, said recently. "In a matter of mo1 my entire life changed."

STRUGGLE TO ADJUST

For the brutal swiftness with which injuries are often incurred, rehabilitation and recovery proces mockingly slow. After spending a mo MUSC Children's Hospital, includin

See 'SPINAL' on Pa

The center of the spinal cord injury clinic grand opening news article
(image one)

SPINAL: First-in-state CSCI program unites treatmen

>> Continued from Page 5

weeks in the Intensive Care Unit, Manigault was admitted to Roper Rehabilitation Hospital.

There, he spent another month acclimating to his stark reality. Finally, he returned to his mother's home where a caregiver continues tending to him five days a week.

COMING TOGETHER

Recently, however, getting the proper medical attention has become easier for Manigault, who for the better part of a decade has navigated a labyrinth of appointments at scattered doctors' offices and medical facilities.

Roper Rehabilitation Hospital, MUSC Health, Carolinas Rehabilitation and the Spinal Cord Injury Research Fund (SCIRF) have developed a new, collaborative program that will improve patient care for hundreds of people in our area living with spinal cord injury.

The Center for Spinal Cord Injury (CSCI) opened July 15 with a special ceremony in the 6th floor rehabilitation gym at Roper Hospital. The facility offers specialized services unique to spinal cord injury patients in one location and during a single appointment.

It's a medical program first in South Carolina, and a boon for patients with spinal cord injuries who often have a range of healthcare needs that are often difficult for a single healthcare system to meet.

"This new Center and our successful collaboration represent an important step forward in the treatment our medical community is now able to offer spinal cord injury patients," said Roper St. Francis Healthcare President and CEO David Dunlap. "It not only fills a void that's been missing, but also demonstrates the value of what we can achieve by working together for our patients."

The tri-county area averages 43 new spiral cord injury cases annually – there are some 12,000 nationwide each year – and about 1,000 people in the area are living with spinal cord injury.

"Too often, when a person with spinal

Wendell Manigault, center, with his mother Pauline Vanderhorst, a PCT in the Roper Rehabilitation Hospital for the past 19 years, and his caretaker Janice Robinson.

ONE-STOP SITE FOR CARE

The Center for Spinal Cord Injury combines a variety of specialists in one convenient location, giving patients easy access to preventive screenings and assessments by making just one appointment.

THE TEAM

Medical Director	Dr. Nancey Tsai
Pain Mgmt.	Dr. Reilly Keffer
Pulmonology	Dr. Steven Sahn
GYN	Dr. David Soper
Neurosurgeons	Dr. Brian Cuddy
	Dr. Sunil Patel
Endocrinology...........	Dr. Sarah Dolven
	Dr. Anita Ramsetti
Urology	Dr. Eric Rovner

cord injury needs medical care, they find themselves in a system that's difficult to navigate because not all healthcare providers have access to specialized equipment and training to treat the unique needs of this population," said Dr. Nancey Tsai, a board certified physiatrist and medical director for CSCI.

Manigault, who is working on a book about his life and is often invited to speak to groups of teenagers, said the new center is a blessing.

"It's a wonderful thing," he said. "It's going to be so much easier for me to make one appointment and know that I'll be able to receive all of the medical attention I need."

GETTING INVOLVED

Charles T. Cole, a retired executive and active member o Charleston community, has seen first the importance of offering spinal injury patients a central place to re care.

Cole, who was left with a devast spinal cord injury following a fall in ? felt fortunate to have received treat from both Roper St. Francis and M and wanted others to have the opportunity. He and his wife, Joa worked with the two hospitals and SQ and successfully spearheaded effor establish the new Center.

"Sitting in a wheelchair, immobil I had a lot of time to think, a lot of tir reflect on how I could turn this injury something that would help others have similar conditions," Cole said. ' Center represents a dream and a v that these two hospital communities collaborate for the common goo spinal injury patients."

The Center for Spinal Cord Inju composed of a team of me specialists from Roper Rehab and M Health, including neurology, management, pulmonology, uro endocrinology, gynecology gastroenterology. Other team men include certified rehabilitation nu wound care nurse, certified wheel and orthotics specialists, pharma registered dietician and board-cert spinal cord injury physiatrists. Phys and nursing assessments, lab v physical and occupational the evaluation and case management among services offered.

Carolinas Rehabilitation, one of busiest rehab centers in the U.S., serv a model in shaping the new Center. O their board certified physiatrists will t regularly to Charleston to lend expertis

Initially, the CSCI will be open o third Friday of each month and will 10 patients on a single day, with patients requiring four or more hou screening, instruction and treatment.

Additional days will be added community awareness of the new C grows.

(image two)

OUTDOOR MEDITATION

Me sitting outside in my yard exercising the outdoor meditation strategy I wrote about

Me sitting in the yard working on my project, in peace.

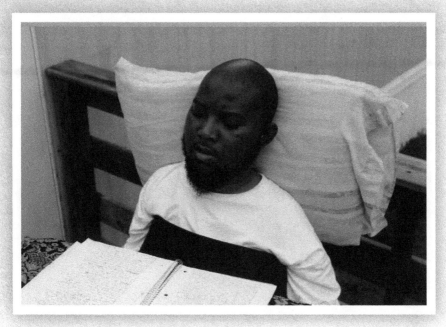

Me sitting on the porch working diligently to complete the writing process of this book

Me sitting in my room with a frown expression on my face as I proceed to write

Me sitting indoors proceeding with my outdoor strategy

LONG LIVE
JAY

The Gentleman whom I had the pleasure of meeting and becoming good friends with through his ole lady Ms. Amy whom I encountered outside of the Medical University of South Carolina around the time he got injured

CPSIA information can be obtained
at www.ICGtesting.com
Printed in the USA
LVHW022133221119
637981LV00015B/493/P

9 781641 114110